FIRMS AND MARKETS

FIRMS AND MARKETS

Essays in Honour of Basil Yamey

Edited by K. TUCKER and C. BADEN FULLER

CROOM HELM
London & Sydney

Croom Helm Ltd, Provident House, Burrell Row,
Beckenham, Kent BR3 1AT
Croom Helm Australia Pty Ltd, Suite 4, 6th Floor,
64–76 Kippax Street, Surry Hills, NSW 2010, Australia

British Library Cataloguing in Publication Data

Firms and markets: essays in honour of Basil Yamey.
1. Industrial economies
I. Yamey, B. S. II. Tucker, Ken
III. Baden Fuller, Charles
338.5 HB201

ISBN 0–7099–2446–1

Printed and bound in Great Britain by
Biddles Ltd, Guildford and King's Lynn

CONTENTS

EDITORS' INTRODUCTION

Professor Basil Yamey is a scholar in many fields and a man of many talents. These essays by former students on economic aspects of firms and markets are offered as a tribute to Basil Yamey's illustrious scholarship in the field of economics.

Basil Yamey

Basil Yamey has established an enviable record of scholarship as is testified by the bibliography of his work listed at the end of this book He was born in 1919 in South Africa where his father was involved in the distributive trades. After graduating from the University of Capetown in 1940 he went to the London School of Economics as a Lecturer. Following the Second World War he spent a brief period at Rhodes University in South Africa and at McGill University, Canada and was made a Reader in Economics at the London School of Economics in 1950. By the mid-1950s he had established his reputation in economics principally through his critical assessment of resale price maintenance as well as his research on the workings of commodity markets and (with Peter Bauer) on the economics of development.

In 1961, he was made a Professor at the London School of Economics. Over the years he has added to our stock of knowledge by publishing on a wide variety of subjects including: the economics of distribution, the economics of commodity markets, the economics of auction markets, industrial economics, competition law and, of course, the economics of development. In addition, he has continuously published on the history of accounting and is considered a leading authority on early accounting practices.

Basil Yamey is, and has always been, concerned with understanding how businessmen make decisions; why firms are successful; what makes markets function, and whether it is appropriate for governments to intervene. It is therefore no surprise that he has also made his mark outside the academic world. For twelve years he was an active and respected member of the Monopolies and Mergers Commission. There he was influential in forming the opinions of the majority but was equally able to write succinct and devastating dissenting opinions in those cases where he felt his colleagues had erred in their logic. His scholarship extended to the history of art. For fifteen years he was a trustee of the National Gallery and for two of those years he was also a trustee of the Tate Gallery. He is a member of the management committees of the Courtauld and the Warburg Institutes.

Basil Yamey has taught many thousands of students from all parts of the world. Attracted by his international reputation they have attended his lectures which have over the years covered foreign trade, development economics, competition law, futures markets and of course industrial economics. They have been taught by him in classes comprising people from countries that were the cradle of ancient civilisation as well as those from nations more recently formed by political and social forces of modern society. Former students currently occupy influential posts in academia, the business world and public institutions in countries both large and small and at all stages of development.

Students who have attended his classes over the years or who have had the privilege of being supervised by him in their post-graduate studies have never been left in any doubt as to his ability as a teacher. His presentation was never based on out-of-date lecture notes; his delivery was suitably succinct; his logic was always robust; and his commentary was packed with challenging and stimulating ideas. When it came to assistance with a manuscript, one could always rely on incisive remarks about the facts and conclusions, a careful scrutiny of the argument and help with re-drafting beyond the normal call of duty as a supervisor.

Former students of Basil are most grateful for his attention to their learning process while at the School. There are many who, while there, came to regard him as a very good friend. Among them are the contributors to this volume. With the support and kindliness of his wife Helen whom he married in 1949 the Yamey household became a 'Home away from Home', renowned for a spirit of lively hospitality and unpretentious conversation. One always learned something from their travels, their keen interest in the arts and their contacts with public life. But friendship was the most memorable element. For those of us who have called on Basil's personal counsel, his professional advice or an objective appraisal of our academic efforts, this friendship in all its dimensions has been extended across time and space.

In 1984, Basil retired from teaching to devote more time to his activities as advisor to companies and to his research into the history of accounting. There is no sign of any diminution of his wit or intellect.

This Book

The ten essays in this book cover a variety of topics in the field of the economics of firms and markets. Each of these essays is associated with the research of Basil Yamey, whose bibliography appears at the end of this volume. For convenience we have grouped the essays into seven sections.

In the first section there are two essays on the **Workings of Commodity Futures Markets**. In the first, Goss and Giles set out a model of price determination and the allocation of available supplies between consumption and storage. They estimate their model using data on the US soybeans market and the Australian wool market. In the second essay, Brasse undertakes a semi-strong test of efficiency for the Tin Futures Market on the London Metal Exchange. She finds that forward pricing errors did exist and that the market has not adjusted perfectly to the receipt of new information. There are close ties between these two essays and the work of Basil Yamey. Basil Yamey and Barry Goss edited the authoritative book *The Economics of Futures Trading* (1976). In addition, Yamey has written a number of scholarly articles on the operations of commodity markets, hedging and the efficiency of futures markets.

In the second section there are two essays on **Competition in Service Industries**. In the first essay, Baden Fuller contributes to the long standing debate on the effect of seller concentration by analysing the causes and consequences of rising concentration in the UK grocery trade from 1970 to 1980. He finds that this rise in concentration has been beneficial to the consumer. In the second essay, Whitehead analyses the structure and conduct of the UK building society movement and the factors which influenced the stability and effectiveness of the rate 'cartel'. These two essays on the evolution of markets and the nature of competition are closely related to the work of Basil Yamey. Basil Yamey is an authority on competition in the distributive trades establishing his reputation in the 1950s through journal articles and his book *The Economics of Retail Price Maintenance* (1954). He continues to write on the subject and is widely known as co-editor (with Ken Tucker) of the Penguin book of readings *Economics of Retailing* (1973).

The third section contains an essay by Webb and de Jong on **Auction Markets**. They model the optimal strategy for winning a single contract offered under the sealed bid or tendering system where competitive behaviour is uncertain. They extend their model to multiple contracts; group tendering behaviour; changing uncertainty and fixed costs, and they discuss the equilibrium. This essay is closely related to the work of Basil Yamey who was interested in the operations of competitive bidding and the Dutch auction, not only through his research into futures markets but also as a scholar contributing on bidding rules (see for example *Journal of Political Economy*, 1972).

The fourth section contains two essays on the subject of **Firm Behaviour**. The essay by Peck examines Gibrat's law of proportional effect and how econometric regressions applied incorrectly can produce misleading results. He models a firm's investment behaviour in an industry under constant returns to scale where all firms are price takers with finite capacity. He shows that although this model is inconsistent with Gibrat's Law, simulation of this model produces data which when subsequently analysed show spurious confirmation of Gibrat's Law. The second essay by Gorecki discusses predatory pricing in the Canadian drug market. He examines Hoffman-La Roche's monopoly position in the Diazepam and Chlordiazepoxide tranquilser markets in Canada prior to 1969. He shows how Roche's tactics to discourage new entry included the promotion of rival products owned by Roche, price cutting and predatory pricing; and that despite these tactics new entry did occur. Of course both these essays are linked to the work of Basil Yamey who established a reputation in industrial economics early on in his career. He was always aware of the problems of interpreting econometric regressions in industrial economics (see for instance his article with Caves in the *Quarterly Journal of Economics*, 1971). His article on predatory pricing (*Journal of Law and Economics*, 1972) is considered a classic. He is perhaps most widely known through his editorship of the Penguin book of readings; *Economics of Industrial Structure* (1973).

In the fifth section of **Law and Economics**, the essay by Markovits discusses monopolistic competition and the second best. He proposes a taxonomy of anaylsis of the distortions to allocative efficiency caused by investment in increasing product quality and variety. He uses the concepts of aggregative, particular and non-additive distortions and shows how these concepts can be related to anti-trust. This essay is also related to the work of Basil Yamey who was (and still is) active in applying the economic precepts to the law. Basil Yamey started to write on law and economics early in his career (see for instance his book *The Economics of Retail Price Maintenance*, 1954, and his monograph with Stephens, *The Restrictive Practices Court*, 1965). Not listed in his bibliography are his contributions in the reports of the Monopolies and Mergers Commission.

In the sixth section in **International Trade**, Snape's essay discusses the effect *on* exporting countries *of* restrictions imposed by importers. He ranks the effects of tariffs, quotas and subsidies under different scenarios. These scenarios include competition or monopoly in either domestic production, domestic importation or foreign production, or combinations of all three. Like so much of Basil Yamey's work in the field of development, this essay deals with a subject which is a matter of concern to both the developed and developing nations. Most of Basil Yamey's prolific and influential writing on the subject of development has been with Peter Bauer, starting with their *Economic Journal* article in 1951 and *Economics of Underdeveloped Countries* (1957).

It is fitting that the final section concerns the **History of Thought** and that it contains an essay in appreciation of Alfred Marshall's *Industry and Trade*. Basil Yamey is an admirer of Marshall and always maintains that much of present-day 'modern economics' can be found in the classics. It is no surprise therefore that in this final essay, Williams argues that Marshall is both analytical and empirical and that he uses innovative methodology giving prominence to the use of long time-series and cross-country comparisons. Marshall's book contains discussions of many topics of relevance to modern economists including horizontal combinations, collusion, vertical integration and the role of the state in lowering industry entry barriers.

Ken Tucker
Chisholm Institute of Technology
Charles Baden Fuller
London Business School

PROFESSOR BASIL S. YAMEY: A TRIBUTE

The essays in this book are by active, busy academics and professional people. Their readiness to write new articles in honour of Basil Yamey reflects the affection and respect in which he is held by those whom he has taught. The quality and range of the publications listed in the bibliography testify to the incisiveness of his mind and the breadth of his interests.

The evidence presented in this volume of his work as a teacher and scholar is impressive. It does not and cannot take account of his contributions to the subject as an editor, colleague and collaborator.

He was Editor of *Economica* from 1960 to 1973. The high level and wide range of the contents of *Economica* over this period reflect the exacting character and the breadth of Basil Yamey's scholarship. They reflect also his unfailing readiness to help contributors ranging from graduate students to senior academics in the revision of their manuscripts, far beyond the call of duty, or the practice of a great majority of journal editors.

The same readiness to help has been conspicuous in his relationship with his colleagues. Informative and helpful comment from fellow academics is a perquisite of a university post, but here again Basil Yamey gives far beyond what is normally expected from a colleague.

I have left to the last his rôle as a collaborator, which I am well placed to assess. We have worked together on and off for more than thirty years. I find it hard to convey my debt to him as collaborator. We have published jointly two books and many articles, but he has been of the greatest help with almost all the books and articles which have appeared under my name since 1951. He usually improved my drafts greatly, at times out of recognition.

I may mention a specific example. In 1973 I wrote a short article for a bank review on the implications of the Link Scheme of foreign aid, the proposal to issue Special Drawing Rights to less developed countries as a form of official foreign aid. Before submitting the article I requested comments from three senior colleagues, all full professors with international reputations, even world standing, in monetary economics and macro economics. In soliciting their opinions I asked them particularly to look for any technical defects in the argument. All three said that they could find no fault with the argument. After receiving their comments I asked Basil Yamey for his opinion. I had not done so at an earlier stage because the article dealt with an area in which he had never worked until then. He promptly detected two gaps in the arguments and helped to close them. He thereby made the article proof against substantive criticisim as became clear subsequently. I mention this episode as an example of his acuteness, and of his ability to exercise it over a wide range, including ground previously unfamiliar to him.

Basil Yamey has thus contributed to economics as scholar, teacher, editor, colleague and collaborator. The extent of his contribution has been exceptional under these headings taken singly, and much more so in combination.

Collections of essays in honour of a scholar are apt to be published at a time when the powers of the person so honoured may be on the decline. Readers of this volume may be assured that this does not apply in the present instance. Basil Yamey's intellectual powers are altogether unimpaired. This is evident to his friends, colleagues and students. It will become evident to others as he continues to publish in the coming years.

Peter Bauer
London School of Economics

PART ONE

WORKINGS OF COMMODITY FUTURES MARKETS

1 PRICE DETERMINATION AND STORAGE IN COMMODITY MARKETS: SOYBEANS AND WOOL

B. A. Goss and D. E. A. Giles
Monash University

1. A Model of Price Determination and Storage

1.1 The Theoretical Model

This paper presents a model of price determination and allocation of available supplies between consumption and storage, based on the theoretical model of Peston and Yamey (1960).[1] Estimates of this model are presented for two commodities: US soybeans and Australian wool. Each country is a major world producer of the respective commodity, and the US soybeans futures market is one of the most active futures markets in the USA, while the Sydney wool futures market is Australia's most developed, and the world's largest such market in wool.

Within the market for each commodity three sub-markets are distinguished: that for storage, for futures, and for present consumption. Storage itself may be hedged or unhedged.[2] Within each sub-market appropriate demand and supply relationships may be distinguished.

The demand for hedged storage comes essentially from long hedgers (FLH_t) who require the commodity at a later date for processing or to fulfil a forward commitment, and who face the risk that the price of this input will rise. They hedge against this risk by a purchase of futures contracts, and, using the cash price as a proxy for the forward actuals price, their demand for hedged storage is assumed to be a decreasing function of the forward premium.[3] The supply of hedged storage (H_t) is assumed to be provided by economic agents who hold inventories and sell futures contracts as a hedge against the risk of a fall in the cash price. In addition, they are assumed to seek gain from their hedging activities, and since a forward premium which declines gives a gain to short hedgers, the volume of short hedging is assumed to be an increasing function of the forward premium (since this premium must decline as the delivery date of the future approaches).

Not all storage is hedged. Some agents, speculators in spot (U_t), hold unhedged inventories in anticipation of a rise in the cash price. Their price expectations are assumed to involve them in a reciprocal demand for, and supply of, unhedged storage. The demand for unhedged storage is assumed to vary inversely with the spot price, and to be unresponsive to the futures price.

The futures market partially overlaps, but is not synonymous with, the storage market. The supply of futures contracts is provided by short hedgers and also by short speculators in futures (SS_t), the latter being economic agents who sell futures because they expect the futures price to fall. Similarly, the demand for futures is provided by long hedgers and by long speculators in futures (FLS_t), the latter being agents who expect the futures price to rise and employ risk capital to purchase futures in support of those expectations. The supply of futures by short speculators is assumed to vary directly with the futures price, while the demand for futures by long speculators is assumed to vary inversely with that price. Both such activities are assumed to be unresponsive to the spot price.

In periods when hedgers are net short, the demand for hedged storage is assumed to be provided by long hedgers and sufficient long speculative positions in futures to balance the hedged storage market. Similarly, in periods when hedgers are net buyers of futures, the supply of hedged storage is assumed to be provided by short hedgers and sufficient short speculative positions in futures to balance the hedged storage market.[4]

The total demand for storage consists of the demand for hedged storage and the demand for unhedged storage; the total supply of storage comprises the supply of hedged storage and the supply of unhedged storage.

The demand for present consumption (C_t), is provided by 'consumers', and their demand for these agricultural products is a derived one because they are really processors of the commodity. Consumers are assumed to carry no stocks in their capacity as consumers; any inventories which they in fact hold are classified as either hedged or unhedged storage. That is, consumers who carry inventories are classified as either hedgers or speculators in spot with respect to their stockholding function (only). Demand for present consumption is assumed to vary inversely with the spot price and to be unresponsive to the futures price. The supply in the sub-market for present consumption is that part of the available supply of the commodity (in a sense to be defined) which is not allocated to storage. The sub-market for present consumption is not the same as the spot market for the commodity, because a spot purchase may be made for either consumption or storage purposes.

The theoretical determination of spot and futures prices and the allocation of available supply between consumption and storage is illustrated in Figure 1.1. In that diagram the futures price (P_t) and the spot price (A_t) are shown on the two parts of the vertical axis, while the quantity of storage is measured from left to right, and consumption is measured in the reverse direction, on the horizontal axis. In the diagram the demand for hedged storage (FLH_t) varies inversely with the futures price and is drawn for a given spot price; similarly, the supply of hedged storage (H_t) varies directly with the futures price and is drawn for a given spot price. The demand for unhedged storage (U_t) is also drawn for a given spot price.

Equality between the total demand for storage ($FLH_t + U_t$) and the total supply of storage ($H_t + U_t$) determines the total volume of storage (OK_t) and the futures price OP'_t. Of this total storage, OB is hedged as given by equality between H_t and FLH_t (for convenience H_t and FLH_t are assumed to be equal at the price OP'_t; otherwise the rule defined above would be employed). The equilibrium futures price may alternatively be seen as determined by equality between the total supply of futures ($SS_t + H_t$) and the total demand for futures ($FLS_t + FLH_t$). That part of the exogenously determined available supply which is not allocated to storage is available for consumption, and is purchased by consumers at the spot price A'_t, which is the spot price for which U_t, FLH_t and H_t are drawn. Theoretically the problem is to find a total demand for storage (D_t) and a total supply of storage (E_t) and hence a futures price (P_t) and carryover (K_t), such that the rest of available supply will be cleared from the market by consumers at the price upon which D_t and E_t are conditional.

1.2 Specification of Equations

Supply of Hedged Storage. As explained above, hedging of inventories by short hedgers can be expected to increase with the price spread. If short hedgers are assumed to pursue the aim of profit maximisation, they may be seen as equating the current forward premium (the return on a unit of hedged stock held to maturity) with the marginal net cost of storage. Hedged stocks may be carried at times of spot premium, but this would be for convenience yield reasons (which can make the marginal cost of storage negative).

A soybeans processor who has bought cash beans may wish to protect the value of his bean inventory by a sale of bean futures. If the price of beans, in relation to the price of soybean oil and soybean meal futures, does not afford an adequate crushing margin, the processor can put on a 'reverse crush' by purchasing oil and meal futures in conjunction with the sale of bean futures. This will be done in the expectation that the market will correct itself, and when a satisfactory margin has appeared, the reverse crush will be unwound by buying bean futures and selling oil and meal futures. A processor pursuing either of these options would be included in our H_t category, and hence the supply of hedged storage can be expected to vary directly with the price spread ($P_t - A_t$), with the ratio of the price of bean futures to that of oil futures, and with the ratio of bean futures prices to meal futures prices. In experimental work with soybeans data, commercial stocks performed better than total stocks as an indicator of inventories eligible for hedging, and better results were obtained with beans' cash and futures prices entered as separate variables.

The specification of this equation is therefore:

$$H_t = \Theta_1 + \Theta_2 P_t + \Theta_3 A_t + \Theta_4 CK_t + \Theta_5 (P_t/P_t^m) + \Theta_6 (P_t/P_t^o) + u_{1t} \qquad (1)$$

and

$$u_{1t} = \rho_1 u_{1t-1} + \varepsilon_{1t},$$

where CK_t is end of month US commercial stocks of soybeans, P_t^m and P_t^o are the prices of soybean meal and oil futures respectively, and ε_{1t} is a well behaved error term. It is expected that Θ_2, Θ_4, Θ_5 and Θ_6 will be positive in sign, while Θ_3 is expected to be negative.

In the case of Australian wool, non-Australian Wool Corporation (AWC) inventories proved to be the best indicator of the volume of raw wool eligible for hedging, outperforming its nearest rival, the monthly output of raw wool. Accordingly, in the wool model, the short hedging equation is

$$H_t = \phi_1 (P_t - A_t) + \phi_2 NK_t + \phi_3 + v_{1t} \qquad (1a)$$

where

$$v_{1t} = \rho_1' v_{1t-1} + e_{1t}.$$

Demand for Hedged Storage. By an argument similar to that employed in Section 1.1 it can be shown that if the forward premium at the time a hedge is lifted is less than the difference between the futures price and the forward actuals price at the time the hedge is opened, there will be a loss to long hedgers. The cash price has been used as a proxy for the forward actuals price, which is generally unobservable, and so it is hypothesised that the demand for hedged storage (and futures) by long hedgers varies inversely with the price spread.

A soybeans processor who believes that the relationship between the futures prices for soybeans, soybean oil and soybean meal offers a satisfactory conversion margin can, in advance of the actuals transactions and crushing operation, 'put on the crush', by buying bean futures and selling oil and meal futures,[5] thus locking in the conversion margin. When the cash transactions are made, the crush hedge is lifted by closing out the futures positions. Processors who put on the crush will be classified in the FLH_t category, and their purchases of bean futures could be expected to vary inversely with the price ratios (P_t/P_t^o) and (P_t/P_t^m). However, attempts to include these variables in this equation were unsuccessful, the estimated coefficient of (P_t/P_t^m) being positive here and negative in equation (1), contrary to our expectations.

Long hedgers usually have commitments to use the commodity in question as an input or to deliver under a forward contracting arrangement. To represent these commitments, in the case of soybeans, variables for planned crushings (consumption) and planned exports have been employed. It has been assumed, in effect, that these plans have been realised, and so consumption and exports each with a lead of two months have been used here, this combination performing better than others in preliminary estimation. This equation therefore appears as

$$FLH_t = \Theta_7 + \Theta_8 (P_t - A_t) + \Theta_9 C_{t+2} + \Theta_{10} X_{t+2} + u_{2t} \qquad (2)$$

and

$$u_{2t} = \rho_2 u_{2t-1} + \varepsilon_{2t},$$

where Θ_8 is expected to be negative and Θ_9, Θ_{10} are expected to be positive in sign.

In the case of Australian wool, the role of long hedgers' forward contract commitments was assumed to be represented by a dummy variable standing for the absence of excess stocks of textiles in Japan. This variable takes the value unity in periods when the Index of Japanese Dealers' Textile Inventory (base 1970 = 100) falls significantly below 160. The corresponding equation for wool is therefore:

$$FLH_t = \phi_4(P_t - A_t) + \phi_5 D_{5t}' + \phi_6 + v_{2t} \qquad (2a)$$

where $D_{5t}' = 1$: January, 1973 to December, 1974 and ϕ_5 is expected to be positive.

Consumption Demand. Soybeans are a high protein feed for beef cattle, and also for poultry and pigs. The demand for soybeans is therefore a derived demand from the demand for beef and poultry meat, and pork. Soybeans are consumed for feed purposes in the form of meal, and we have taken soybeans crushings as synonymous with consumption,[6] which during the sample period occupies about 56 per cent of US production.

Concentrating on the impact of beef cattle and poultry requirements on the consumption demand for soybeans, this demand has been treated as a function of the cash price of soybeans, the parameters of the demand functions for finished beef and poultry, and the parameters of the supply functions of other productive factors in beef and poultry production.

Lacking a comprehensive empirical analysis of these parameters, real national income has been used as a parameter of both beef and poultry demand, the cash price of live beef and the slaughter of beef as proxies for the other beef demand parameters, and the cash price of broilers as a proxy for the other poultry demand parameters. In addition, the cash price of corn has been used as a proxy for the effect of parameters of the supply of other factors. Experimental work suggested retention of the consumption of pig meat as a proxy for the parameters of the demand for pork, although the consumption of poultry and the cash price of hogs were deleted on the same grounds.

It was not clear *a priori* whether corn is a substitute or a complement for soybeans in the production of these meats, and so we have no expectation of the sign of the coefficient of this variable. The cash prices of beef, corn and broilers were expressed in relative price terms, so the consumption demand equation for soybeans is

$$C_t = \Theta_{11} + \Theta_{12}(A_t/B_t) + \Theta_{13}Y_t + \Theta_{14}(A_t/D_t) + \Theta_{15}(A_t/J_t) + \Theta_{16}L_t + \Theta_{17}S_t + u_{3t} \quad (3)$$

and

$$u_{3t} = \rho_3 u_{3t-1} + \varepsilon_{3t},$$

where B_t, D_t and J_t are the cash prices of live beef cattle, corn and broilers respectively, Y_t is real US net national income, L_t is the consumption of pig meat and S_t is the slaughter of beef. It is expected that Θ_{13}, Θ_{16} and Θ_{17} will be of positive sign, while Θ_{12}, Θ_{14} and Θ_{15} are expected to be negative (assuming that changes in B_t and J_t are demand induced).

In the case of Australian wool we are fortunate in being able to draw on a study of the demand for raw wool in the United Kingdom by the Bureau of Agricultural Economics (1967). Their log-linear relationship was adapted by deleting their demand for wool tops inventories (because consumers are assumed to carry no stocks), by substituting a synthetics price variable for their synthetics quantity variable (which was assumed not to set the upper limit to market penetration by synthetics during the sample period), and by using an index of textile production to represent changes in tastes and population. Seasonal dummy variables were also found to be significant in this equation. The resulting consumption demand for raw wool is:

$$lnC_t = \phi_7 ln(A_t/S_t) + \phi_8 lnM_t + \sum_{j=9}^{19} \phi_j = 9\ SEAS_{(j-8)t} + \phi_{20} + v_{3t} \quad (3a)$$

and

$$v_{3t} = \rho'_3 v_{3t-1} + e_{3t},$$

where S_t is the price of synthetic fibres, M_t is an index of textile production and $SEAS_{it}$ is the seasonal dummy variable for the *i*th month of the calendar year. The coefficient ϕ_7 is expected to be negative, while ϕ_8 is expected to be positive.

Unhedged Storage. Unhedged inventories are held by speculators who purchase stocks spot in the expectation of a rise in the spot price. Assuming their expectations are held with uncertainty, these traders may be seen as extending their spot purchases until their expected price equals the sum of the current spot price plus the marginal net cost of storage and the marginal risk premium,[7] r_t. Yet in preliminary work the storage cost variable failed to perform in the case of soybeans, while in the case of wool both the storage cost and risk premium variables failed to perform; and the representation of price expectations by an adaptive expectations hypothesis performed better than a series of expectational dummies, for both soybeans and wool. This hypothesis, based on the work of Nerlove (1958) and others, assumes that the current revision of expectations is a proportion of the immediately prior expectational error:

$$A_t^* - A_{t-1}^* = \alpha(A_t - A_{t-1}^*) \; ; 0 < \alpha < 1$$

where A_t^* is the expectation, currently formed, of the spot price for the following period. Employing this hypothesis in conjunction with the simple relationship (as indicated by preliminary work) for soybeans:

$$U_t = \beta_0 + \beta_1 A_t + \beta_2 A_t^* + \beta_3 r_t + w_t$$

with expected parameter signs β_1, β_3, < 0 and $\beta_2 > 0$, gives

$$U_t = \alpha\beta_0 + (1-\alpha)U_{t-1} + (\beta_1 + \alpha\beta_2)A_t + \beta_1(\alpha - 1)A_{t-1} + \beta_3 r_t + \beta_3(\alpha - 1)r_{t-1} + [e_t + (\alpha - 1)e_{t-1}],$$

which becomes:

$$U_t = \theta_{18} + \theta_{19}U_{t-1} + \theta_{20}A_t + \theta_{21}A_{t-1} + \theta_{22}r_t + \theta_{23}r_{t-1} + u_{4t} \qquad (4)$$

For computational reasons, the moving average process in u_{4t} is replaced by the autoregressive process:

$$u_{4t} = \rho_4 u_{4t-1} + \varepsilon_{4t}.$$

The expected signs of the coefficients of (4) implied by the above restrictions are $0 < \theta_{19} < 1$; $\theta_{21}, \theta_{23} > 0$; $\theta_{22} < 0$; and the sign of

Θ_{20} depends on the relative magnitudes of α, β_1 and β_2. The corresponding equation for the Australian wool model is:

$$U_t = \phi_{21}U_{t-1} + \phi_{22}A_t + \phi_{23}A_{t-1} + \phi_{24} + v_{4t} \qquad (4a)$$

and

$$v_{4t} = \rho_4' v_{4t-1} + e_{4t}.$$

The adaptive expectations hypothesis has been used previously in the context of commodity storage by Brennan (1958).

Demand for Futures by Long Speculators. These traders purchase futures in expectation of a rise in the futures price, and so preliminary work centred around a function of the form

$$FLS_t = \alpha + \beta_1 P_t + \beta_2 P_t^* + \beta_3 r_t + w_t'$$

where P_t^* is the expected futures price, and r_t is again the marginal risk premium to accommodate the likely case where expectations are held with uncertainty by risk-averse traders. Representation of price expectations by an adaptive expectations hypothesis failed to perform satisfactorily in this equation both for soybeans and wool, as did the risk premium variable. Accordingly, shifts in expectations in this equation are represented by a series of dummy variables.[8]

In the case of soybeans, demand for futures by long speculators is given by

$$FLS_t = \Theta_{24} + \Theta_{25}P_t + \Theta_{26}D_{5t} + \Theta_{27}D_{6t} + \Theta_{28}D_{7t} + \Theta_{29}D_{8t} + u_{5t} \quad (5)$$

and

$$u_{5t} = \rho_5 u_{5t-1} + \varepsilon_{5t},$$

where $D_{5t} = 1$: April, 1972 to December, 1972 to represent the international commodity boom; $= 0$ elsewhere.

$D_{6t} = 1$: January, 1975 to August, 1975, to represent the international slump; $= 0$ elsewhere.

D_{7t} = 1 : May, 1976 to April, 1977, for a period of revival; = 0 elsewhere.

D_{8t} = 1 : May, 1977 to July, 1978, for a period of stagnation; = 0 elsewhere.

The expected signs therefore are as follows: $\Theta_{26}, \Theta_{28} > 0$; Θ_{25}, Θ_{27} $\Theta_{29} < 0$.

In the case of wool, only two expectational dummies representing boom or revival conditions performed satisfactorily, and the corresponding equation for wool is:

$$FLS_t = \phi_{25}P_t + \phi_{26}D_{1t}' + \phi_{27}D_{3t}' + \phi_{28} + v_{5t} \tag{5a}$$

where D_{1t}' = 1 : January, 1972 to March, 1974 to represent the international commodity boom; = 0; elsewhere.

D_{3t}' = 1 : March, 1976 to December, 1976 to represent the textile consumption revival; = 0 elsewhere.

The coefficient ϕ_{25} is expected to be negative in sign, while ϕ_{26} and ϕ_{27} are expected to be positive.

Short Speculation in Futures. Future contracts are also sold by economic agents without actuals commitments who expect the futures price to fall. They may be seen as extending their sold positions to the point where the current futures price does not exceed their expected futures price plus marginal risk premium. Nevertheless, the risk premium variable did not perform in preliminary estimation, nor did the adaptive expectations hypothesis as a representation of short speculators' expectations. Recourse was then had to a series of dummy variables to represent shifts in expectations. In the case of soybeans, only one commodity boom variable and one recession variable performed satisfactorily, while in the case of wool only the recession and stagnation variables performed and the commodity boom and consumption revival variables did not. Hence the equation representing the supply of futures by short speculators, for soybeans is:

$$SS_t = \Theta_{30} + \Theta_{31}P_t + \Theta_{32}D_{9t} + \Theta_{33}D_{10t} + u_{6t} \tag{6}$$

and

$$u_{6t} = \rho_6 u_{6t-1} + \varepsilon_{6t}.$$

where D_{9t} = 1 : January, 1973 to March, 1974 for the international commodity boom; = 0 elsewhere;

D_{10t} = 1 : October, 1975 to December, 1976 for an expected slump; = 0 elsewhere.

Sales of futures by short speculators are expected to vary directly with the current futures price and inversely with the expected price, so that the expected signs of the coefficients are $\Theta_{31} > 0$, $\Theta_{32} < 0$, and $\Theta_{33} > 0$.

For wool the corresponding equation is:

$$SS_t = \phi_{29}P_t + \phi_{30}D_{6t}' + \phi_{31} D_{7t}' + \phi_{32} + v_{6t} \tag{6a}$$

where D_{6t}' = 1 : March, 1974 to March, 1975 for general recession; = 0 elsewhere.

D_{7t}' = 1 : May, 1976 to April, 1977 for stagnation in textile consumption; = 0 elsewhere.

All coefficients in this last relationship (6a) are expected to be positive.

Identities. In the accounting identity

$$K_t + C_t \equiv K_{t-1} + Z_t - X_t \tag{7a}$$

where Z_t = current production;
X_t = current exports;
K_t = closing stock in period t,

we define the left side of (7a) as the disposal of available domestic supply, and the right side as the domestic availability of the commodity (assuming imports zero). Hence we assume that the left side of (7a) is synonymous with the horizontal axis in Figure 1.1.

In periods where FLH_t is greater than H_t it is necessary to include sufficient (Q_t) of SS_t in the supply of hedged storage to balance the hedged storage market. Similarly when H_t exceeds FLH_t, sufficient (W_t) of FLS_t must be included in the demand for hedged storage to balance the hedged storage market. Hence equilibrium in the consumption and storage markets requires

$$C_t + H_t + U_t + Q_t = C_t + FLH_t + U_t + W_t \qquad (7b)$$

where $W_t = 0$, when $FLH_t \geqslant H_t$
$\quad = H_t - FLH_t$, when $H_t > FLH_t$;

and $Q_t = 0$, when $H_t \geqslant FLH_t$
$\quad = FLH_t - H_t$, when $FLH_t > H_t$.

The left side of (7b) represents quantities supplied, while the right side represents quantities demanded. Subtracting C_t from both sides gives the equilibrium condition in the storage market; each side is then equal to K_t, the quantity of stock in existence. It is assumed that the storage market achieves equilibrium every trading period, so that only equilibrium values are observed. Hence either side may be employed to derive the identity (7) below. We have chosen the right side giving:

$$K_t \equiv U_t + FLH_t + W_t \qquad (7)$$

This expression is not an accounting identity in the sense that it holds even at times of disequilibrium; it is an identity of observed values which holds every trading period. We can also write

$$H_t + SS_t \equiv FLH_t + FLS_t \qquad (8)$$

which is the equilibrium condition in the futures market, and can also be interpreted as an identity of observed values in the same sense as (7).

The complete model has eight endogenous variables: H_t, FLH_t, C_t, U_t, FLS_t, SS_t, P_t and A_t, with six behavioural equations and two identities (7) and (8). This applies to both the soybeans and wool models. In the case of soybeans the variables CK_t, P_t^m, P_t^o, X_t, B_t, Y_t, D_t, J_t, L_t, S_t, r_t, K_t and the dummy variables are treated as exogenous, while in the case of wool NK_t, M_t, S_t, K_t and the dummy variables are exogenous variables.

2. Data

This section discusses the definition, the collection and generation, and the interpretation of data employed in estimating the model discussed in Section 1. The data are discussed, for both soybeans and wool, under the headings 'Spot and Futures Prices', 'Other Endogenous Variables' and 'Other Variables'. Details of the data used are available on request.

2.1 Spot and Futures Prices

Soybeans futures prices (P_t) are monthly averages in US dollars per bushel of daily closing prices for a six months futures quotation[9] at the Chicago Board of Trade, as published in their *Statistical Annual* for the years 1972–79. Data on A_t are monthly average cash prices in US dollars per bushel for soybeans (No. 1 yellow) at Chicago, as published in the Chicago Board of Trade *Statistical Annual* 1979, and derived from USDA Economic Research Service, *Grain Market News*.

For wool, the spot price (A_t) is the monthly average of weekly auction quotations for 22 micron in 1977 (21 micron in 1976, 'average 64s' prior to 1976) provided by the Australian Wool Corporation in *Wool Market News*. It is quoted in Aust. cents per kilogram, clean basis. The wool futures price (P_t) is the monthly average of daily prices for a futures contract approximately six months from maturity, in Aust. cents per kilogram, clean basis, provided in the weekly *Statistical Report* of the Sydney Futures Exchange.[10] Futures price quotations refer to 'standard wool' which is 22 micron type 78 (64 type 78 prior to 1976).

2.2 Other Endogenous Variables

The demand for and supply of hedged storage (FLH_t and H_t respectively) of soybeans is assumed to be measured by the end-of-month open interest (in thousand bushels) of 'large' (reporting) hedgers at the Chicago Board of Trade as published by the US Commodity Futures Trading Commission in *Commitments of Traders* and *Databook* for the years 1972 to 1978. The reporting levels in soybeans were 200,000 bushels until 1 June, 1977 and 500,000 bushels after that date. The CFTC reports open position data, both long and short, for large hedgers, large (reporting) speculators and for non-reporting traders, who are usually assumed to be 'small' speculators (see Rockwell, 1967), a convention we have followed here. The classification (as between hedging and speculation) reported by the CFTC is that employed by traders themselves in meeting US government regulatory requirements.

These open position data were also used to measure the supply of and demand for soybeans futures contracts by hedgers, because a corresponding classification by type of transaction is not available for turnover. This last procedure is somewhat unsatisfactory for open positions instituted outside the current month, although in this case no better alternative is available.

The demand for and supply of soybeans futures contracts by long and short speculators (FLS_t and SS_t) is also measured by the end-of-month open interest for both 'large' and 'small' speculators as reported by the CFTC. As mentioned above, this procedure is not optimal for open positions created prior to the current month, but is the best alternative available with the given data.

In periods when FLH_t exceeded H_t, values of U_t were obtained by subtracting FLH_t from K_t; similarly, when H_t exceeded FLH_t, U_t was generated as a residual by subtracting H_t from K_t. Due to the high hedging-to-inventories ratio characteristic of the US soybeans market, this procedure sometimes generated negative values for U_t. Such values are inconsistent with the theoretical model presented in Section 1, and so all observations with negative values for U_t were deleted. In the sample period April 1972 to September 1978, eight such observations were deleted, leaving 70 observations.

Data on soybean consumption (C_t) are monthly observations, in thousand bushels, on factory crushings in the US, as published in the *Commodity Year Book* (1979), and derived from US Bureau of the Census.

No disaggregated data on turnover or commitments are published for Australian futures markets, nor do the data exist in the records of the Sydney Futures Exchange or the Clearing House. Therefore we have attempted to collect and generate data on turnover on the Sydney wool futures market, classified according to whether transactions are hedging or speculation, and whether they are on the long or short side of the market. First all Floor Members of the Exchange who traded during our sample period were interviewed and asked the proportionate composition of their business in the categories 'short hedging', 'long hedging' and 'speculation', taking into account any sub-periods they wished to distinguish. Floor Members' replies were based on their records and on their knowledge of clients' businesses. Clearing House records of monthly turnover were then obtained for each Floor Member, and for other Clearing House members, the turnover of the latter being allocated to the appropriate Floor Members.

The proportionate breakdown of business for each Floor Member was then applied to that Member's monthly turnover, so that monthly aggregates of 'long hedging', 'short hedging' and 'speculation' were obtained. The volume of speculation was then divided between long and short so as to balance the futures market for each month. Data on H_t, FLH_t, SS_t and FLS_t for wool were generated by this procedure.

The supply of hedged storage has therefore been measured by an estimate of sales of futures by short hedgers each month, rather than by open interest as in the case of US soybeans. Similarly the demand for hedged storage has been measured by an estimate of monthly purchases of futures by long hedgers. This procedure has the disadvantage that it is accurate only for hedges with a duration of one month. The validity of the procedure depends on whether changes in turnover, classified by type of transaction, are a reasonable proxy for changes in open interest, similarly broken down.

Sales of futures contracts by short speculators (SS_t) and purchases of futures by long speculators (FLS_t) are measured by estimates of the appropriate monthly turnover variable, which do not suffer from the shortcomings of open interest data (in this context) used in the case of US soybeans. U_t data on wool were again generated by subtracting from monthly data on K_t the greater of H_t or FLH_t, although in this case no negative values were generated because most stocks of raw wool in Australia are held by the AWC, and all the Corporation's inventories are unhedged.

Consumption of wool data (C_t) are quarterly data on Australian consumption of raw wool from Australian Bureau of Statistics' sources made available by the AWC and interpolated on a monthly basis, using the program TRANSF (Wymer, 1977b). Consumption data were converted from million kilograms, clean basis, to contracts ('lots') traded on the Exchange, where a contract refers to a quantity of greasy wool which is the equivalent of 1500 kilograms clean basis.

2.3 Other Variables

Data on US soybeans stocks (K_t) are end-of-quarter data interpolated to a monthly basis using the program TRANSF (Wymer, 1977b). Data on commercial stocks of soybeans (CK_t) are end-of-month data, while X_t represents monthly soybeans exports from the US. These three sets of data are published in the *Commodity Year Book* 1979, the first two being from USDA sources and the third from the US Bureau of the Census. Data on B_t are monthly average wholesale cash prices of choice beef steers at Omaha in US dollars per 100 pounds, from USDA sources and published in the *Commodity Year Book* (1979) while D_t represents the monthly average cash price of corn at Chicago in US dollars per bushel as published in the Chicago Board of Trade *Statistical Annual*.

The prices of soybean meal futures (P^m_t) and soybean oil futures (P^o_t) are monthly averages calculated from daily data, for futures contracts approximately six months prior to delivery (using a definition similar to that employed for soybeans as explained in Note 7), quoted in US dollars per ton and US dollars per hundred pounds respectively at the Chicago Board of Trade, and published in the *Statistical Annual* of that exchange.

The cash price of iced broilers data (J_t) are monthly averages calculated from weekly average quotations in US dollars per hundred pounds at Chicago, and published in the Chicago Board of Trade *Statistical Annual*. Slaughter of beef data (S_t) are Federally Inspected Slaughterings of Cattle in US in thousands of head; the data for L_t comprise Average Live Weight of Hogs Slaughtered Under Federal Inspection in the US, in pounds per head, both as published in the *Commodity Year Book* and derived from the USDA.

The marginal risk premium (r_t) is defined as the Commercial Paper rate (90-day) less the Treasury Bill rate (90-day) in per cent per annum, as published in *International Financial Statistics* of the International Monetary Fund. The data series on income (Y_t) consists of monthly observations on US Real and Personal Income in billions of 1975 US dollars, derived from *International Financial Statistics*.

Total Australian stocks of wool (K_t) were obtained by adding AWC month-end inventories to data on non-AWC stock (NK_t), the latter being obtained by interpolation (using TRANSF) from annual data on NK_t drawn from Commonwealth Secretariat sources. NK_t is measured in million kilograms, clean basis.

The index of manufacturing activity in Australian wool textiles (M_t) which appears in equation (5a) is published in the ANZ Bank's *Quarterly Survey*. The price of synthetic fibres (S_t), which also appears in equation (3a), is the monthly average price in UK pence per pound, of acrylic tow in the USA, Japan and the EEC, weighted according to production. Data on S_t were drawn from the International Wool Secretariat report *Competition from Synthetic Fibres*.

3. Estimation and Results

3.1 Estimation of the Model

The six stochastic relationships in the model have been estimated from monthly time-series data covering the period January 1973 to December 1977 for wool, and April 1972 to September 1978 for soybeans. Eight observations were omitted from the soybeans sample, these data points corresponding to months in which U_t took negative values. As a result, the wool sample comprises 60 observations, while the soybeans sample comprises 70. Each equation is overidentified and each model is only mildly non-linear in the endogenous variables. The non-linearities in equations (1) and (3) of the soybeans model arise in connection with various relative prices involving the endogenous variable P_t, and to simplify the estimation of the parameters, these relationships were linearised by means of a first-order Taylor approximation about sample mean values. The resulting restrictions on the intercepts of the equations were taken into account in the subsequent estimation of the model. The wool model is non-linear in the endogenous variable A_t, which appears in level form in parts of the model, but in logarithmic form in equation (3a). Although lnC_t appears in equation (3a), C_t itself does not appear elsewhere in the wool model, so this system may be treated as being linear in the logarithm of this variable. Equation (3a) was also linearised with respect to A_t by means of a first-order Taylor approximation about sample mean values, the resulting restrictions on the intercept term being retained in subsequent estimation.

Preliminary estimation by both Ordinary Least Squares (OLS) and Full Information Maximum Likelihood (FIML) suggested the

Table 1.1: FIML Parameter Estimates: Soybeans

Parameter	Equation/ Dependent Variable	Variable	Estimate	Asymptotic Standard Error
θ_1	(1)	Constant	−107.646	295.882
θ_2	H_t	P_t	4.461	2.252
θ_3		A_t	−2.219	5.305
θ_4		CK_t	0.760	0.375
θ_5		(P_t/P^m_t)	6.114	102.086
θ_6		(P_t/P^o_t)	0.511	10.465
θ_7	(2)	Constant	121.161	23.728
θ_8	FLH_t	(P_t-A_t)	−0.113	1.068
θ_9		C_{t+2}	0.484	0.390
θ_{10}		X_{t+2}	0.023	0.166
θ_{11}	(3)	Constant	39.171	61.363
θ_{12}	C_t	(A_t/B_t)	−3.397	5.878
θ_{13}		Y_t	0.076	0.271
θ_{14}		(A_t/D_t)	−0.282	0.148
θ_{15}		(A_t/J_t)	8.811	6.497
θ_{16}		L_t	0.023	0.196
θ_{17}		S_t	0.103	0.027
θ_{18}	(4)	Constant	6.333×10^4	4.884×10^5
θ_{19}	U_t	U_{t-1}	0.788	5.928
θ_{20}		A_t	-1.278×10^3	9.857×10^3
θ_{21}		A_{t-1}	56.653	491.243
θ_{22}		r_t	−897.908	7.293×10^3
θ_{23}		r_{t-1}	1.140×10^3	8.829×10^3
θ_{24}	(5)	Constant	381.817	233.678
θ_{25}	FLS_t	P_t	−1.706	3.193
θ_{26}		D_{5t}	0.226	0.227
θ_{27}		D_{6t}	−0.454	0.241
θ_{28}		D_{7t}	0.336	0.239
θ_{29}		D_{8t}	−0.328	0.235
θ_{30}	(6)	Constant	154.838	159.565
θ_{31}	SS_t	P_t	2.003	2.192
θ_{32}		D_{9t}	−0.096	0.181
θ_{33}		D_{10t}	0.177	0.062
ρ_1	(1)		0.847	0.062
ρ_3	(2)		0.705	0.091
ρ_3	(3)		0.858	0.091
ρ_4	(4)		0.805	0.076
ρ_5	(5)		0.865	0.040
ρ_6	(6)		0.849	0.047

need to allow for first-order autoregressive processes in most of the structural error terms. Accordingly, these structural equations were transformed in the usual way[11] prior to estimation, the res-

Table 1.1A: FIML Parameter Estimates: Wool

Parameter	Equation/ Dependent Variable	Variable	Estimate	Asymptotic Standard Error
ϕ_1	(1a)	(P_t-A_t)	0.067	0.023
ϕ_2	H_t	NK_t	0.887	0.375
ϕ_3		Constant	− 9.713	5.613
ϕ_4	(2a)	(P_t-A_t)	−0.025	0.005
ϕ_5	FLH_t	D'_{5t}	1.409	0.328
ϕ_6		Constant	3.452	0.199
ϕ_7	(3a)	$ln\ (A_t/S_t)$	−0.662	0.185
ϕ_8	$ln\ C_t$	$ln\ M_t$	0.039	0.060
ϕ_9		$SEAS_{1t}$	-0.386×10^{-3}	0.234×10^{-3}
ϕ_{10}		$SEAS_{2t}$	-0.285×10^{-3}	0.595×10^{-3}
ϕ_{11}		$SEAS_{3t}$	0.196×10^{-4}	0.773×10^{-3}
ϕ_{12}		$SEAS_{4t}$	0.114×10^{-2}	0.908×10^{-3}
ϕ_{13}		$SEAS_{5t}$	0.193×10^{-2}	0.109×10^{-2}
ϕ_{14}		$SEAS_{6t}$	0.248×10^{-2}	0.124×10^{-2}
ϕ_{15}		$SEAS_{7t}$	0.310×10^{-2}	0.140×10^{-2}
ϕ_{16}		$SEAS_{8t}$	0.343×10^{-2}	0.152×10^{-2}
ϕ_{17}		$SEAS_{9t}$	0.354×10^{-2}	0.164×10^{-2}
ϕ_{18}		$SEAS_{10t}$	0.317×10^{-2}	0.179×10^{-2}
ϕ_{19}		$SEAS_{11t}$	0.304×10^{-2}	0.190×10^{-2}
ϕ_{20}		Constant	8.061	0.594
ϕ_{21}	(4a)	U_{t-1}	0.763	0.181
ϕ_{22}	U_t	A_t	−1.527	0.924
ϕ_{23}		A_{t-1}	1.343	0.871
ϕ_{24}		Constant	82.773	50.376
ϕ_{25}	(5a)	P_t	−0.005	0.110×10^{-2}
ϕ_{26}	FLS_t	D'_{1t}	1.473	0.134
ϕ_{27}		$D'_{3\,t}$	0.025	0.110
ϕ_{28}		Constant	0.393	0.378
ϕ_{29}	(6a)	P_t	0.203×10^{-2}	0.110×10^{-2}
ϕ_{30}	SS_t	$D'_{6\,t}$	1.473	0.134
ϕ_{31}		$D'_{7\,t}$	0.025	0.110
ϕ_{32}		Constant	0.393	0.378
ρ'_1	(1a)		0.850	0.054
ρ'_3	(3a)		0.939	0.026
ρ'_4	(4a)		−0.082	0.075
ρ'_5	(5a)		0.296	0.109

ulting non-linear restrictions on the parameters being imposed directly when the model was estimated by non-linear FIML using Wymer's (1977a) RESIMUL package. The OLS estimates were used as initial values for the FIML algorithm, and the convergence tolerance was set to 0.1 per cent. After some initial experimentation the inequality restrictions $\hat{\Theta}_{10} > 0$ and $0 < \hat{\Theta}_{19} < 1$ were imposed in obtaining the results reported in Table 1.1 for soybeans. Similarly, with the wool model inequality restrictions were placed on three parameters to ensure that $\phi_{21} > 0$, $\phi_{23} > 0$ and to constrain the price elasticity implied by ϕ_1 to a magnitude consistent with prior information.[12]

3.2 Results

The results for the models as a whole are discussed first, and then the estimates for each individual equation are considered. The FIML estimates of the 33 structural parameters of the soybeans model and the six autocorrelation parameters are given in Table 1.1, together with the associated asymptotic standard errors. All of these estimates have the anticipated signs.[13] The standard errors are based on the asymptotic covariance matrix, and asymptotically the quantity $(\hat{\Theta}_i - \Theta_i)$ / a.s.e. $(\hat{\Theta}_i)$ is approximately standard normal in distribution. On this basis, many of the structural parameter estimates in this model are not significantly different from zero at the 5 per cent level, which is a rather disappointing feature of these results. The estimates of the autocorrelation parameters, and their significance, suggest that the structural relationships (particularly the speculative futures equations) may be under- specified to some extent. The Sign Reversal Test statistics reported in Table 1.2 indicate that the autocorrelation transformations have been quite successful in eliminating simple autocorrelation from the structural disturbances. These statistics are based on sign changes in the structural residuals between periods t and $(t-\tau)$ in the sample, and are asymptotically $\chi^2(1)$ in distribution. Only the structural residuals of equation (1) exhibit significant remaining serial correlation, this test suggesting some first-order autocorrelation (at the 1 per cent significance level) and second-order autocorrelation (at the 5 per cent level).

The estimated short-run price elasticities associated with each equation of the soybeans model appear in Table 1.3. These elasticities are calculated at the sample mean values of the relevant

Table 1.2: Sign Reversal Test Statistics: Soybeans

	Equation					
τ	(1)	(2)	(3)	(4)	(5)	(6)
1	8.25*	1.05	3.00	2.05	1.25	1.28
2	4.96	2.12	2.73	1.98	1.22	1.25
3	1.76	2.37	2.40	1.89	1.16	1.27
4	1.10	2.50	2.29	1.85	1.11	1.23
5	0.76	2.85	2.20	1.72	1.15	1.19
6	0.56	2.55	1.96	1.61	1.18	1.22
7	0.43	2.70	1.82	1.48	1.14	1.18
8	0.26	2.61	1.72	1.38	1.11	1.12
9	0.33	2.44	1.59	1.30	1.07	1.11
10	0.31	2.44	1.53	1.25	1.07	1.12
11	0.54	2.30	1.53	1.14	1.08	1.09
12	0.51	2.26	1.59	1.02	1.08	1.09

Note: *Significant at the 1% level.

Table 1.2A: Sign Reversal Test Statistics: Wool

	Equation					
τ	(1a)	(2a)	(3a)	(4a)	(5a)	(6a)
1	1.11	1.38	13.34*	8.31*	0.11	1.36
2	0.01	3.42	2.58	0.33	1.84	0.07
3	0.73	1.38	0.18	0.02	4.89	0.43
4	0.21	1.24	0.09	0.00	0.56	0.26
5	0.35	0.01	0.51	0.16	0.20	0.54
6	0.04	0.73	0.47	1.10	0.05	2.87
7	0.00	2.27	2.81	7.22*	0.53	0.01
8	1.08	0.32	0.40	0.29	0.12	1.26
9	0.25	2.37	3.54	0.23	0.60	0.16
10	0.59	0.08	4.73	0.87	0.06	1.21
11	0.06	2.46	1.74	0.18	1.17	1.54
12	0.90	0.34	0.01	1.62	0.01	2.29

Note: *Significant at the 1% level.

variables, and asymptotic standard errors for the elasticities are reported in parentheses. In general, these elasticities are quite plausible, although some are smaller than might have been anticipated, *a priori*.

The within-sample predictions of each restricted reduced form equation of the soybeans model are summarised in Table 1.4 in terms of percentage root mean squared error, and Figures 1.2 to 1.5 compare the within-sample prediction paths with the corresponding actual paths for a selection of the endogenous variables. Although the volume of unhedged storage is least well explained

Figure 1.1 Determination of Spot and Futures Prices

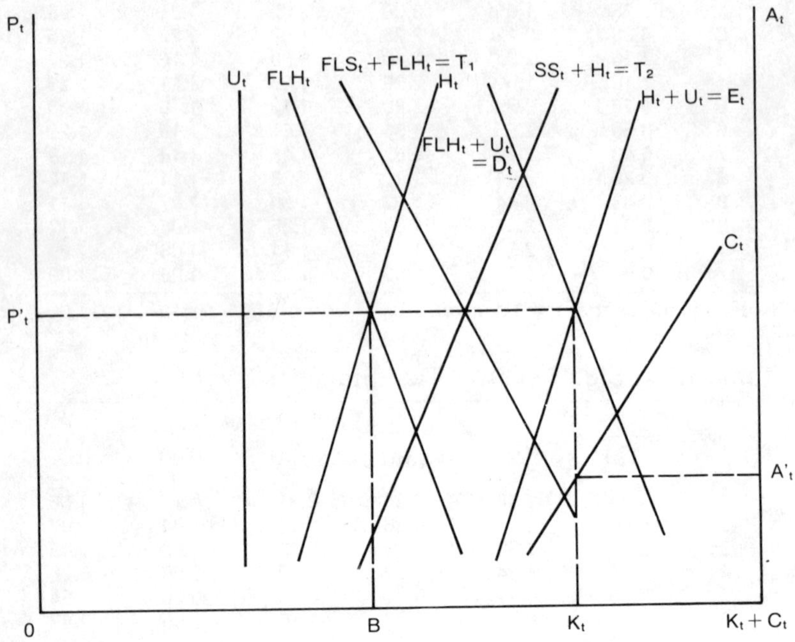

Source: Peston and Yamey, 1960

by the full simultaneous system, this should be interpreted in the light of the frequent high hedging ratio in this market (which is understated in this model because of our decision to include 'non-reporting traders' in the speculative futures categories), and the enormous variation exhibited by the U_t variable during the sample period. The performance of the model in predicting values of U_t is no doubt affected by the method of generating that variable as a residual, which, as explained in Section 2, resulted in the omission of eight data points because of negative U_t values, such values being beyond the scope of the model.

The relatively good performance of the model in predicting values of the futures price (P_t) is particularly encouraging in view

Figure 1.2: Soybeans Model: Futures Price

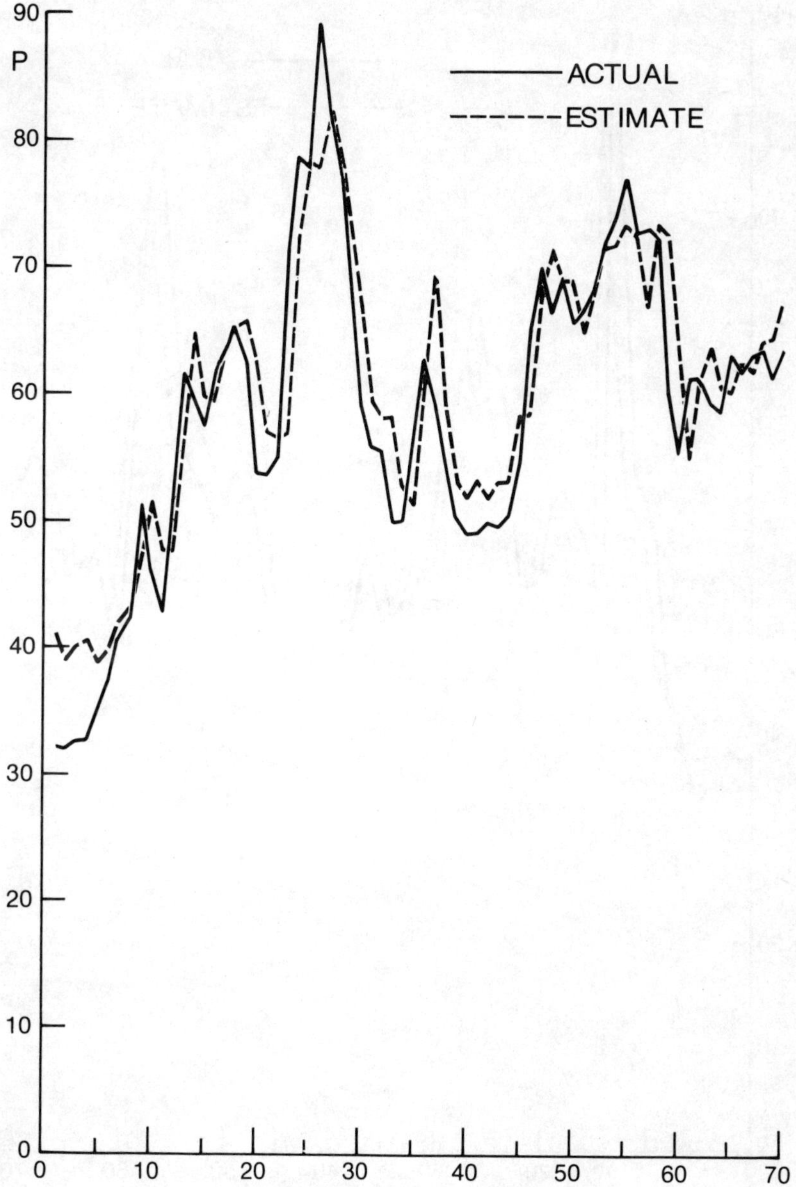

Note: Specific dates are not given, due to omitted observations. (See Section 3.1.)

Figure 1.3: Soybeans Model: Spot (Cash) Price

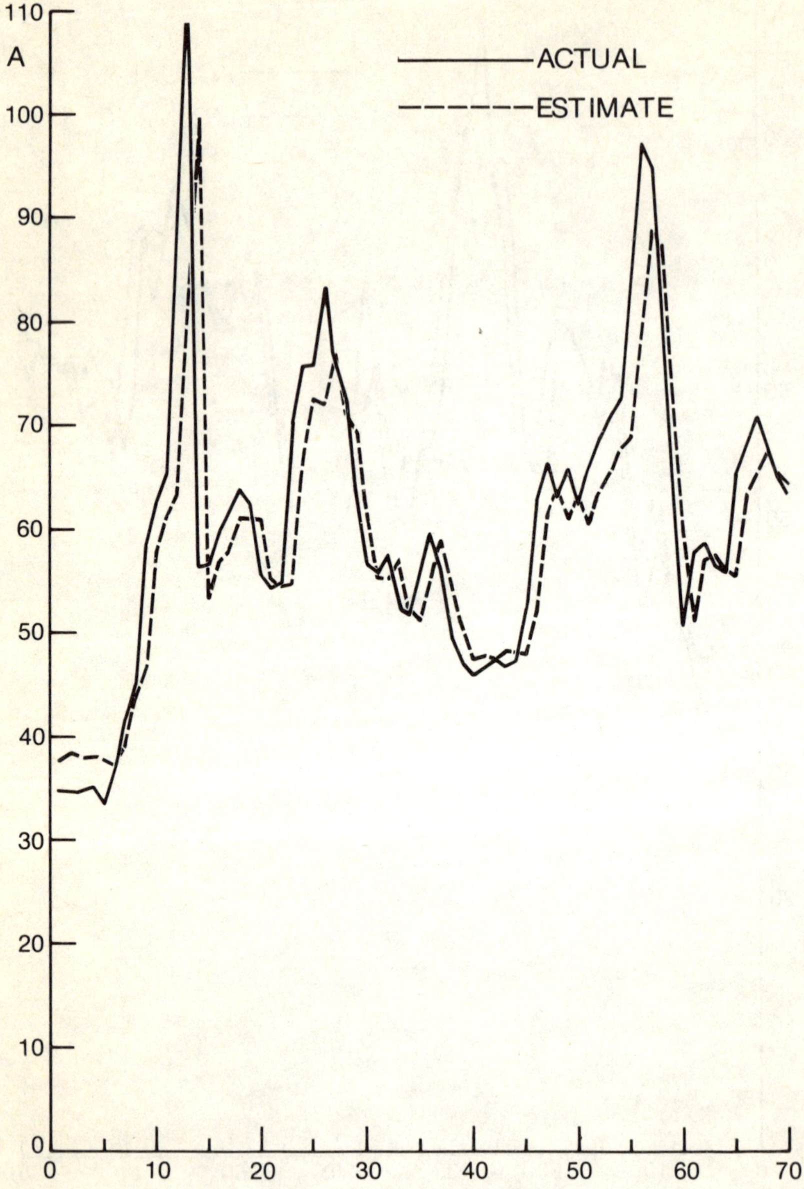

Note: Specific dates are not given, due to omitted observations. (See Section 3.1.)

Figure 1.4: Soybeans Model: Consumption

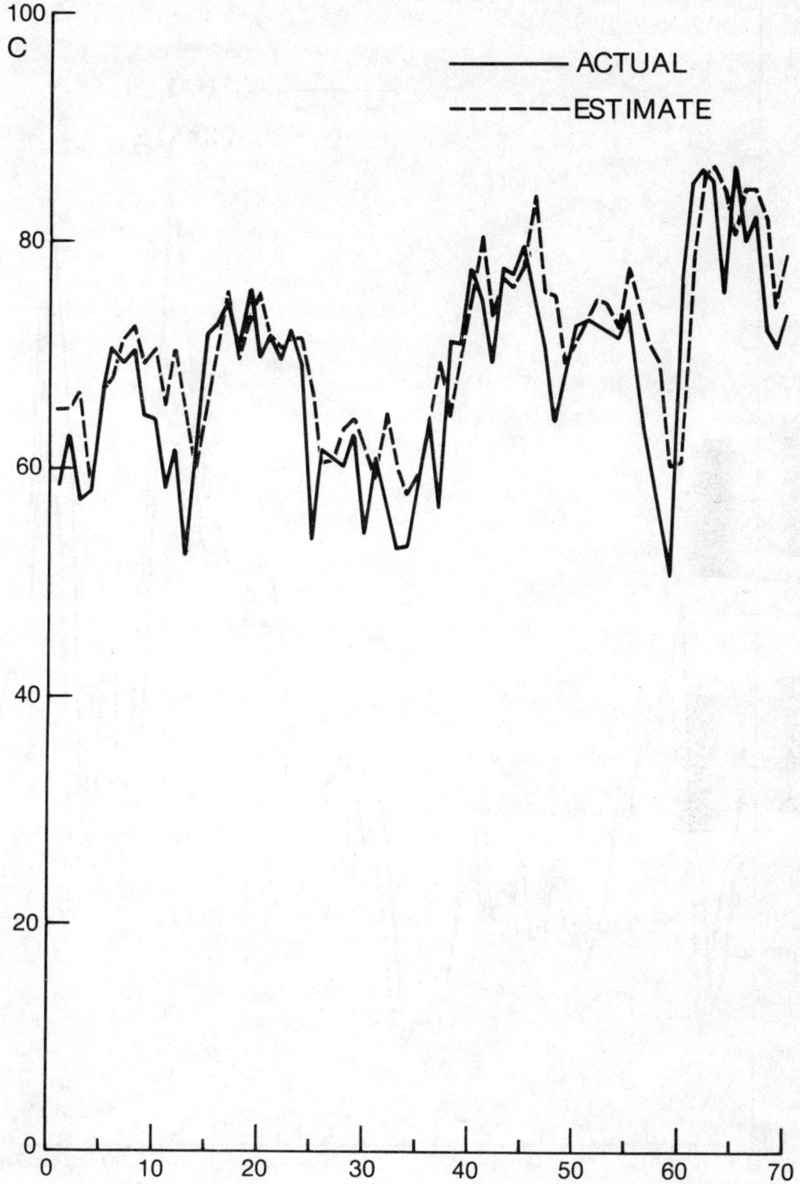

Note: Specific dates are not given, due to omitted observations. (See Section 3.1.)

Figure 1.5: Soybeans Model: Hedged Storage

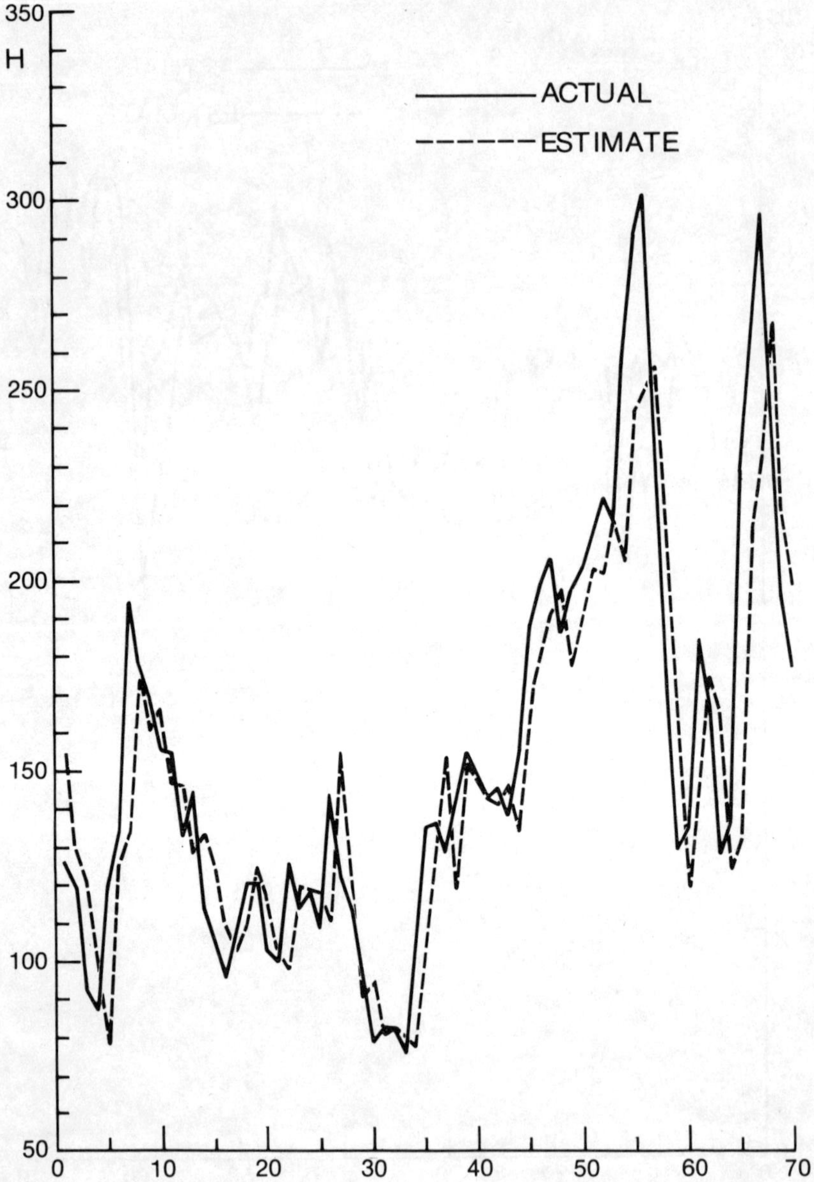

Note: Specific dates are not given, due to omitted observations. (See Section 3.1.)

of the fact that the soybeans market is one of the most active commodity futures markets in the United States. The futures speculation variables are less well predicted than the other endogenous variables, and this presumably reflects the need for a more sophisticated modelling of price expectations than employed here (such as rational expectations).

The FIML parameter estimates for the wool model are reported in Table 1.1A. All of the estimated parameters have the expected signs, and on the same distributional assumption with respect to $(\hat{\phi}_i - \phi_i) / \text{a.s.e}\ (\hat{\phi}_i)$ as was used with the soybeans results, many are significant at the 5 per cent level.

Table 1.3: Estimated Price Elasticities: Soybeans

Equation	Price						
	P	A	D	B	J	P^m	P^o
(1)	1.72 (*)	− 0.87 (2.09)				−0.02 (0.25)	−0.01 (0.18)
(2)	−0.05 (0.44)	0.05 (0.44)					
(3)		0.03 (*)	0.10 (0.05)	0.07 (0.12)	−0.20 (0.15)		
(4)		−166.94 (1287.99)					
(5)	−0.45 (0.83)						
(6)	0.55 (0.60)						

Note: *Covariance information not available.

In Table 1.2A, which reports the results of the sign reversal test, there is little evidence of autocorrelation except in equations (3a) and (4a). In the latter equation, this may be the result of the moving average (rather than autoregressive) process implicit in the error structure after the adaptive expectations hypothesis is taken into account. The estimation procedure used cannot allow for the possibility of this type of departure from serial independence.

Table 1.3A gives short-run price elasticities for the wool model estimated at sample mean values (except for equation (3a)), together with their asymptotic standard errors. These price elasticity estimates agree approximately with information provided in discussions with some major Floor Members, and are

Table 1.3A: Estimated Price Elasticities: Wool

Equation	Price		
	P	A	(A/S)
(1a)	5.99 (4.44)	−6.04 (4.48)	
(2a)	−1.86 (0.40)	1.87 (0.40)	
(3a)			−0.57 (0.18)
(4a)		−5.08 (2.14)	
(5a)	−2.30 (0.79)		
(6a)	0.32 (0.25)		

clearly much larger than those obtained for the soybeans model, although we are unable to explain this difference at this stage.

Table 1.4: Within-sample Percentage RMSE from Restricted Reduced Forms

Endogenous Variable	% RMSE Soybeans	% RMSE Wool
H	16.12	48.70
FLH	13.42	50.29
C	9.81	4.69
U	86.15	5.92
FLS	20.82	111.07
SS	20.32	90.05
P	9.82	6.71
A	13.46	8.25

The within-sample predictive performance of the wool model is compared with that of the soybeans model in Table 1.4, and time-paths for some of the variables appear in Figures 1.6 to 1.9. In contrast with the soybeans model, the explanation of unhedged storage is relatively satisfactory in the wool model. This is especially pleasing, as the majority of inventories are held unhedged in this market. Again, the futures speculation variables are explained less satisfactorily, and a second common feature of

Figure 1.6: Wool Model: Spot (Cash) Price

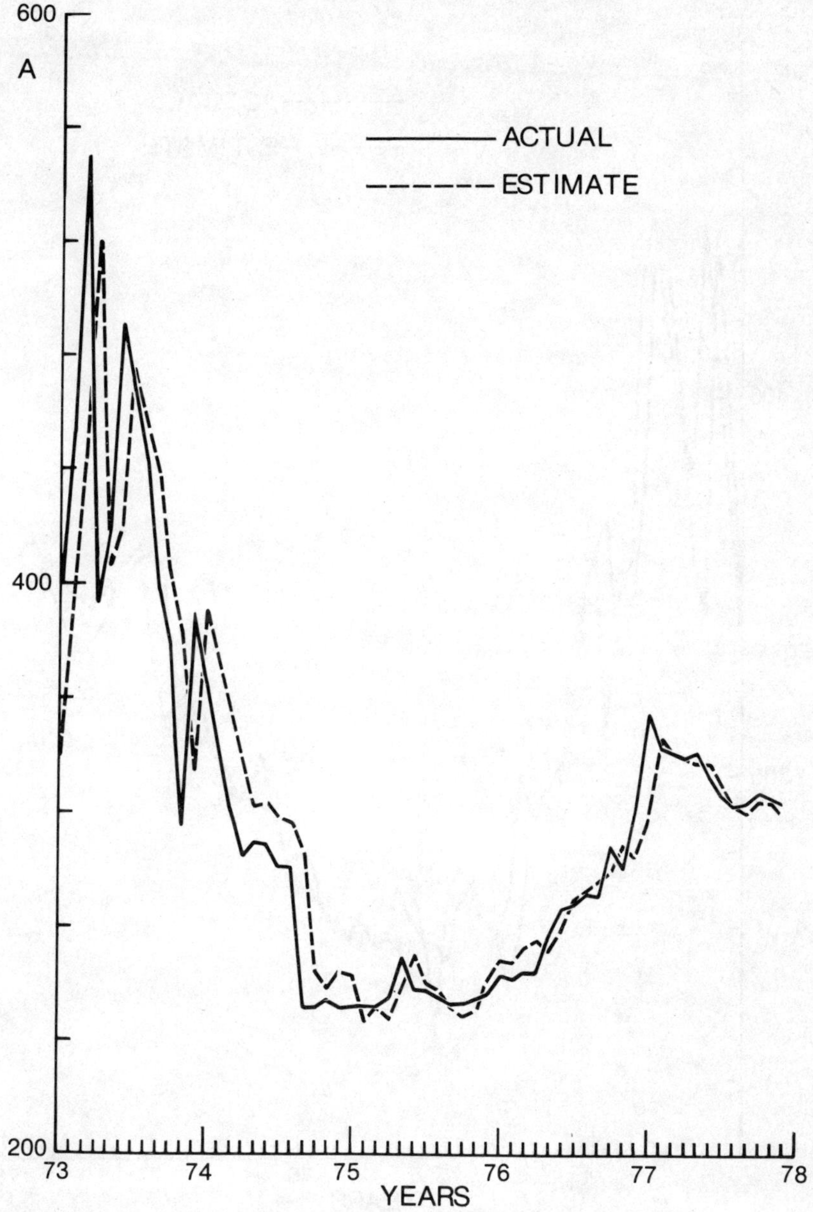

Figure 1.7: Wool Model: Futures Price

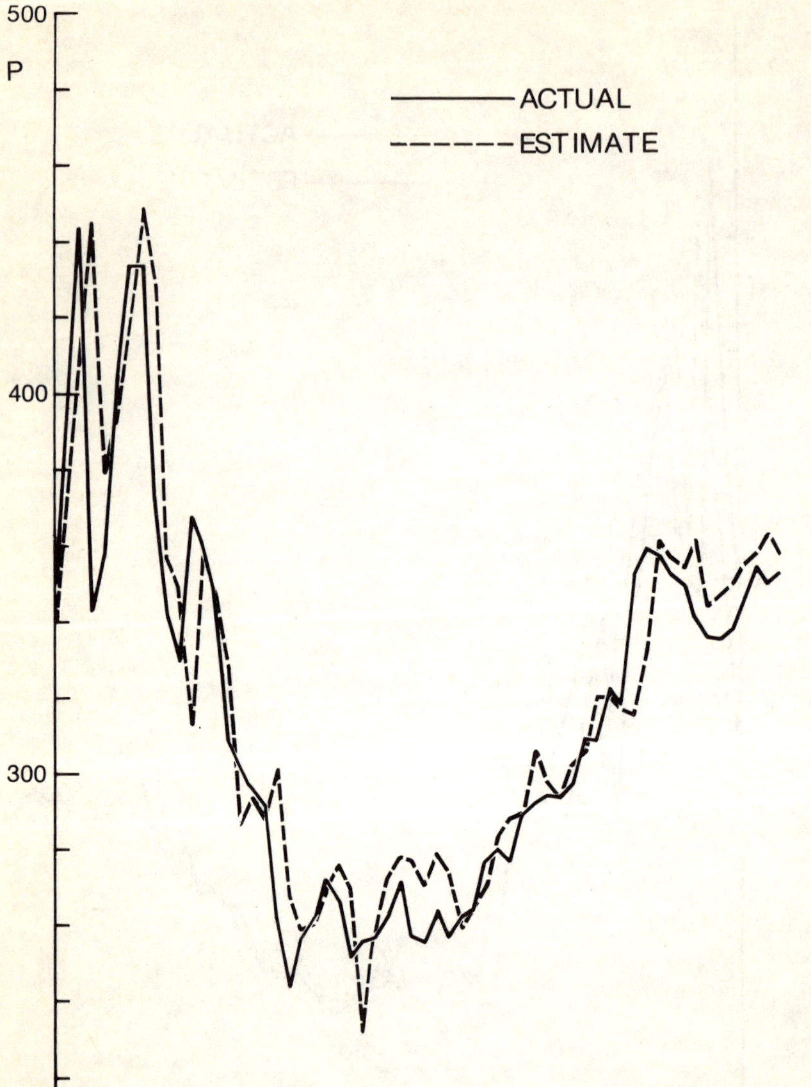

Figure 1.8: Wool Model: Unhedged Storage

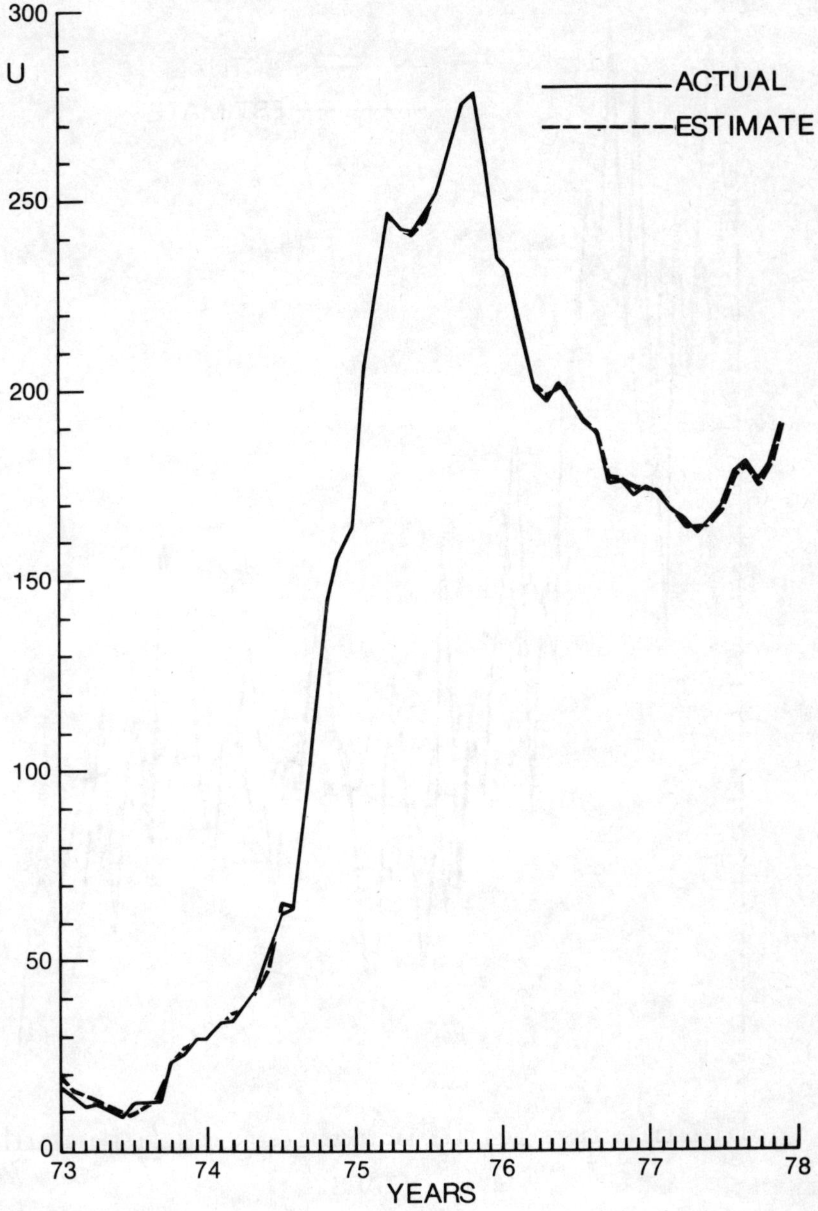

Figure 1.9: Wool Model: Hedged Storage

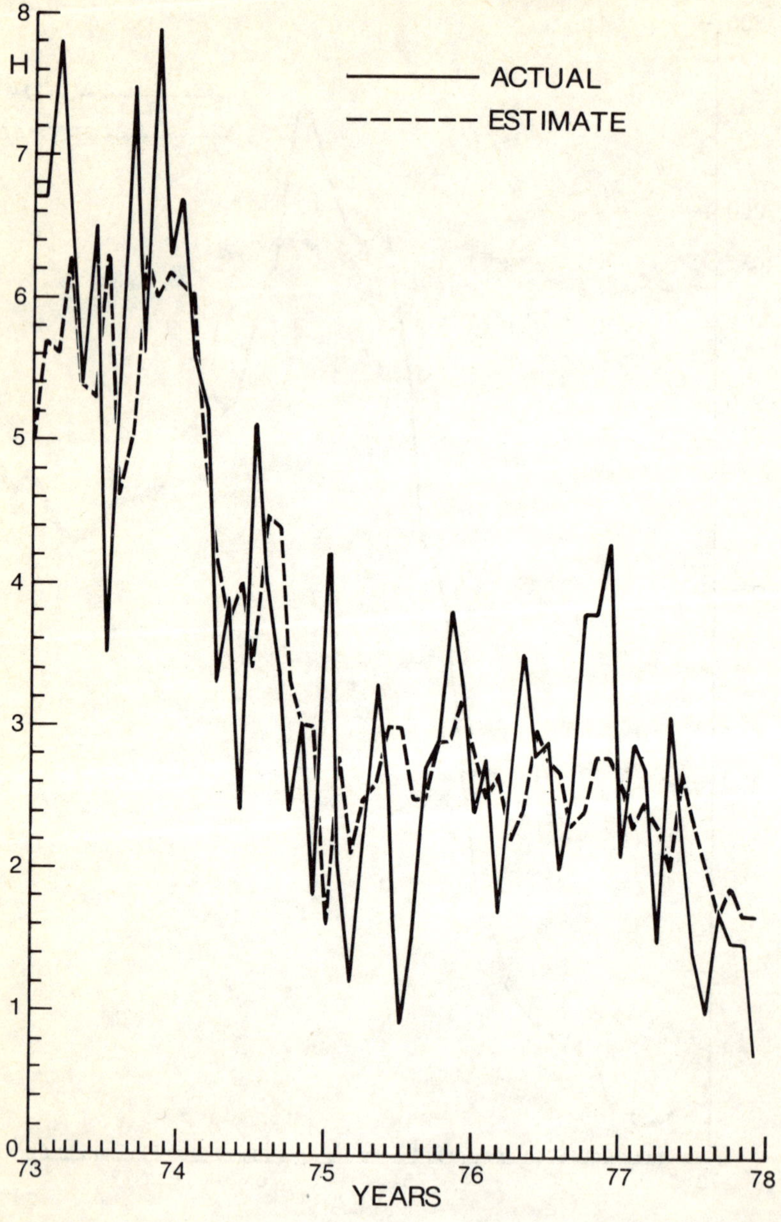

both models' performances is that consumption and both cash and futures price variables are well determined. Overall, the results for the soybeans model in Table 1.4 are markedly superior to those for the wool model, the averages of the per cent RMSE figures being 23.77 per cent and 40.71 per cent respectively. However, there is equal variability in the explanation of the endogenous variables in the two models, the corresponding coefficients of variation for these per cent RMSE figures being 1.08 and 1.03 respectively.[14]

The results for each equation in turn can now be considered. In equation (1) for soybeans, which represents the supply of hedged storage and futures by short hedgers, the estimates support the view that these economic agents adjust their supply of hedged storage directly in response to changes in the futures price, and inversely with changes in the spot price, a result which would seem to be consistent with that obtained by Rutledge (1972) for a portfolio based model. The estimates also support the view that short hedgers adjust their positions directly with changes in the ratio of the price of bean futures to that of meal futures, and directly with the ratio of bean futures to soybean oil futures prices, a result which is consistent with the 'reverse crush' hypothesis (although neither of these estimates is significant). In addition, the commercial stocks variable, which represents the influence of inventories eligible for hedging, enters with a significant coefficient.

The estimates support the view that short hedgers in the case of wool (equation (1a)) also vary their supply of storage directly with the price spread, a result which evidently had not been obtained previously for Australian wool, and the associated parameter estimate is significant. Non-AWC stocks represent wool inventories eligible for hedging, and the estimate of this coefficient is significant.

In Section 1.2 it was suggested that it is reasonable to expect the demand for hedged storage by long hedgers (equation (2)) to vary inversely with the spread between the futures price and the forward actuals price (for which the cash price has been used as a proxy) for reasons of prospective gain from price spread changes. The estimates for soybeans tend to support this hypothesis, with the estimate of the coefficient of the price spread in equation (2) having the correct sign, although lacking significance. The other variables, which represent the forward commitments of long hedgers, also lack significance. Although the crush hedge is an important option for soybean processors, the preliminary estimation of the simultaneous system did not support this hypothesis, possibly because, as suggested by Andreas (1955), opportunities for such a hedge may exist only for a few days each year. The hypothesis of the crush hedge, it will be recalled, requires these agents to adjust their positions inversely with the ratios of bean to meal futures prices and bean to oil futures prices.

In the long hedging equation for Australian wool (equation (2a)), the parameter estimate for the price spread also has the predicted sign and is significant, as is the estimate of the dummy variable (D_5') representing the impact of the Japanese textile industry on the Australian wool market. While economic theory is relatively uninformative about the behaviour of long hedgers (which is reflected in the dearth of statistical evidence on this issue), the results reported here may be one of the first empirical contributions to the analysis of long hedger behaviour.

It was hypothesised in Section 1.2 that the consumption of soybeans varies directly with income, and with the consumption of beef, poultry and pig meat, inversely with the price of soybeans and in a direction unspecified *a priori*, with the price of corn. The estimates obtained for equation (3) suggest that the consumption of soybeans varies directly with the slaughter of beef, with income, and with the consumption of pig meat.

The estimates also suggest that consumption of soybeans varies inversely with the cash price of soybeans relative to that of beef, and inversely with the price of soybeans relative to that of corn, which is consistent with the view that soybeans and corn are substitutes in production. The positive coefficient on the price of soybeans relative to that of broilers suggests that consumption of soybeans varies directly with the consumption of broilers only if changes in broiler prices are predominantly supply induced, although the coefficient on the relative price of beef is consistent with the view that changes in beef prices are demand induced. Only the very first of this group of estimates is clearly significant, although the estimate of the coefficient of the relative price of corn borders on significance.

The consumption equation for soybeans performs the best of all soybeans equations in terms of intra-sample prediction, as shown in Table 1.4. Nevertheless, the consumption equation for wool (equation (3a)) performs the best of all twelve behavioural relationships, with its significant estimate of relative price elasticities, its jointly significant seasonal dummies, and a textile production index to capture changes in tastes and population.

Preliminary estimation suggested that the demand for unhedged storage (U_t) is an inverse function of the current spot price and, in the case of soybeans, of the marginal risk premium; and a direct function of the expected spot price, where the price expectations of this group of agents were represented by the adaptive expectations hypothesis. For soybeans, none of the parameters is statistically significant, which suggests that an alternative expectations hypothesis, possibly that of rational expectations, may be more appropriate for this market. In the case of wool, the unhedged storage relationship (equation (4a)), and in particular the adaptive expectations hypothesis, has performed better with parameter estimates showing anticipated signs and significance. The wool result is encouraging in that most wool inventories are unhedged, compared with the soybeans market, which has a higher hedging ratio.

Thus, the adaptive expectations hypothesis, although devised by Nerlove to explain 'normal' or long-term expectations, has performed reasonably well in the explanation of short- and medium-term behaviour of holders of unhedged inventories in the markets studied here. In both equations the estimate of the coefficient of U_{t-1}, which is the adaptive expectations adjustment coefficient, lies between zero and unity as required, and is significant in the wool model. It is interesting that very similar rates of adjustment have been estimated in each case. We are aware of the limitations of this hypothesis, in particular that if current expectations are correct, no revision will be made to expectations even in the face of new information. In the short run however, such new information is likely to affect the expectational error and, if random, should not lead to bias in the parameter estimates of expectational variables. Moreover, the tendency of the adaptive expectations hypothesis to understate (in times of persistent inflation) or overstate (during persistent deflation) the true expectation should not affect the estimates, because the sample period exhibited neither of these phenomena.

It is convenient to discuss together the equations for long speculative positions (FLS_t) and short speculative positions (SS_t) in futures. As outlined in Section 1.2, it is hypothesised that these speculative positions are functions of the current futures price and a series of dummy variables representing shifts in expectations. While the expectational dummies do not contain any information about the way in which expectations are formed or revised, they do at least present a refutable hypothesis. It is expected that FLS_t will be inversely related to the current futures price and recession dummies, and directly related to dummies representing the expectation of a boom. In the case of soybeans, all estimates of coefficients have the expected signs, although only one, that attached to a stagnation dummy variable near the middle of the sample period, approaches significance. In the corresponding wool equation only the boom and textile consumption revival dummy variables were retained after preliminary estimation. In this case, significance is confined to the coefficients of the futures price and the international commodity boom dummy variable.

The function representing short speculative positions in futures (SS_t) was hypothesised to be directly related to the current futures price and recession expectational dummies, and inversely related to boom dummy variables. In the soybeans equation only the international boom and recession dummies for the period to December 1976 were retained after the preliminary analysis, and only the second of these is significant. All parameter estimates for the SS_t function for wool have the expected signs. The coefficients of the futures price and recession dummies are significant. In the case of wool, only the international recession and textile consumption stagnation variables survived preliminary estimation.

4. Conclusions

This paper analyses a simultaneous equations model of price determination and market allocation between storage and consumption. The model is based on the theoretical treatment by Peston and Yamey (1960), and also draws on the analysis of Goss and Giles (1980). The paper presents the comparative specification and parameter estimates of this system for the US soybeans and Australian wool markets, two large international markets, each of which performs its forward pricing function in an unbiased fashion (Tomek and Gray, 1970; Giles and Goss, 1980).

This model has shown itself to be a potentially complete and sensitive vehicle for analysing commodity market phenomena, although our investigation of alternative expectations hypotheses, especially for speculative futures relationships, is still in its early stages.

The model pays particular attention to hedging behaviour and speculation in both cash and futures markets, as well as consumption relationships. In the comparative empirical exercise reported here, the first to be undertaken on the Peston-Yamey model, the system performs better for soybeans than for wool, and in the case of soybeans, better for the futures market than for the cash market (although the consumption equation performs well). The soybeans results, while not optimal, are encouraging as the soybeans futures market is one of the most active futures markets in the United States. Moreover, for the soybeans futures market, the model has performed better with the relationships for long and short hedgers than with those for speculators, which is helpful in view of the high hedging ratio in this market.

In the case of wool, the model has performed better in the cash market than in the futures market, and both the consumption and unhedged inventory relationships perform quite well. This is again helpful, as most wool inventories are held unhedged.

In conclusion, these results are sufficiently encouraging to warrant further refinement of the individual equations, especially the speculative futures relationships, and the application of the model to other commodity futures markets.

Notes

1. It also draws on the model of the Australian wool market estimated in Goss and Giles (1980).

2. We do not imply that hedging is done primarily for the purpose of risk reduction. Indeed, in general, hedging may be defined as a position in futures, in conjunction with an actuals position of opposite sign, in pursuit of gain subject to a risk constraint. Nevertheless, hedgers in this model are assumed to hold actuals and futures in a one-for-one ratio, except for (unknown) errors of measurement in the data. Futures positions not matched by actuals commitments, or actuals positions not hedged are assumed to be included in the appropriate speculative category.

3. This does not imply that these traders plan to take delivery under the futures contracts. They are said to demand storage because they plan to acquire the physical commodity in the following period. These traders are using the futures contract as a substitute for a merchandising contract (see Working, 1953).

4. The original Peston-Yamey model did not distinguish separate categories for long hedgers and short speculators, so that the supply of hedged storage was provided by short hedgers, while the demand for hedged storage was assumed to be provided by long speculators in futures.

5. These futures positions would be taken in appropriate proportions. The crushing operation yields, from one bushel (60 lb) of soybeans, 48 lb of meal and 11 lb of oil, one pound being lost in processing. Hence a crush hedge for each 100,000 bushels of beans would require the purchase of 20 bean contracts (5,000 bushels each) and the sale of 24 meal contracts (100 tons each) together with the sale of 18.3 oil contracts (60,000 lb each). (See also Andreas, 1955; Williams, 1956; and Parrott, 1977.)

6. The soybean oil which is also produced is used in food products and has industrial uses.

7. This statement assumes that there is not marked diversity of individual expectations. (See Kaldor, 1939, 1961; Goss, 1972.)

8. It is intended that later work will focus on the rational expectations hypothesis in this context.

9. For soybeans a six months future is defined as follows:

when the month is January, the future is July;
when the month is February, the future is August;
when the month is March, the future is September;
when the month is April, May, the future is November;
when the month is June, July, the future is January;
when the month is August, September, the future is March;
when the month is October, November, the future is May;
when the month is December, the future is July.

10. Our enquiries reveal that the typical duration of a hedge in wool on the Sydney Futures Exchange is approximately four and a half months, most frequently in a future approximately six months from maturity. The definition of a six months future is:

when the month is January, February the future is July;
when the month is March, April, the future is October;
when the month is May, June, July, the future is December;
when the month is August, September, the future is March;
when the month is October, November, the future is May;
when the month is December, the future is July.

11. For example, equation (2) becomes:

$$FLH_t = \rho_2 FLH_{t-1} + \theta_7(1 - \rho_2) + \theta_8(P_t - A_t) - \rho_2\theta_8 (P_{t-1} - A_{t-1}) + \theta_9 C_{t+2} - \rho_2\theta_9 C_{t+1} + \theta_{10} X_{t+2} - \rho_2\theta_{10} X_{t+1} + \varepsilon_{2t}$$

12. Discussions with some major Floor Members on the Sydney Futures Exchange indicated that they would have expected long and short hedgers each to adjust their market positions by at least 200 contracts in response to a price change of three cents, during the period studied.

13. In the discussion of equation (3) in Section 1.2, the prior sign of θ_{15} was hypothesised to be negative. The estimated positive parameter is interpreted in the subsequent discussion.

14. The authors have recently re-assessed the wool consuption and stocks data used in this study, and the wool model is being re-estimated with the revised data. No substatial change in the nature of the results is expected. Interested readers should contact the authors for details of these results.

References

Andreas, D. (1955), 'Commodity Markets and the Processor', paper presented at the Eighth Annual Symposium of the Chicago Board of Trade; reprinted in A. E. Peck (ed.), *Views from the Trade: Readings in Futures Markets* Book 3, Chicago, Board of Trade, 1978

Brennan, M. J. (1958), 'The Supply of Storage', *American Economic Review, 48*, 50–72

Bureau of Agricultural Economics (1967), *The Price Elasticity of Demand for Wool in the United Kingdom*, Wool Economic Research Report No. 11, Canberra

Commodity Year Book (1979), New York, Commodity Research Bureau

Giles, D. E. A. and Goss, B. A. (1980), 'The Predictive Quality of Futures Prices, with an Application to the Sydney Wool Futures Market', *Australian Economic Papers, 19*(35), 291–300

Goss, B. A. (1972), *The Theory of Futures Trading*, London, Routledge and Kegan Paul

Goss, B. A. and Giles, D. E. A. (1980), 'Price Determination and Storage in the Australian Wool Market', Monash University, Department of Economics, Seminar Paper No. 12/80

Kaldor, N. (1939, 1961), 'Speculation and Economic Stability', *Review of Economic Studies*, 7. Reprinted in N. Kaldor (ed.), *Essays on Economic Stability and Growth*, London, Duckworth

Nerlove, M. (1958), 'Adaptive Expectations and Cobweb Pheonomena', *Quarterly Journal of Economics, 72*, 227–40

Parrott, R. B. (1977), 'The Practice of Business: A Professional's View of Hedging', *Business Horizons*, June; reprinted in A. E. Peck (ed.), *Views from the Trade: Readings in Futures Markets* Book 3, Chicago, Board of Trade, 1978

Peston, M. H. and Yamey, B. S. (1960), 'Intertemporal Price Relationships with Forward Markets: a Method of Analysis', *Economica, 27*, 355–67

Rockwell, C. S. (1967), 'Normal Backwardation, Forecasting, and the Returns to Commodity Futures Traders', *Food Research Institute Studies, 7*, Supplement, 107–30.

Rutledge, D. J. S. (1972), 'Hedgers' Demand for Futures Contracts: A Theoretical Framework with Applications to the United States Soybean Complex', *Food Research Institute Studies, 11*(3), 237–56

Tomek, W. G. and Gray, R. W. (1970), 'Temporal Relationships Among Prices on Commodity Futures Markets', *American Journal of Agricultural Economics, 52*(3), 372–80

Williams, R. (1956), 'How a Soybean Processor Makes Use of Futures Markets', paper presented at the Ninth Annual Symposium of the Chicago Board of Trade; reprinted in A. E. Peck (ed.), *Views from the Trade: Readings in Futures Markets* Book 3, Chicago, Board of Trade, 1978

Working, H. (1953), 'Futures Trading and Hedging', *American Economic Review, 43*, 314–43

Wymer, C. R. (1977a), *Computer Programs: RESIMUL Manual*, Washington DC, International Monetary Fund, mimeo

Wymer, C. R. (1977b), *Computer Programs: TRANSF Manual*, Washington DC, International Monetary Fund, mimeo

2 TESTING THE EFFICIENCY OF THE TIN FUTURES MARKET ON THE LONDON METAL EXCHANGE

Valerie G. Brasse
City University, London

Successful trading in futures markets of contracts for such varied commodities as grains, livestock, metals, foreign currencies and financial instruments has prompted prolific analysis into these markets' major functions. These are considered to be principally the provision of facilities for risk management as well as the guidance of inventory levels and the establishment of forward prices. In the past much emphasis has been placed on the first of these functions whilst the literature has treated the remaining two as so closely entwined that evidence of their separate performance has rarely been stressed. Yet clearly their relative importance differs for different commodities. Inventory guidance is crucial for the efficient working of most soft commodity markets but has little or no role to play in the money markets.

This paper, however, concentrates on the rational price formation function of futures markets with respect to the LME tin market. If metal traders, rather than producers, in fact use futures prices as expected output prices when allocating resources, an assessment of the 'quality'[1] of these prices is essential. In other words, we are concerned with the efficiency of the market in the sense first used by Fama.

Briefly, a market is said to be efficient when prices fully reflect all available information. Thus at any point in time, t, an actuals price will emerge that reflects current information on supply and demand. Simultaneously, current expectations concerning future levels of supply and demand will be fed into the today's futures price of a contract maturing in time t+j. If the market is efficient then the futures price ${}_tP_{t+j}$ may differ from the actuals price of the contract maturing in period t+j, A_{t+j} for two reasons; first because the futures price may reflect the presence of a market premium;[2] second because of the receipt of new information. This will change traders' expectations, and impinge on the whole range of prices in the market. This in no sense implies that the expired future was incorrectly priced before its expiration, nor that the pre-existing intertemporal price relationship was in error; this may or may not have been correct in relation to information then available. But new information and events may simply make the previous period's forecasts obsolete. Moreover, since in competitive markets this new information is generated randomly, the difference between the futures price in period t and the actuals price that emerges in period t+j will be a purely random number incapable of estimation by a study of previous prices.

Thus, if the market is efficient futures prices will exhibit two separate though related characteristics. First futures prices will follow a random walk (indeed Samuelson (1965) has shown that in a perfect market futures prices will behave as a martingale model); and second, futures prices will provide the best available estimates of the subsequent actuals prices (or more precisely of the matured futures prices).[3]

Just how well futures markets perform their forward pricing function, and whether futures prices are unbiased predictors of subsequent actuals prices remain empirical issues. In the past, two main methods of testing the unbiased estimation hypothesis have been employed. The first (and most common) is to use simple linear regression.

Typically in these studies the final actuals price is regressed on some futures price j months prior to maturity and the joint hypothesis tested that the intercept equals zero and the slope equals 1.

Such a function, however, tends to be seriously misspecified due to the classic error in the variables bias and there will usually be considerable autocorrelation among the residuals if ordinary least squares regression is employed. To circumvent this, econometricians have opted for instrumental variable estimation (Goss, 1981). Alternatively mean squared error techniques have been used.

The evidence to date tends to support the view that lagged futures prices are unbiased predictors of actual prices for a range of US continuous inventory agricultural commodities, such as corn, soya beans and coffee (Tomek and Gray, 1970; Kofi, 1973), for Australian wool (Giles and Goss, 1980) and for some currencies (Hansen and Hodrick, 1980). However, the evidence does not support the unbiased prediction hypothesis for discontinuous inventory commodities such as potatoes (Kofi, 1973) or non-inventory commodities such as finished live beef cattle

(Leuthold, 1974). Indeed the evidence is rather mixed. For example, Yamey (1977) finds the predictive performance of futures prices in the Liverpool cotton market to have been no better than that of futures prices in the US potatoes market even though the former commodity is a continuous inventory commodity and the latter is not.

In the only published study of metals futures Goss (1981) found that over the years 1971–78 the tin market[4] on the London Metal Exchange performed its forward pricing role quite well, copper and zinc markets were a qualified success but that the lead market failed the unbiased prediction test altogether.

What these 'weak' form tests of the efficient market hypothesis fail to establish is whether the forecast error, where it exists, between the current period futures price and the subsequent actuals price is due to uncertainty (that is lack of information), to poor speculation (that is lack of judgement and/or lack of capital) or to the presence of a market premium. No useful normative policy implications can therefore be drawn on the finding of bias unless we can determine its source.

Holbrook Working wrote, as early as 1949, that the sources of market mistakes are information and judgement and he classified the market inaccuracies as either 'necessary' or 'objectionable'. An efficient market contains only necessary inaccuracy: price changes are due to new information. Any error beyond that is objectionable inaccuracy, often termed speculative error and it is likely to result from the bad judgement of traders or from non-competitive market situations.

The simple linear regression mentioned earlier in the 'weak' form test of the efficient market hypothesis lacks a performance norm with which to compare results. If prices reflect all publicly available information as it is released, the market is said to be semi-strong efficient. The efficiency of the market in this sense is tested by examining whether the expectations formed reflect currently available information.

There have been few published empirical semi-strong form tests applied to commodities. The first was conducted by Leuthold and Hartmann (1979) for the live hog futures market. In this study they designed an econometric model using relevant available information to forecast hog prices. Using two alternative methods of evaluation they found that on occasion their econometric model forecast more accurately subsequent actuals prices than did the futures market. This suggests the presence of objectionable inaccuracies in the hog futures market.

Hansen and Hodrick (1980) carried out a semi-strong form test for several currencies in the foreign exchange market and found the simple efficiency hypothesis to be suspect for some currencies. Using commercial econometric models Rausser and Just (1979) observed that futures prices performed better for soya bean oil and meal, econometric forecasts were preferable for livestock commodities while results for other commodities were mixed.

This paper draws on the Leuthold and Hartmann technique and applies it to the tin futures market. The econometric model developed here serves several purposes. First, it acts as a performance norm with which to compare the forward pricing record of tin futures prices. Second, it provides a test as to whether the marked fluctuations in the price of this internationally traded primary commodity can be explained by systematic variation in supply and demand. Third, the exercise throws light on how a competitive model of price adjustment fares when used to explain short-run price behaviour. In serving the first purpose the design of the model is deliberately kept simple. If a simple model shows the market to be inefficient, further elaboration becomes unnecessary to test the efficient market hypothesis.[5]

For a storable commodity like tin, a stock disequilibrium model of price adjustment may be set out as follows:[6]

$$C_t = aP_t + bX_t + u_t \qquad a < 0 \qquad (1)$$
$$Q_t = cP_t + dY_t + v_t \qquad c > \qquad (2)$$
$$S^d_t = f(P^e_{t+1} - P_t) + gZ_t + w_t \qquad f > 0 \qquad (3)$$
$$S_t = S_{t-1} + Q_t - C_t - (BS_t + G_t) \qquad (4)$$
$$\Delta P_t = \sigma_1 \, \Delta \, P^d_{t-1} + \sigma_2 \, (P^d_{t-1} - P_{t-1}) \qquad (5)$$

where C_t is the rate of tin consumption in period t; Q_t is the rate of production in period t; S^d_t is the desired level of stock in period t; S_t is the actual stock at the end of period t[7]; P_t is the commodity price in period t; P^e_{t+1} is the price expected to prevail at time t+1 in time t; P^d_t is some 'equilibrium' price that equates S^d_t and S_t; u_t, v_t and w_t are disturbance terms in the consumption, production and demand for stock equations respectively; X_t Y_t and Z_t are shifting variables in the same, the full specification of which will be discussed later. The model thus has five equations with five unknowns, C_t, Q_t, S_t, P_t and P^e_{t+1}. Equations (1) and (2) are the familiar demand and supply equations; equation (3) is a desired demand equation for stock and equation (4) is a stock identity. Equation (5) shows the adjustment mechanism by which prices adjust to market disequilibrium. The error correction mechanism was chosen in preference to the partial adjustment model on the ground that operators in a highly competitive market would be expected to learn quickly from their mistakes and revise their expectations accordingly. Partial adjustment never allows this learning or catching up process to be completed.

The price level that balances the short-run desired demand for stock and the short run supply may be found by inserting equations (1), (2) and (3) into equation (4)

$$S_t^d = S_t$$

or

$$P_t^d = \frac{1}{c+f+|a|}(fP_{t+1}^e + gZ_t + bX_t - dY_t - S_{t-1} + \eta_t) \qquad (6)$$

where $\eta_t = u_t + v_t + w_t$

Subtracting equation (3) from (4) and substituting equation (6) into the resulting expression yields

$$P_t^d - P_t = \frac{1}{c+f+|a|}(S_t^d - S_t) \qquad (7)$$

Equation (7) shows that the deviation of the market price from its desired (equilibrium) level is positively related to the deviation of the actual stock from its desired (equilibrium) level and is negatively related to the absolute sum of short run elasticities of supply and demand.[8] Furthermore stock and price must achieve their respective equilibria simultaneously.

If the adjustment model is to be consistent then substituting equation (7) into the price correction mechanism

$$\Delta P_t = \sigma_1 \Delta P_t^d + \sigma_2(P_{t-1}^d - P_{t-1})$$

gives

$$\Delta P_t = \sigma_1 \Delta P_t^d + \frac{\sigma_2}{c+f+|a|}(S_{t-1}^d - S_{t-1}) \qquad (8)$$

i.e. the change in prices in any period t is equal to some combination of the change in equilibrium price in that period and the deviation of actual stock from the equilibrium stock levels of the previous period.

The price adjustment mechanism may be re-written as

$$\Delta P_t = (\sigma_1 - (\sigma_1 - \sigma_2)L)\ P_t^d - \sigma_2 P_{t-1}$$

where L is the lag operator such that $Lx_t = x_{t-1}$

Thus

$$P_t = (\sigma_1 - (\sigma_1 - \sigma_2)L)P_t^d + (1 - \sigma_2)P_{t-1} \qquad (9)$$

Substituting equation (6) into equation (9) our model explains price as[9]

$$P_t = (1-\sigma_2)P_{t-1} + (\sigma_1 - (\sigma_1 - \sigma_2)L \times \left\{\frac{1}{c+f+a}(FP^e_{t+1} + gZ_t + bX_t - dY_t - S_{t-1} + \eta_t\right\} \qquad (10)$$

So while stock disequilibrium acts as a trigger for price change the actual magnitude of the change for a given amount of stock excess/shortfall depends on the determinants of P_t^d in the manner described.

Equation (10) cannot be estimated directly as it stands because several of the variables have yet to be fully specified. In particular gZ_t, which itself is a determinant of the unobservable S_t^d needs further clarification. At its simplest level there is the transaction demand for stock. To producers, stocks are final products and are held as a buffer against the imperfect synchronisation of production and consumption. Producers' demand for stock may be postulated as a positive function of the rate of consumption. To consumers, stocks are intermediate products or raw materials and are held to ensure smooth production into other final goods. Consumers' demand for stock may therefore also be expressed as a positive function of the rate of consumption, i.e. the rate of consumption of tin represents both consumers' and producers' transaction demands for stock.

The supply of storage literature emphasises the expected change in prices ($P^e_{t+1} - P_t$) as a suitable variable to be included in Z_t and hence a determinant of S_t^d. According to this the desired (optimal) level of inventory of a competitive firm that maximises its present value is $P^e_{t+1} - P_t = F(H^d_t)$ where $F(H^d_t)$ is a marginal storage cost function with $F' > 0$ and $F(0) < 0$.

Other variables included in Z_t are a trend term to take into account more efficient inventory control, dummy variables to represent, respectively, periods of unusually heavy speculation and periods when export controls imposed by the International Tin Council were in operation. It was considered that S^d_t would be positively related to the rate of inflation and negatively related to the rate of interest and the exchange rate.

The theory and practice of futures markets suggested at least two other candidates as determinants of S^d_t. One was the degree of backwardation, through its role in inventory guidance. The greater the backwardation (i.e. the greater the amount by which the actuals price exceeds the forward futures price), the greater is the reflected relative scarcity of current physical stock and the greater is the incentive for anyone holding stocks to release them before the period of relative scarcity comes to an end. The converse is also true. So, *ceteris paribus*, desired stocks will be positively related to the size of contango (backwardation being negative contango).

Finally, given the precise degree of arbitrage that occurs between London and Penang and given that our model attempts to explain prices on the LME, it might be expected that desired stock by traders on the LME would be negatively related to the ratio of the London to Penang sterling equivalent. To summarise, our complete specification of S^d_t may be represented as follows:

$$S_t = \Omega \left\{(P^e_{t+1} - P_t), C_t, T, SPEC,. EXPCON, \dot{P}/P, r, \dot{P}_f - P_s, EXCHR, \frac{\text{LME spot}}{\text{Penang}}\right\}$$

where T is a trend term

SPEC is a dummy variable to allow for excess speculation

EXPCON is a dummy variable to represent export control

$\dot{P}/P$ is the rate of inflation

r is the rate of interest

EXCHR is the effective sterling exchange rate

$P_f - P_s$ is contango (or forward premium)

$\frac{\text{LME spot}}{\text{Penang}}$ is the ratio of the LME tin spot price to its sterling equivalent ruling in Penang.

As it stands the model still contains a variable for which no suitable data can be found namely P^e_{t+1}.[10] To remedy this, it is assumed that prices in commodity markets are generated according to the rational expectations hypothesis developed by Muth (1961).[11] The relevant information set should consist only of the values of the predetermined variables in the model at the time t, i.e. we require knowledge of the complete model outlined in the set of equations (1) – (3).

The world consumption function of a commodity is postulated to depend on its own price, the price of close substitutes[12] and world money income.

$$C_t = \Phi_1 (P_t, PM_t, Y_t, P_s) \quad \frac{dC_t}{dP_t} < 0 \quad \frac{dC_t}{dPM_t} > 0$$

$$\frac{dC_t}{dY_t} > 0 \quad \frac{dC_t}{dP_s} < 0$$

This equation derives from the optimising behaviour of the consumer under a budget constraint. The exact functional form will depend on an explicit utility function, knowledge of which is not necessary for our purpose.

Similarly the level of output that maximises a short run profit function subject to the constraint of a production function under perfect competitive conditions on both the product and factor markets will depend on prices lagged one period and a trend term to account for increased productive capacity or capital stock in the production function.

Thus

$$Q_t = (P_{t-1}, T) \quad \frac{dQ_t}{dP_{t-1}} > 0 \quad \frac{dQ_t}{dT} > 0$$

Short-run variable costs such as labour and raw materials are ignored. Expected price may therefore be presented by the following linear equation:

$$P^e_{t+1} = a_0 + a_1 PM_t + a_2 Y + a_3 P_A + a_4 P_{t-1} \tag{11}$$

where PM is a world price, Y is world income, P_A is the price of aluminium and P_{t-1} is the lagged commodity price.[13,14] From the mathematical expression of the rational expectations hypothesis we have that $P_{t+1} = P^e_{t+1} + e_t$, where e_t is a stochastic disturbance with zero mean and is uncorrelated with P^e_{t+1}. A simple test of equation (11) can be made using the actual observed price in the next period, P_{t+1}, as the dependent variable.

From the results (see Appendix 2.1) it can be shown that only the price of aluminium and world money income generate significant coefficients. For this reason and to mitigate the multi-collinearity between the stock trend term and world income, only the former variable, the price of aluminium, was used to represent price expectations, P^e_{t+1}, in the main model.

Before proceeding further with our estimation of the model a word is in order about the data. Reliable data existed for most variables with the exception of tin stocks. Whenever these stocks, as reported in the International Tin Council's Statistical bulletin, appeared inconsistent with movements in consumption and production, the following identity was adopted: the change in stocks in every period equals the difference between production and consumption: This procedure requires stock data for at least one year, and the year selected was one for which data on consumption, production and stocks were in closest agreement.

The main model was estimated using monthly data, but to do this we must make a simple assumption concerning buffer stock net purchases/sales. These figures are released quarterly so for our purposes the quarter's activity is deemed to occur in the last month of that quarter. This procedure seems acceptable since with the exception of periods when buffer stock intervention is great and its direction therefore known, as when the tin price approaches the International Tin Agreement's floor/ceiling price, market participants have little knowledge of the buffer stock manager's activities and these cannot therefore enter into their own decision making. Moreover, between January 1977 when the buffer stock ran out of tin altogether, and the end of our sample period it has stopped being a market influence.

Equation (10) was estimated several times in an attempt to reduce the problem of multi-collinearity between some of the independent variables, in particular the exchange rate, interest rate and rate of inflation. The inclusion of all three monetary variables had a dampening effect on at least two of the coefficients. Since the inflation variable consistently performed better than the other two, this was retained.

Moreover, in early runs of the model, the coefficient of the lagged stock variable, though usually of the right sign was rarely significant. This can be explained by noticing that the coefficient of backwardation was always highly significant. The degree of backwardation, as pointed out earlier, bears a direct relationship to the level of stocks. By removing the former the coefficient of the latter becomes significant, as the theory of the model dictates.

All the equations were estimated using Hendry's GIVE program, and were tested for autoregressive restrictions. These, however, proved to be invalid and the inclusion of lagged variables in the unrestricted form added little or nothing to the significance of the regression as a whole. The coefficients of the lagged parameters have not therefore been included in the results shown. One of the best estimates obtained that was consistent with the theory was explained as follows: (see Appendix 2.1)

$$P_t = b_0 + b_1 S_{t-1} + b_2 P_{t-1} + b_3 EXPCON + b_4 SPEC + b_5 \dot{P}/P + b_6 T + b_7 \frac{LMESPOT}{Penang} \qquad (12)$$

Plots were undertaken of the residuals. The inclusion of a dummy variable to represent speculation failed to capture all the unusual extranous events of 1974. But the really large discrepancies appear in the second half of 1977 and continue through 1978 when the fitted actuals price lay continually below the path of the actual actuals price. This is reflected in the poor predictive test statistics (Chow Test F (20,91) = 5.57) such that the equation fails this ex-post predictive test.

The explanation is not hard to find. The 20 months chosen to test for parameter stability coincide with a period in the international tin market when traders' expectations were continuously frustrated. The US GSA program was officially suspended in June 1978 but rumours were rife from the previous year onwards of a new Bill to be passed through Congress authorising the sale of another 30,000 tons of tin (roughly one-sixth of world annual consumption of tin) out of a stockpile of 200,629 tons. The Bill was not in fact passed until December 1979. The result of these misplaced expectations and the consequent running down of industrial stocks was a dramatic rise in the price of tin which this model could not have foreseen.

Our primary purpose in setting up this econometric model has been to provide a performance norm with which to evaluate the forward pricing ability of the tin futures market in a semi-strong form context. As equation (10) was finally estimated (in the format of equation (12)) several of the variables appeared in the current period to explain the current price. Ideally we require an equation which uses information available in period t–1 to estimate the price in period t. So equation (12) was re-estimated using the data lagged one month (see Appendix 2.1). A comparison of the two equations shows little difference in either the significance of the whole regression or its ability to predict the spot price over the sample period. Armed with the knowledge of the relevant variables in period t–1 it is now possible to judge whether the tin futures price in period t–1[15] can better predict the actuals price in period t than can the econometric model. The tin futures price, measured as the monthly average of daily closing prices, can be interpreted as the expectation of the future actuals price or as a 'forecast'. From this it can be inferred if the futures market appears to be using all the information available and conforming to the expectations hypothesis.

Drawing on Leuthold and Hartmann, two statistical measures were chosen to evaluate the two 'forecasts'. The first is the root mean squared error, computed as

$$\text{RMSE} = (\Sigma(P-A)^2/n)^{1/2}$$

where P is the predicted value and A is the actual value. It is a good approximation of the size of the unsigned errors, with large errors carrying more weight than small errors through the squaring process.

The second measure is a composite prediction evaluation. Leuthold and Hartmann explain the procedure as follows, 'Predictions from the futures market and the econometric model are essentially conditional expectations of subsequent cash prices as implied by the structure of the model and sets of information available. If these two predictors are combined and they utilise the available information with equal efficiency they should then contribute equally to the accuracy of the composite prediction. If one explanatory variable contributes more to the variation of the dependent variable than the other explanatory variable the former can be said to be from the more efficient price discovery model or market' (p.485).

Assuming that the futures market and econometric model are individually unbiased predictors of the subsequent cash price the following composite prediction model can be specified:

$$PT_t = b({}_{t-i}FPT)_t + (1-b)({}_{t-i}PPT)_t + e_t$$

Where PT_t is the realised cash price of tin at time t, $({}_{t-i}FPT)_t$ is the futures price of tin for t observed at time t-i (here i=1) and

Table 2.1: RMSE and Composite Regression Weights, 1969–78

Time Period	RMSE		Composite Regression Weights	
	FPT	PPT	FPT	PPT
1969	29.3	40.1	1.73 (4.17)	−0.72 (−1.73)
1970	43.4	66.7	0.89 (3.3)	0.1 (0.39)
1971	20.1	30.9	1.34 (3.12)	−0.35 (−0.81)
1972	27.5	33.5	0.67 (1.52)	0.34 (0.77)
1973	161.6	123.8	1.07 (1.24)	−0.01 (−0.01)
1974	297.4	227.4	0.15 (2.94)	0.87 (17.82)
1975	95.0	93.2	0.31 (1.42)	0.68 (3.15)
1976	186.8	141.0	−0.08 (−0.4)	1.07 (5.73)
1977	338.4	405.1	−0.06 (−0.17)	1.1 (2.99)
1978	357.4	584.7	−0.43 (−1.08)	1.53 (3.67)
1969–1978	201.1	247.9	0.19 (4.08)	0.84 (17.8)

Note: All figures in parentheses are t-ratios.

$({}_{t-i}PPT)_t$ is the predicted cash price for t observed at time $t-i$ and generated from the econometric model. Theoretically if both forecasts are equally efficient b should equal 0.5 The coefficients reflect the weights of the individual predictors and their marginal contribution to the composite predictor. The composite model is estimated by Ordinary Least Squares.

Table 2.1 shows for annual forecast periods and the combined ten-year period the RMSE and the composite regression weights as defined. Unfortunately the results for the whole period (as given on the bottom line of each table) are contradictory. The RMSE for the futures market is considerably less than for the econometric model, suggesting the former is more efficient. However, the futures market exhibits a smaller composite weight suggesting that the contrary is true. Examination of the results year by year shows that the econometric model has a smaller RMSE in four out of ten years. In 1977 and 1978 the RMSE for the econometric model is enormous, confirming our earlier observations that the model's predictions were well off course. Judging by the composite weights, the econometric model was the better performer in five out of the ten years.[16] It is worthwhile noticing that in the highly volatile years of 1974 and 1976 both measures indicate the econometric model to be the more efficient.[17]

Conclusions

This paper concludes that the tin futures market has not consistently used all the available market information. At times it has reacted quite slowly to the receipt of new information such that forward price changes have been predictable and the presence of objectionable inaccuracies confirmed.[18] Tin futures prices cannot therefore be consistently relied upon to reflect accurately subsequent actuals prices.

There are no institutional rules to be blamed for this. The most likely explanation is the poor quality of speculation, corroborated by earlier observations that the econometric model outperforms the futures market (by both criteria) when prices are highly volatile. During world economic and political crises the base metals have, in the wake of the precious metals, become refuges for speculative cash.[19] Such movements in and out of commodity futures markets may be effected by people with little or no knowledge of the relevant markets and with interests that differ from those of commodity speculators as such. Whether these errors cause resources to be misallocated in production decisions is beyond this analysis owing to the short time horizon involved. But reliance by producers and traders on inaccurate futures prices as expected cash prices may cause them to lose confidence in the market and so ignore its potential in risk management (even though successful hedging can be effected in inefficient markets). Finally a comment on the nature of the semi-strong form test of efficiency. Our underlying concern throughout is to establish whether a market with futures trading fares better than one without. But it may be that the results obtained using an econometric model are affected by the presence (or absence) of futures trading. In particular, futures markets yield a basis (contango or backwardation), which is a price for storage and which therefore influences stocks. More generally, if the participants in a market typically interpret fundamentals in supply and demand correctly, futures prices will tend to predict eventual actuals prices well. And economic models which take account of market fundamentals will also yield good price forecasts. But if market participants behave irrationally and ignore market fundamentals this will be reflected in market prices. The same model will now 'forecast' poorly since market prices reflect only the immediate market fundamentals together with the market's irrational views regarding the next period. In this respect the performance of economic models and futures prices as forecasts of eventual prices are likely to be strongly inter-related. It should thus be borne in mind when performing this type of test that a reasonably functioning futures market may cause prices to be more predictable by means of models.

Appendix 2.1: Selected Regression Results

Equation 12 using monthly data for the years 1968–78

	1	2
Constant	1619.8	1673.1
	(3.73)	(3.77)
S_{t-1}	−0.0066	−0.0096
	(2.02)	(2.74)
P_{t-1}	0.75	0.71
	(12.25)	(10.7)
EXPCON	−143.7	−163.9
	(3.50)	(3.56)
SPEC	129.5	145.1
	(2.46)	(2.57)
·P/P	4.85	5.78
	(4.79)	(4.99)
PENANG	−119.9	−107.4
	(3.11)	(2.69)
T	−6.84	−8.43
	(3.51)	(3.78)
R^2	0.99	0.99
Durbin-Watson	1.75	1.71
CHOW F (20, 91)	5.57	5.4

Col. 1 shows the coefficients of equation (12) as set out in the text.
Col. 2 shows the coefficients of the same equation when all the observations are lagged one period.
(The t-ratios are in parentheses below their respective coefficient)

Equation (11) was estimated using annual data as follows:

$$P_{t+1} = \underset{(-1.73)}{0.76}\, P_{t-1} - \underset{(-1.52)}{46.48}\, PM_t + \underset{(3.7)}{214.0}\, P_A + \underset{(2.78)}{4.31}\, Y_t$$

Appendix 2.2: Definitions

TINCON — World monthly rate of consumption of primary tin metal (ooo's tons) as reported in the International Tin Council's Statistical Bulletin.

S_t — Tin metal stocks as defined by the following identity: S_{t-1} + (excess of tin production less consumption) − (BS–G) where

BS	is the quarterly net purchase of tin metal by the Buffer Stock manager in ooo's tons as reported in the ITC Statistical Bulletin.
G	is the net monthly US General Services Administration purchase (source as above).
EXP CON	is a dummy variable for export control =0 Jan. 1968 – Sept. 1968, Jan. 1970 – Mar. 1975, Apr. 1976 – Dec. 1978. = 1 Oct. 1968 – Dec. 1969, Apr. 1975 – Mar. 1976
SPEC	is a dummy variable representing speculative activity = 1 for 1974 = 0 for all other years.
P_t	is the monthly average LME actuals price for standard tin.
$P_f - P_s$	is the monthly average backwardation (– ve)/contango (+ ve) using monthly average futures and actuals prices for LME standard tin.
P/P	is a measure of inflation using the UK monthly wholesale price index 1963 =100.
P_A	is the monthly average producer price of 99.5% virgin ingot aluminium (in cents per lb) in New York according to American Metal Market quote.
EXCHR	is the Sterling effective exchange rate on the Smithsonian basis 1971= 100.
r	is the Treasury Bill yield/average discount expressed as a rate at which interest is earned during the life of the Bills.
PM_t	is the UN export price index of manufactures as a proxy for world prices.
Y_t	is the OECD GDP at average 1975 prices and exhange rates.

All data gathered monthly, quarterly or annually over the period 1968 – 1978.

(Equation 12 estimated using monthly data)

Notes

1. 'Quality' here refers to the extent that futures prices accurately predict subsequent actuals prices.
2. We use the term market premium to stress that its source may not derive from risk consideration alone.
3. There are technical reasons for a non-zero or non-random *maturity* basis, see Goss and Yamey (1976). However, the range of this basis is likely to be so small that for the purpose of this discussion it has been assumed away altogether.
4. Goss observed that the tin actuals price was poorly estimated by its own three month futures using OLS estimates but fared considerably better when using instrumental variable estimation.
5. The converse is not, however, true. A simple model which appears to suggest that the market is efficient may in fact reflect a poor model with misspecification errors.
6. Specific assumptions of the model are that agents operate in a competitive market, are risk neutral, enjoy no transactions costs and use information rationally.
7. S_t is a measure of private stocks, i.e. those held by private traders and excludes stocks held by national and international buffer stock agencies. The tin market has for long been influenced by the International Tin Agreement (ITA) through its operation of a buffer stock, coupled, where necessary, with export controls. It has also been subject to intervention by the managers of US strategic stockpile, the General Services Administration (GSA). In equation (4) BS_t therefore refers to net purchases by the tin buffer stock and G_t denotes net purchases of stock by the GSA in period t.
8. If equations (1) to (3) are log-linear functions, then c, f and a are elasticities.
9. Equation (10) is a condensed structural form equation since the endogenous variable P_t is not just a function of the exogenous variables in the model as a reduced form equation requires. The coefficients of (10) are functions of the parameters of (1) to (5). Estimates of the coefficients of (10) will be unbiased and consistent but not the most efficient.
10. A natural candidate for P^e_{t+1} would seem to be the futures price but as we have already pointed out the futures price is not always a very useful predictor.
11. The rational expectations hypothesis is usually represented by $P^e_{t+1} = E(P_{t+1}/Inf_t)$ i.e. the predicted price for the period t+1 is equal to the expected price predicted by the model conditional on all the information available at the time the prediction was made (t). E is the expected value operator and Inf_t denotes the information set available as of time t. The rational expectations hypothesis is not perfect, however. It may ascribe to market participants more information than they are actually likely to possess.
12. The price of aluminium was chosen as the close substitute.
13. The time trend variable has been excluded from equation (11) since it is highly correlated with world income.
14. A detailed list of all data sources appears in Appendix 2.2.
15. The most obvious choice of predictor of a spot price in period t would be its own three month future price quoted in period t−3. But this would bias the comparison between the two alternative forecasts. The re-estimated equation uses information available in period t−1 which could not be known in period t−3. Hence a futures price lagged one month must be chosen, i.e. the three month price of a futures contract maturing two months after the particular cash price under consideration.
16. Because of the potential multi-collinearity problems the t-test may be distorted, but other things being equal the larger weights always have higher t-ratios.
17. Leuthold and Hartmann made the same observation with their live hog

model. It should be borne in mind, however, that the yearly results are based on only 12 observations and therefore carry less weight than the overall results.

18. Remember we ignore risk aversion in the discussion. This is not unreasonable on the basis of empirical evidence available (see also Brasse, 1982).

19. See W. C. Labys and H. C. Thomas 'Speculation, Hedging and Commodity Price Behaviour', *Applied Economics*, 1975. They calculate that the index of the volume of futures trading in tin rose from 112 in 1972 (1970=100) to 163 in 1974.

References

Brasse, V. G. (1982) 'Aspects of the Post War International Tin Market with special reference to Futures Trading', unpublished thesis of University of London

Fama, E. F. (1970) 'Efficient Capital Markets: A Review of Theory and Empirical Work', *Journal of Finance, 25*, 383–417

Giles, D. E. A. and Goss, B. A. (1980) 'The Predictive Quality of Futures Prices, with an Application to the Sydney Wool Futures Market'. *Australian Economic Papers, 19*, 291–300

Goss, B. A. (1981) 'The Forward Pricing Function of the London Metal Exchange', Monash University, Department of Economics, *Applied Economics, 13*, 133–50

Goss, B. A. and Yamey, B. S. (eds.) (1976) '*The Economics of Futures Trading*, London, Macmillan

Hansen, L. P. and L. R. Hodrick (1980) 'Forward Exchange Rates as Optimal Predictors of Futures Spot Rates: An Econometric Analysis', *Journal of Political Economy, 88*, 829–53

Hendry, B. F. (1976) 'General Instrumental Variable Estimation of Linear Equations with Endogenous and Lagged Endogenous Regressors and Autoregressive Errors', London School of Economics, mimeo

Kofi, T. A. (1973) 'A Framework for Comparing the Efficiency of Futures Markets', *American Journal of Agricultural Economics, 55*, 584–94

Leuthold, R. M. (1974) 'The Price Performance on the Futures Market of a Nonstorable Commodity: Live Beef Cattle', *American Journal of Agricultural Economics, 56*, 271–9

Leuthold, R. M. and P. A. Hartmann (1979) 'A Semi-Strong Form Evaluation of the Efficiency of the Hog Futures Market', *American Journal of Agricultural Economics, 61*, 482–9

Muth, J. F. (1961) 'Rational Expectations and the Theory of Price Movements', *Econometrica, 29*, 315–35

Rausser, G. C. and R. E. Just (1979) 'Agricultural and Commodity Price Forecasting Accuracy: Futures Markets and Commercial Econometric Models', *International Futures Trading Seminar* Chicago: Chicago Board of Trade

Samuelson, P.A. (1965) 'Proof that Properly Anticipated Prices Fluctuate Randomly', Industrial Management Review *6*, 41–50

Tomek, W. G. and Gray, R. W. (1970) 'Temporal Relationships among Prices on Commodity Futures Markets: XX Their Allocative and Stabilising Roles; *American Journal of Agricultural Economics, 52,* 372–80

Working, H. (1949) 'The Investigation of Economic Expectations', *American Economic Review, 39*, 150–66

Yamey, B. S. (1977) 'Continuous Inventories, Futures Prices and Self-fulfilling Prophecies', mimeo, London School of Economics

PART TWO

COMPETITION IN SERVICE INDUSTRIES

3 RISING CONCENTRATION: THE UK GROCERY TRADE 1970–1980[1]

C. W. F. Baden Fuller
London Business School

Introduction

Industrial economists among others have feared that an increase in concentration among sellers is likely to be detrimental to the public interest. Rising concentration is said to bring higher prices, higher barriers against new competitors and the dissipation of resources in non-price competition. Are these fears justified? Theory cannot fully justify or refute these fears; the argument hinges on evidence. Most empirical work on this issue has examined statistical relationships across samples of manufacturing (and mining) industries. Less work has been done examining industries over time, and very little work has been done on the service sector. The last omission is serious; in most Western economies the service sector is the largest and fastest growing. An examination of the UK grocery retailing trade between 1970 and 1980 casts doubt on the theory that rising concentration is always against the public interest. Some of the evidence used to support these conclusions has been drawn from the recently published Monopolies and Mergers Commission (MMC) Report on Discounts to Retailers (1981), but much has not been generally available before.

Brief Review of Theory

The economics literature suggests that rising concentration may be accompanied by some gains and costs. The gains may come from the greater efficiency in the utilisation of resources; the costs from

[1] The author alone is responsible for errors, all of which are unintentional. Grateful thanks to AGB; Michael Beesley; Mike Dent; Institute of Grocery Distribution, members of the trade; John McGee; Mary Morgan; Nielsen; Ken Tucker; Robin Wensley and Philip Williams.

the welfare losses of the higher margins which may be charged by the sellers.

Since the writing of J. S. Mill's *Principles* it has been recognised that increases in concentration may be associated with efficiency gains. These gains may occur within the industry. For example, if there were significant economies of scale or experience effects such that the most efficient firm size was larger than the current firm size, then were some firms to increase their size to take account of these unexploited gains, rises in their market share would occur. Such rises might translate into a rise in seller concentration and yet be associated with more efficient utilisation of resources. (See, for instance, Peltzman, 1977.) It will be suggested in this paper that in the UK grocery trade, such internal efficiencies have occurred but are relatively small.

Efficiency gains from rising concentration may occur outside the industry among suppliers. For example an increase in seller concentration may be accompanied by an increase in buyer concentration viewed from the suppliers' side. I shall call this effect 'buying power'. Lustgarten (1975) has observed this phenomenon in US manufacturing industry. In the UK grocery trade, the UK Monopolies and Mergers Commission (1981) has concluded that rising concentration has been associated with buying power; this paper will re-examine that evidence.

A number of economists have argued that rising concentration may bring undesirable effects. The arguments can be divided into two parts; those which consider the direct effect of increasing concentration on raising prices and those which consider the indirect effects of increasing concentration on prices by the raising of existing entry barriers.

It has been argued by Spence (1977) and others that increases in concentration may cause industry members to invest more resources in entry-deterring assets such as capacity, advertising or product differentiation. If this were so, and if the industry members were using some static or dynamic 'limit pricing' rule, then rising concentration might raise margins by this indirect route. This paper will examine the barriers facing entrants into UK grocery retailing generally, with special attention to the phenomenon of increased retailer advertising expenditures.

G Stigler (1964) and K Cowling and M Waterson (1976) among others have argued that, ignoring any effect on existing entry barriers, an increase in concentration may make industry members more aware of their interdependence and more able to coordinate their actions so raising margins.[1]

A number of counter-arguments have been advanced that stress the many circumstances where it may be difficult or impossible to coordinate the raising of margins. Three of these are relevant here. The recent literature on contestability (see Baumol, 1982) emphasises that in the absence of entry barriers, existing firms may neither wish nor be able to raise margins. In retailing generally, entry is a credible threat as Hood and Yamey (1951) point out: 'Competition from new firms is not the only source of danger . . . retailers in other trades can take up items . . . the flexibility of merchandise is a potent contribution to price competition in retailing.'[2]

Peltzman (1977) among others stressed that the ability to coordinate actions may also depend on how the increase in concentration had arisen. If it had occurred by internal growth of the firms and was accompanied by changes in their rankings then coordinated actions between firms may be less likely.

Scherer (1980, pp. 224–5) stressed that management styles may also play a role. Where each firm's managers are drawn from different backgrounds then it may be harder to coordinate the raising of prices.

Since the pioneering work of Bain, it has been argued that concentration may work in a non-linear fashion. There may be thresholds below which increasing concentration has little effect; above these thresholds it may be accompanied by increasingly significant increases in market power. (For a survey see Scherer, 1980).

It is generally thought that, as far as retailing is concerned, the relevant thresholds in concentration (measured on a national basis) are quite small; smaller than those for manufacturing. For instance, Marion, Mueller *et al.* (1979, p. 7) noted that in the USA for grocery retailing in 1976 the four-firm concentration ratio was 19 per cent and the eight-firm 26 per cent. They (Chapter 6) expressed concern over the recent mergers that have caused national concentration to rise. Caves, Porter *et al.* (1980, p. 117) noted that in Canadian grocery retailing the four-firm concentration ratio in 1975 was 65 per cent; they (Chapter 14) commented that increasing concentration in sectors 'not subject to international trade' (of which retailing must be one) should cause concern.

In the UK in the last decade there has been a significant increase in concentration in grocery retailing. The four-firm concentration ratio has risen from 26 per cent in 1970 to 40 per cent in 1980 (or from 37 per cent to 51 per cent if the Cooperative stores are treated as one firm). This paper will now examine the causes and effects of this rise in concentration.

The UK Grocery Trade 1970–1980

UK grocery retailing is but one of many industries experiencing a rise in concentration. This increase has been large; the average market share of the top four or eight firms has grown by more than 40 per cent in the period 1970–1980. The significant rise in concentration has come about through internal growth of the firms and not by combination; moreover Allied Suppliers, the largest grocery retailer in 1970, fell to seventh place by 1980. The rising concentration has been encouraged and accompanied by fierce competition between the retailers. As a result grocery supplier margins and grocery retailer margins have fallen over the decade.

For those unfamiliar with the UK, here is a short description of the four types of retailers: multiples, cooperatives (cooperative retail societies), voluntary groups (retailers associated with wholesale buying organisations) and independents. Independent store operators are distinguished by operating fewer than ten outlets. Whilst there are a few large independent stores such as Carrefour, they are mostly small 'corner' grocers. Voluntary group members usually trade under the name of their buying group such as Spar, VG or Mace. While member stores are encouraged to purchase their goods from the federation, they are not obliged to do so; they frequently purchase from other wholesalers or independently. Most cooperative outlets are part of one of the large cooperative retail chains, which can purchase through the CWS (Cooperative Wholesale Society). However, many cooperative chains negotiate individually with suppliers and the CWS does not exercise central authority. In contrast, the outlets of multiple retailers are controlled centrally.

When examining the trade it should be realised that there is no general agreement as to whether the cooperative movement should be treated as one entity, or many; likewise for the voluntary groups. As the largest voluntary group, Spar, controls less than 2½ per cent of packaged grocery sales, differing treatments of individual voluntary groups should not have material effect. The opposite is the case for cooperatives, whose share exceeds 15 per cent. Fortunately the trends in concentration are the same regardless of the treatment of cooperatives.

Trends in Concentration

There is no full agreement about the relevant market upon which to measure concentration. From the suppliers' viewpoint the national measure is probably appropriate. (UK food suppliers face minimal import competition.) From the buying public's viewpoint, the relevant market is certainly small. (Although increasing car ownership and lengthening of shop hours have extended the consumers' search area, almost all grocery products are purchased locally.) From the viewpoint of the retailers, competition takes place on many fronts; for larger retailers, local markets overlap and even regional ones are not clearly defined. Ideally an analysis of local, regional and national markets would be in order; alas trends of market shares (and hence concentration) are only available on a national basis. I am informed by those who have seen regional data on a time series basis that national trends reflect regional trends.

Market share data come from two sources: Nielsen and AGB. Nielsen (combining the Census reports into its statistics) calculates the sales of grocery retailers from data supplied by the firms. AGB, using a consumer panel, only measures the sales of major packaged grocery items. Differences exist between AGB and Nielsen data as different grocers sell differing product mixes; some emphasise products such as clothes, durables and fresh foods, whereas others stress packaged grocery items. AGB data permit calculation of Herfindahl indices and concentration ratios. Both AGB and Nielsen data ignore the sales of grocery items by non-grocery stores such as Marks and Spencer. (AGB have estimated that 85 to 90 per cent of all retail grocery sales go through grocers.)

Table 3.1, based on *Nielsen* data, shows that between 1950 and 1961 multiples gained little ground. It should be remembered that this was the period during which Retail Price Maintenance (RPM) was enforced. After RPM was abandoned around 1964, multiples and voluntary groups gained ground (mainly) at the expense of independent stores and cooperatives. For the period 1971 to 1981, *Nielsen's* data show a significant decline in the role of independent stores (21 per cent in 1971 to 11 per cent in 1981) and voluntary groups (22 per cent in 1971 to 17 per cent in 1981); a static role for cooperatives (15 per cent) and a significant gain in the role of multiples (44 per cent in 1971 to 58 per cent in 1981).

Table 3.1: Shares of U.K. Grocery Store Sales by Type of Store 1950–1981: Percentages

	1950	1961	1966	1971	1975	1976	1977	1978	1979	1980	1981
Multiples	24	27	36	44	48	48	50	52	54	55	58
Cooperatives	22	21	17	15	16	16	16	15	15	15	15
Voluntary Groups	54	13	21	22	20	21	20	19	18	17	17
Independents		40	26	21	16	15	14	13	13	12	11

Note: The columns may not add to 100% because of rounding.
Source: Nielsen

Table 3.2, based on *AGB's* figures, also shows a significant decline in the role of independent stores and voluntary groups and a significant gain for multiples. Differences exist between AGB and Nielsen data; AGB's figures show a higher market share for multiples for 1970, and a faster growth in market share. The differences are explained by the fact that in 1970 multiples sold proportionately more packaged groceries than other stores and this proportion has been increasing over the decade.[3] These

Table 3.2: Shares of Packed Grocery Sales by Grocers 1970–1981: Percentages[a]

	1970	1974	1975	1976	1977	1978	1979	1980	1981
Multiples	49[b]	53	55	57	60	64	65	68	70
Cooperatives	19	21	20	20	19	18	18	18	17
Voluntary Groups	16	14	14	13	12	10	9	8	7
Independent stores	18[b]	13	11	10	9	8	8	7	6
H8[c] with Cooperatives	.055	.057	.063	.059	.059	.066	.072	.076	.083
C4[d] with Cooperatives	37	41	42	41	42	46	48	51	53
C8[d] with Cooperatives	50	54	58	56	58	62	66	71	72
H8[c] without Cooperatives	.019	.021	.023	.023	.027	.037	.043	.048	.057
C4[d] without Cooperatives	26	27	27	27	30	34	36	40	42

Notes: a. The columns may not add to 100% because of rounding.
b. = approximate.
c. H8 = Herfindahl's indices based on leading eight stores.
d. C4, C8 = Four-firm and eight-firm concentration indices.
Sources: AGB/TCA

factors are reflected in AGB's figures which are based on sales of packaged groceries whereas Nielsen's are based on all sales.

The firm concentration ratios and Herfindahl indices computed on the basis of AGB data show that concentration increased very markedly over the decade. For instance the four-firm concentration ratio rose by 16 per cent, and the Herfindahl by 0.03.[4] (These increases were not significantly affected by including or excluding cooperatives.) The dramatic increases in concentration took place mainly after 1976, and had not stopped in 1980 as the 1981 figures show.

Sources of Increasing Concentration

Most of the increases in concentration can be attributed to internal expansion by the firms in the industry; only a small part was the result of merger activity. This is more remarkable given that the increase in concentration has been accompanied by a decline in one of the leading firms and the emergence of two new large retailers.

At the beginning of the decade (1970), the largest multiples (with market shares) were the Allied Group (7.9), Tesco (7.2), Sainsbury (6.1), Fine Fare (4.8), and International Stores (3.2). At the end of the decade (1980) they were Sainsbury (13.4), Tesco (13.4), Asda (8.5), Fine Fare (5.5), Kwik Save (5.4) and International Stores (4.7). Over the decade, Allied Suppliers fell from No. 1 to No. 7, losing nearly half its market share through closing unprofitable stores.[5] Tesco and Sainsbury, which in the period about doubled their shares, expanded mainly by opening new large stores.[6] Asda, the northern based superstore group, increased its market share about sixfold by a prolonged programme of rapid store openings outside town centres.[7] Kwik Save, also northern based, captured nearly 5 per cent of the market in ten years from an almost insignificant position in 1971; its policy was to offer cut-priced packaged groceries from smaller locations near town centres. Kwik Save has used acquisitions as a means of helping growth.[8] Similarly, International Stores has used acquisitions to help growth and it has increased market share by about 50 per cent over the same period.[9]

The cooperative movement has experienced little overall change in market share; however within the movement there have been many mergers, rationalisations and closures of smaller outlets, and building of many superstores. Even so it is thought that no individual retail society accounts for more than 1 per cent of grocery sales.

Effects of Increasing Concentration on Suppliers

The major force behind increasing concentration has probably been the desire to exploit 'buying power'. Retailing managers believe that a larger market share enables them to extract lower prices from suppliers. It has been said that Daisy Hyams, one time Chief Buyer of groceries at Tesco, was the bane of the grocery manufacturing industry because she was able to negotiate terms very favourable for Tesco. Suppliers also believe that increases in grocery concentration have resulted in greater buying power for the retailers causing manufacturers' margins to fall. The evidence generally supports this view.

In their 1981 report on Discounts to Retailers, the Monopolies and Mergers Commission (MMC) surveyed twelve major suppliers (manufacturers) of groceries supplying a range of nationally available brands valued at £960 millions. The report revealed that on average, the top four grocery multiples paid 1.5 per cent less than the next ten grocery multiples which in turn paid 2.0 per cent less than the rest of the trade. Some of these lower prices reflected services provided by the largest retailers in the form of in-store promotion etc., but in the opinion of the Commission the larger part reflected purchasing power. The Commission also examined discounts given to the three largest retailers Sainsbury, Tesco, and Asda, and showed that Tesco (by a small margin) obtained the best terms. Tesco, at that time, was the largest retailer, Sainsbury being a very close second.

Increases in buying power are evidenced by the downward trends over the decade in profitability of UK food manufacturing. Before examining the trends, it is appropriate to ask what determines the level and trend of profitability of food manufacturers. As regards the level of profits, the food manufacturing industry is highly concentrated and benefits from high entry barriers; in the absence of 'buying power' one might expect a higher than average rate of profit. As regards the trend, the movements of the value of sterling would not be a very important variable in this industry as there is little opportunity for import substitution. Food products such as cornflakes and biscuits are not easily transported long distances; and the generality of the proposition is confirmed by the share of UK manufacturing output going to export and very stable shares of imports as a share of UK consumption. Likewise, the state of the economy would be unlikely to have great effect on the trends; generally food products have low income elasticities. Increased retailer buying power would adversely affect profitability trends especially if at the beginning of the period manufacturing had market power.

Figures on profitability are reported in Table 3.3. Those for food manufacturing are published by the Food and Drink Industries' Council and the Food Manufacturers' Federation and are based on a survey of 30 firms; the figures for all UK manufacturing are based on Department of Industry figures. Despite being adjusted for the effects of inflation, the data have limitations. Apparently no attempt has been made to separate out earnings from exports or from overseas subsidiaries which means that movements in exchange rates will affect the data. Also, the data are drawn from financial accounts and not managerial records so

Table 3.3 Profitability[a] of UK Food Manufacturers and all UK Manufacturers on a Current Cost Accounting Basis 1965 – 1977

Year	UK Food Manufacturers	All UK Manufacturers	Difference
1965	14.7	11.0	3.7
1966	11.4	9.2	2.2
1967	11.6	9.6	2.0
1968	10.5	9.9	0.6
1969	9.2	8.7	0.5
1970	6.5	5.8	0.7
1971	6.6	7.2	−0.6
1972	9.8	8.9	0.9
1973	1.3	7.1	−5.8
1974	3.5	3.5	0.0
1975	5.5	2.1	3.4
1976	5.4	4.4	0.9
1977	4.9	4.7	0.2
Mean 1965–1977	7.8	7.1	0.7

Note: a. Profitability is measured profits divided by capital employed 'net trading income before interest and less depreciation, and capital employed is averaged and includes net current assets other than investments, bank overdrafts and loans, together with tangible fixed assets at written down value'.

Sources: *Food and Drink Industries' Council* and *Food Manufacturers' Federation* cited in MMC (1981) p.197

their validity as measures of economic rates of return is subject to the usual caveats. (For a full discussion of this point see Fisher and McGowan 1983.)

As shown in Table 3.3, the profitability of food manufacturers measured on a *current cost* accounting basis, has fallen from 14.7 per cent in 1965 to 4.9 per cent in 1977. (1977 is the last year data were available.) This decline has been continuous, except for the years 1972–74 where the average of these three years is below the trend. Whilst year to year movements in profitability are not correlated with changes in retailing concentration, the overall declining trend is consistent with the view that buyers have become more 'powerful' over the decade.

Table 3.3 also gives figures comparing food manufacturers' profits with those of all manufacturers. They show that in the late 1960s food manufacturers were on average considerably more profitable than all manufacturing; and that between 1968 and 1974 the differences steadily vanished so that the rates of profit equalised. In 1975 and 1976 there was a reversal of the trend but the change was not great, and could be explained by the fact that UK manufacturing generally has had to compete with tougher international competition than food manufacturers. Once again, year on year changes in profitability differences are not correlated with changes in retail concentration, but the overall picture is consistent with the hypothesis that buying power has caused a decline in food manufacturers' profits, from a level which was greater than average to a level which is now average.

Economies of Scale and Increasing Concentration

In gauging the importance of 'buying power' and the potential importance of economies of scale it is useful to bear in mind the cost structure of a typical multiple grocery retailer. The value of sales is made up roughly as follows: cost of purchases 80 per cent; cost of labour 10 per cent (most of which is store labour); rent and rates 4 per cent (most of which is the cost of stores); other expenses 4 per cent; net margin 2 per cent.

Several writers have stressed the cost advantages from operating larger stores (see, for instance, Tucker, 1978). Such benefits come from higher labour and capital productivity. In recent years the 'most efficient store size' appears to have increased.[10] But this change cannot have 'caused' increases in concentration as even the largest stores (35,000 square feet) account for no more than 0.2 per cent of national grocery sales.

At the firm level, the benefits traditionally associated with scale have been improved reporting and control systems, reduced training costs and lowered warehousing costs. Training costs are not a large expense for grocery retailing as most of the labour is unskilled; reporting and control costs are not large either; in these areas benefits of scale can be small at most. Centralised warehousing used to be an important benefit of scale; however, not only do the newer large stores usually have a warehouse as an integral part of the premises eliminating the need for centralised warehousing but many of the packaged grocery items such as biscuits, cake, frozen foods, bread and milk are delivered direct from supplier to the branches. In summary, the benefits of large scale do not seem to explain the dramatic increases in concentration.

The Effects of Increasing Concentration on the Role of Price

Competition in the grocery industry takes place on many fronts; these include advertising, store location, store cleanliness, opening hours, range of products stocked, quality of own label goods and last but not least price. Contrary to what might be expected the increase in concentration over the decade has been associated with greater emphasis on price. This is evidenced by the trend towards centralisation of price decisions, Tesco's decision to stop using trading stamps and changes in firms' marketing expenditures.

Most major grocery multiples make pricing decisions regarding packaged groceries centrally and frequently. Commonly the board of directors meets weekly on Monday to decide price policy and in many cases to fix the prices of key high volume items such as baked beans. After such meetings the central office will issue price lists to branches. Within any organisation there may be several different lists. Usually, the highest prices are charged in the lowest volume outlets. Asda, having only large stores, most of whose area is greater than 20,000 square feet, has one price list; Sainsbury, which has stores up to 25,000 square feet, has two (sometimes three) price lists and Tesco, which has stores of all sizes, has three price lists.

Some firms such as Tesco permit regional or branch managers to alter some prices to suit local conditions; others such as Asda allow no deviations. In Asda's case, freedom to alter price is curtailed by the policy of asking suppliers to price the goods in the factory. Trade sources suggest that the general trend of the industry has been towards fewer lists and less local latitude. The benefits of this policy are greater control over price and a focusing of the store manager's role away from price towards operations. The greater centralisation of price decisions suggests that retailers view control of price as more important than they did before.

There is also evidence that there is an increasing willingness to use price as a central competitive weapon. One of the key elements of Tesco's strategy in the late 1960s and early 1970s was its use of trading stamps. Customers could redeem the stamps for products offered by Green Shield. Because of Tesco's national position, the giving of stamps was an important form of non-price competition for the trade. Tesco was not the only store giving stamps, the cooperatives also gave stamps redeemable for cash or purchases in cooperative stores. In June 1977 Tesco stopped providing stamps, valued at 2½ per cent of sales, and cut its prices by an average of 4 per cent. Not surprisingly this provoked competitors to cut prices too. Around the same time, the cooperative movement stopped providing stamps in its large stores. These moves of dropping stamps increased the role of price in competition.

There has been a significant change in the advertising mix of grocery products over the last decade. In real terms, retailer advertising has risen and manufacturers' advertising has fallen. Between 1970 and 1980, retail advertising expenditures by grocery and other food retailers rose to eightfold from £5 millions to £41 millions in comparison to a rise in the advertising price index of four times and the overall trend in advertising expenditures by all UK firms which rose three and a quarter times. But, over the same decade, food manufacturers' advertising merely doubled from £66 millions to £137 millions. Combining the two sets of expenditures we see that the total of expenditures on grocery and other food items rose about two and a half times from £71 millions to £178 millions. The combined total considered as a proportion of all advertising or viewed in relation to the price index has fallen over the decade.

There are two reasons for supposing that this change in marketing mix has increased the role of price in retailing. First, as retailer advertising tends to focus more on price than manufacturers' advertising, the changing mix increases the role of price. Secondly, the consumer, indifferent as to who pays for what advertising, now receives fewer advertising messages than before. Unless the persuasiveness of these messages has increased, the consumer is probably viewing prices more carefully than before.

The Effects of Increasing Concentration on Collusion

The increasing emphasis by grocery retailers on price is *not* proof of increasing competition; price as a weapon could have become more recognised but less used. One of the chief arguments concerning the supposed dangers of rising concentration makes just this point. In addition to evidence on profit margins which are discussed in the next section, there are three reasons for believing that price 'collusion' has not taken place. First, new entry has been a continuous phenomenon in grocery retailing; secondly the evidence suggests that each firm faces a highly elastic short run demand curve suggesting that the incentives to cut price are high, and thirdly price coordination does not seem to have taken place for firms manifestly take differing views on price levels and price changes.

Besides the continuous stream of new entry into small single-outlet grocers from aspiring would-be entrepreneurs, during the 1970s there have been a number of occurrences of entry and expansion on a sizeable scale. Already noted was the massive expansion of Asda which increased its market share from 1.5 per cent in 1971 to 8.5 per cent in 1981, and expansion by Kwik Save from an insignificant position in 1971 to nearly 5 per cent in 1981.

If a firm faces a highly elastic demand curve, there is a greater temptation to cut price when margins are believed to be high; a highly elastic demand curve means that the gains from price cutting can be large. That grocery retailers face a highly elastic demand curve is well asserted and can be shown.

AGB has collected price data for groceries offered by major multiples and the cooperative societies. The price data have been compiled into an index based on the weighted average charged for a basket of packaged groceries (which is the same basket used for their market share statistics). These monthly price data for the period March 1977 to March 1978, together with some monthly market share data, have been made available to this researcher. Using these monthly data an estimate of demand elasticity can be computed, see Appendix 3.1.

For the data for Tesco, the major national retailer, the fits were good and the results robust, and indicate an elasticity of four. When one considers that the data are monthly, this is a high number. Relationships between price and market share were not robust for Asda, Sainsbury or the cooperative stores; this is hardly surprising as the data were computed on a national basis whereas

Sainsbury and Asda are regional companies, and the cooperatives operate a variety of stores and price lists.

The management of the four most important retailers Asda, Sainsbury, Tesco and the cooperatives have come from differing backgrounds and run firms very differently. In particular, Asda's top management was recruited from outside the grocery industry and until 1965 its parent company Associated Dairies had no significant association with grocery retailing. Sainsbury is a family firm; its board of directors controls 45 per cent of the voting stock. Tesco, formerly a family firm, is publicly owned.

In conclusion, analysis of the data provides little support for the theory that there was price collusion.

Effects of Increasing Concentration on Performance

Thus far the paper has considered the effect of increasing concentration on the conduct of firms. It has been noted that more emphasis has been placed on price competition and it has been suggested that price collusion is not taking place. The evidence also suggests that firms face a high price elasticity in the short run and that entry barriers are low (but perhaps rising). All these observations combine to suggest that grocery retailing is becoming more competitive.

The evidence also suggests that grocery retailers are exercising buying power against suppliers, forcing their profit margins down to a level on a par with the rest of UK manufacturing. Are the discounts received by multiple retailers being passed on to the public at large, or are they being kept and dissipated in unnecessary expenditures or distributed as higher profits? Executives of the food manufacturers often say that the discounts are not being passed on, and they cite the high profitability of multiples such as Sainsbury, Kwik Save and Asda. Executives of retailers say these high profits are exceptional and caused by unusual operating efficiency and that the discounts are being passed on. Theory lends support to the retailers' view, namely that consumers should benefit from discounts received being passed on in the form of lower prices.[12] The evidence goes further, it suggests that not only are discounts passed on but that increased competition has taken place forcing retailer margins down too.

The MMC (1981) examined the prices paid by grocery retailers and the prices charged to consumers in three towns in April 1979. The sample contained 170 retail outlets; one each of the top four retailing multiples, eight of the cooperatives and 53 of other multiples. The products surveyed included 25 brands of eight packaged grocery products. On average, one-half of the variance in output prices could be explained by the variance of input prices. Simple correlations showed that a 1 per cent fall in input prices produced a 1 per cent fall in output prices; this relationship was statistically significant. These results lend *some* support to the notion that lower input prices are passed on.

It was remarked earlier that the major multiples charge different mark-ups by size of store; the MMC made no attempt to control for the variable 'size of store'; moreover its sample was strongly biased towards independents and smaller multiples. These are serious deficiencies and the MMC findings cannot be considered as conclusive; another test is needed.

Examining changes in gross and net margins of all grocery retailers over the decade provides further, stronger, support for the view that lower input prices have been passed on in the form of lower output prices, and support for the view that the industry has become more rather than less competitive.

Data on gross margins have been collected by the Office of the Census and the Institute of Grocery Distribution (IGD). For independent grocers (which include voluntary groups), the Census data reveal that margins were 20.1 per cent in 1971, falling to 15.7 per cent by 1979 (see Table 3.4). Margin trends for multiples are harder to ascertain. In 1971, the Census excluded cooperatives from its data, and included them for the data for 1976 through 1979. Further difficulty was caused by the fact that in 1976 and 1977, several large grocery retailers (such as Asda) appear to have been excluded on the basis that they sold significant amounts of non-grocery type products such as durables and clothes. Even

Table 3.4: Gross Margins of Grocers 1971 – 1979

	1971	1976	1977	1978	1979
Independent Grocers (including Voluntary Groups) (1 – 9 Outlets)	20.1	15.1	15.4	15.3	15.7
Multiple Grocers	19.9[a]	18.4[b]	17.0[b]	17.1	18.0

Notes: a. Includes cooperative stores.
b. In 1976 and 1977 large general foods retailers were excluded whose sales comprised around one third of large multiple retailers.

Source: Census of Distribution (1971); Retail Enquiries 1976–79

allowing for these changes, the Census statistics are clear: the gross margins of multiples in the late 1970s were well below the figure for 1971.

A further analysis of Table 3.4 shows that margins for multiples in 1977 and 1978 were below those of 1976 and 1979. The lower figures for 1977 and 1978 are properly interpreted as the result of the price cut initiated by Tesco in June 1977. Was the figure for 1971 typical? It seems that it was, as is shown by other margin data.

IGD have compiled estimates on gross margins for multiples. These data covering the years 1972/3 to 1978/9 confirm the declining trend in gross margins for multiples (see Table 3.5). Data for years after 1978/9 have not been released; apparently they have risen a little over 1977/8 but are nowhere near the 1972/3 levels.

Table 3.5: Gross Margins and Net Margins of Multiple Grocers 1973–1982

Year ending April	1973	1974	1975	1976	1977	1978	1979	1980	1981	1982
Gross Margins	20.0	19.5	18.8	18.5	18.9	18.1	17.8	n.a.	n.a.	n.a.
Net Margins	3.5	3.5	2.5	1.7	2.1	1.8	1.7	1.9	1.8	2.1
Difference	16.5	16.0	16.3	16.8	16.8	16.3	16.1	n.a.	n.a.	n.a.

Note: n.a. not disclosable, but 'above 1979 levels and well below 1973 levels'.
Source: IGD

The IGD have also compiled estimates of net margins for multiples (see Table 3.5). These data show that from 1972/3 to 1981/2 net margins have almost halved. It is apparent therefore, that there has been a significant reduction in gross margins and net margins. (It is not possible to give any data on net margins or on returns to capital for independent grocers.)

When comparison is made between the UK experience and that of the US the trends described above become more remarkable. Marion, Mueller *et al.* (1979) report that the gross margin for US grocery multiples averaged about 18 per cent between 1965 and 1977 with almost no change between the beginning and end of the period. Likewise, net margins remained constant around 1½ per cent.

The Future

The trend towards increasing concentration has not shown any sign of reversing. If the past has no reason to cause concern, should the future be considered differently? Until now, there appear to have been low entry barriers into retailing. If these barriers were to rise then there might be cause for concern.

One future barrier to entry might be imminent changes in retailing technology involving laser checkout systems. These new systems may confer considerable advantages on larger firms in the industry especially those with larger stores. Electronic point of sale systems, of which laser scanning is a part, confer advantages in stock control as well as reducing the need for labour to price goods individually. Early users may gain advantages through learning effects that make late entry less attractive.

Members of the trade frequently point out that entry by building new stores is becoming increasingly difficult. The number of potential sites is in decline partly due to market saturation and partly because of the absence of land. Even where sites exist, local authorities appear less willing to grant planning permission — partly as a result of the opposition of the local small retailer lobbies. But this supposed entry barrier can in part be overcome by taking over existing retail sites vacated by exiting grocery or other retailers; it is doubtful whether site availability will be a serious entry barrier to new firms.

There have been two notable mergers in recent years, one between Allied Suppliers (the eighth-largest retailer) and Argyll Foods and the other between Linfood (the ninth-largest retailer) and Key Markets. In each case the market shares of the acquired firms were less than 2 per cent and the combined firms less than 6 per cent. Clearly a wave of mergers among the lead firms might give rise for concern, but these two recent mergers would not appear to be significant.

Conclusion

This paper has examined the UK grocery trade. It has revealed a substantial increase in concentration over the years 1970–1980, which trend appears to be continuing into the 1980s. The increased concentration, achieved by internal expansion of firms, was chiefly attributed to the benefits of centralised buying allowing larger retailers to purchase more cheaply than smaller ones. The increases in concentration, and buying power, appear to have had an appreciable effect on suppliers. Supplier profitability in the early

1960s was considerably higher than the average for manufacturing; by the late 1970s profitability had fallen, and had reached a level equal to that of all manufacturing.

Because of the low entry barriers and high firm price elasticities, it was suggested that increasing concentration among grocery retailers would be associated with greater price competition. The abandonment of the use of trading stamps and the changing mix of advertising expenditures point to this. As a consequence, one would expect highly competitive behaviour and this was confirmed by the evidence. Over the period 1970–1980 retailers' gross margins and net margins fell indicating that not only were lower input prices being passed on, but that retail margins were falling as well.

Appendix 3.1

To calculate the elasticity of demand for Tesco, multiple regressions were run using market share (MS) as the dependent variable and price (P), lagged price (LP) and lagged market share (LMS) as the independent variables. In the model given below, the relationship between price and market share is dynamic:

$$MS = aP + bLP + cLMS + error.$$

The long run effect of price on market share is given by the equation $(a + b) / (1 - c)$. The model may be restricted by omitting

Table A3.1: Relationship Between Tesco's Market Share and Tesco's Price for the Period March 1977 to March 1978

	Constant	P	LP	LMS	df	Implied Elasticity
(1)	49 (6.9)	−0.24 (4.0)	−0.15 (2.4)	0.047 (0.7)	11	3.9
(2)	52 (12.4)	−0.25 (4.4)	−0.17 (3.3)		12	4.0
(3)	70 (4.7)	−0.62 (4.0)			14	5.9

Notes: Figures in brackets are Student 't' statistics; the mean price was 100 and mean market share 10.5.

Data Source: AGB/TCA see text.

the variables LP and LMS. It can be seen from the results shown in Table A3.1 that (statistically) equation (2) provides the best fit and the long run elasticity in this case is 4.0. This is the best equation because the 't' statistic on LMS is insignificant, unlike the 't' statistic on LP. (However regardless of the restriction imposed, all the estimates yield high elasticities.)

Notes

1. From time to time antitrust policy has been based seemingly on analysis of concentration effects alone, for example the policy of the US Federal Trade Commission towards mergers in the late 1960s.
2. Some local authorities are said to favour planning applications from existing well-established firms. If this were the case then there could be an entry barrier to new firms to retailing generally.
3. The Census figures on commodity line sales of grocery retailers confirm this; compare the 1971 *Report on Census of Distribution* with the 1979 *Retail Enquiry*.
4. The Herfindahl index is the sum of the squared market shares; in this case it is based on the shares of the largest eight firms.
5. Allied Suppliers originally rose to No. 1 position by acquiring Moores Stores.
6. Tesco acquired Cartiers Stores in 1979; Cartiers had 0.5 per cent market share. Sainsbury made no significant grocery retail acquisitions in the decade.
7. Associated Dairies, the parent company of Asda, made no acquisitions in the grocery trade in the decade.
8. Kwik Save acquired Cee-N-Cee in 1979; Cee-N-Cee had 1 per cent market share.
9. International Stores is owned by BAT.
10. Between 1974 and 1979 the average size of new stores opened by multiples rose from 11,000 square feet to 21,000 square feet and the average size of store closed rose from 1,500 square feet to 2,200 square feet.
11. For a brief description of the origins of the firms and their management see the London Business School '*Tesco*' unpublished case study.
12. In theory, the monopolist takes both cost and demand into account when setting price; a fall in cost of an input causes a profit-maximising monopolist to lower prices unless the input is not used in variable proportions.

References

Baumol, W. J. (1982) 'Contestable Markets: An Uprising in the Theory of Industry Structure', *American Economic Review, 72*, 1–16.
Caves, R. E., Porter, M. E., Spence, A. M. and Scott, J. T. (1980) '*Competition in the Open Economy*' Harvard University Press, Harvard, Conn.
Cowling, K. and Waterson, M. (1976) 'Price Cost Margins and Market Structure,' *Economica, 43*, 267–74
Fisher, F. M. and McGowan, J. J. (1983) 'On the Misuse of Accounting Rates of Return to Infer Monopoly Profits', *American Economic Review, 73*, 82–98
Hood, J. and Yamey, B. S. (1951) 'Imperfect Competition in Retail Trade'

Economica, 18, reprinted in K. A. Tucker and B. S. Yamey *Economics of Retailing*, Penguin 1973

Lustgarten, S. H. (1975) 'The Impact of Buyer Concentration in Manufacturing Industries', *Review of Economics and Statistics, 57*, 125–32

Marion, B. W., Mueller, W. F., Cotterill, R. W., Geithman, F. E. and Schmelzer, J. R. (1979) *The Food Retailing Industry*, Praeger, New York

Peltzman, S. (1977) 'The Gains and Losses from Industrial Concentration', *Journal of Law and Economics, 20*, 229–63

Scherer, F. M. (1980) *Industrial Market Structure and Economic Performance*, Rand McNally, Chicago.

Spence, M. (1977) 'Entry, Capacity, Investment and Oligopolistic Pricing' *Bell Journal of Economics, 8*, 534–44

Stigler, G. (1964) *Theory of Price*, second edn., Macmillan, London

Stigler, G. (1982) 'A Theory of Oligopoly' *Journal of Political Economy, 72*, 1–16

Tucker, K. A. (1978) *Concentration and Costs in Retailing*, Saxon House, Farnborough

UK Government, Monopolies and Mergers Commission (1981) *Report on Discount to Retailers*, London, HMSO

4 THE STRUCTURE AND BEHAVIOUR OF THE BRITISH BUILDING SOCIETY MOVEMENT

C. Whitehead
London School of Economics

Introduction

Building societies are non-profit organisations, subject to the 1962 Building Societies Act. All societies are registered under the Chief Registrar of Friendly Societies whose role is to ensure that societies are prudently managed and operate securely in their members' interests.[1] Societies must be financially independent, i.e. neither owning subsidiaries nor being a subsidiary of another institution. Their business is restricted to raising funds and making loans which are fully secured against property. They are required to keep certain reserve and liquid asset ratios and to limit the bulk of their loans to a maximum of £60,000. They play an important part in both the savings market, where they attract over 45 per cent of short-term personal sector savings, and the mortgage market where they have usually provided over 80 per cent of house purchase finance.

Building societies have been the subject of many studies in recent years. These have described and analysed their objectives, their method of operation in the mortgage and finance markets and, in particular, their impact on the housing market. In these discussions the behavioural assumption that building societies act as a price fixing 'cartel' has been a relevant factor. Indeed one recent work specifically analysed the benefits and particularly the costs of acting in this way (Gough and Taylor, 1979). However, there has been little examination of the reasons why this cartel exists or of why it has remained stable for so long. These are important questions both in the analysis of the way in which the housing finance market operates and in the determination of policy towards that market. They are particularly relevant at the present time because competitive pressures on building societies have increased with respect to both the inflow of funds and the provision of mortgages.

In this paper we first examine different views of the importance of the cartel. Next we look at how the cartel operated in the relatively uncompetitive environment which obtained until the late

1970s and in the more competitive environment which followed. We then describe the structure of the industry within which the cartel has operated. Relevant models of oligopoly are next examined to determine the conditions necessary for an agreement to be either desirable or effective, given the existing industrial structure. Finally, we look at the extent to which these conditions apply to the housing finance market and in particular to the building society cartel.

Current Views of the Cartel

No-one discussing the building societies doubts that they have operated for many years as a price-fixing cartel, through their representative body the Building Societies Association (BSA). Yet, the formal objectives and functions of the Association make no specific mention of price setting, nor even of any discussion of interest rate determination.[2] Rather, they state that they offer information and advice to members and outside bodies, act on behalf of members in discussions with other representative bodies, the Government and the Bank of England, involve themselves in education and research and provide a forum for discussion and policy formulation. Official studies of the building societies reflect this view, placing little or no emphasis on the role the Association plays in setting interest rates and considerable emphasis on its role as a voluntary association through which constituent bodies meet together for discussion and in order to act as a pressure group.[3]

Boléat (1979), currently Deputy Secretary General of the BSA, does however detail the Association's price setting role in relation to both savings and mortgage rates. He states that the Council meets monthly to provide a forum for discussion and policy making.[4] At these meetings it may make recommendations as well as give information and advice. These recommendations require a two-thirds majority vote of the Council. Member societies usually follow the agreed rates 'although they are not obliged to do so' (Boléat, 1979, p. 14). Boléat suggests that rate determination is only a small part of even the policy formulation element of the Association's business and emphasises instead their involvement in specifying legislation and in responding to external variables, particularly government initiatives. Further, he points out that the Labour Government's Housing Policy Review (Department of

Environment, 1977) was in sympathy with the recommended rate system and the Conservative Government did not accept the Wilson Committee (1980) recommendations that it be abolished. Thus the price setting agreement appears to have government sanction.

The impression given by the official descriptions, of a voluntary, relatively unimportant but beneficial agreement, is in sharp contrast to that to be found in the academic analyses of building society behaviour. Gough and Taylor (1979), for instance, concentrate their discussion entirely on the restrictive arrangements of the cartel with respect to interest rates, efficiency, the distribution of benefits and the extent and price of home ownership. They argue that there are significant costs with respect to each of these aspects and that the increased competition which they suggest would arise from its abandonment would lead to a cheaper, more effective, housing finance market. They are in no doubt that the cartel has been both important to the running of the system and effective in restraining trade. Wider ranging discussions such as that by Maclennan (1982) agree with the view that the cartel has modified savings and mortgage market behaviour significantly, helping the societies at the expense of at least some groups of consumers. Econometric analyses, by e.g. Mayes (1979), Hadjimatheou (1976) and Ghosh (1974), which model the behaviour of societies and the housing market all include as a major assumption that the cartel operates to hold the mortgage rate below its market clearing level. As a result the existence and effective functioning of the cartel is a major factor in their explanations of institutional and market behaviour. To determine the relative merits of these two strongly opposing views of the cartel it is necessary to examine both how the agreement actually operates and what would be the likely behaviour of societies without such a formal agreement.

Operation of the Cartel

As we have already seen the cartel operates through the Building Societies Association (BSA). This found its final form in 1940, amalgamating two associations which had grown up in the 1930s as part of a period of extreme inter-society competition. The objective of the BSA was to agree a code of practice specifying prudential requirements and limiting competition via a range of agreements including the recommended rate system.

At the end of 1982 only 174 of the 227 societies registered with the Chief Registrar of Friendly Societies (i.e. the organisations that make up the building society movement) belonged to the Association. However, these represented almost 99.9 per cent of the assets of registered societies. Furthermore, only one major society, the Halifax, has ever left the Association, for a period of eight years between 1956 and 1964. The BSA can therefore be said to act for the whole movement.

The Council of the BSA makes recommendations in relation to both borrowing and lending rates. It specifies the interest rate to be paid on fully paid up shares. On the mortgage side it recommends the rate to be charged on new annuity mortgages made on the security of private dwellings and suggests the timing and extent of changes for existing mortgages. In this way the Association determines not only the price of the product but also the main element of cost (interest payments) and the margin above this available to cover expenses, taxation and increases in reserves. Formally, it does not determine market shares although the chosen mark-up affects the relative capacity of societies to expand.

Most price setting agreements aim to restrict output and increase price to the resultant market clearing level in order to maximise or at least improve profitability. The BSA recommended rate system is apparently very different, first because societies are non-profit organisations, second because mortgage rates are held down rather than increased, and third because the resulting rate does not clear the market. However, the effect on output is similar: the quantity of mortgage funds made available is lower than it would otherwise be.

Recommendations made by the Association are not mandatory on members and no society has been expelled for non-compliance. Yet a significant proportion of members do not comply with all the recommendations at all times. A survey undertaken by Gough and Taylor in 1978 (reprinted in Gough and Taylor, 1979), showed that about 25 per cent of BSA members were not using the recommended mortgage rate while over 40 per cent were not using the recommended share rate. In all cases the rates charged or offered were higher than the recommended rates. Among non-BSA members few chose to adhere to the recommended rate. However, the effect of non-compliance on overall mortgage and savings rates was limited because non-compliance was concentrated among the smaller societies. Higher rates at that time probably applied to less than 5 per cent of the total assets of the movement and the vast majority of rates charged were within 1 per cent of the recommended rate. Most societies also change their rates at the times of changes in the BSA rate and by similar amounts. The relative structure thus remains fairly constant (Boléat, 1982).

When setting the savings rate the Association's stated aim is to bring in enough funds to maintain 'the desired level of new lending' (BSA, 1982a, p. 15). The mortgage rate is then calculated by adding on margins to cover the societies' tax liabilities, their management expenses and enough surplus to at least maintain their reserve ratios (BSA, 1982a). As the same mark-up applies to all societies it has to allow for their very different circumstances and levels of efficiency. In practice by complying with the recommendations the vast majority of member societies have been able to add to reserves almost every year. The mark-up included is thus generally large enough to allow the less efficient societies to cover their costs.

The savings rate resulting from these calculations has traditionally been such that the flow of funds has been inadequate to meet demand. The system thus ensured that, while other institutions did not enter the market, all societies were always able to lend out all their funds to secure borrowers. Other objectives were also relevant, in particular the provision of a stable flow of funds for house purchase to ensure a buoyant housing market.[5]

Since 1979 however, there have been significant changes in the way the system has operated. First an Association report (BSA, 1979) urged that societies should move towards market interest rates in order to make sure that adequate building society funds were available to meet all reasonably secure demand. Secondly, the large scale entry of the banks into mortgage provision, together with greater integration with other financial markets on the savings side, increased competition so that the BSA argued that 'it is unlikely that the mortgage rate can be maintained significantly below market rates in the future' (BSA, 1979).

On the savings side the greater competitive pressure has led to more inter-society competition. Although there is still an agreed share rate, most societies now also offer term shares and other higher interest rate savings schemes which compete with those offered by other societies as well as with the banks and national savings. As a result there was a net outflow of funds attracting the basic share rate in 1982 and higher rates now apply to almost half of total assets. Yet the effect on the overall cost of borrowing is still quite small. In early 1983 these higher rates added about 0.65 per cent to the average cost of shares and deposits, increasing the overall cost of funds by less than 10 per cent.

These changes have undoubtedly put pressure on the BSA cartel, reducing the capacity of member societies to choose their mortgagors and the terms and conditions on which mortgages are issued. However, the framework remains intact and there is as yet no example of non-compliance by a large institution in relation to either the share rate or the mortgage rate. Thus we observe an agreement that has operated with little change for 40 years, but now appears to be under a certain amount of pressure.[6]

The Structure of the Industry

The product provided by building societies is finance for house purchase and improvement. In this market the building societies are the only specialist suppliers but other institutions such as commercial banks, insurance companies and local authorities are also involved to varying degrees. On average these other sources have been relatively unimportant, accounting for little more than 20 per cent of the stock of mortgages (Table 4.1). Until the late 1970s, these institutions acted mainly in a residual role, filling gaps in the market in which the societies had little interest. As such they hardly impinged on the decision-making process of societies. It was therefore reasonable to speak of 'the building society industry'.

Table 4.1: Mortgage Loans Outstanding

	End 1973 %	End 1977 %	End 1982 %
Building Societies	77.2	80.3	75.1
Local Authorities	8.4	8.9	5.9
Insurance Companies etc.	6.9	4.8	3.1
Banking Sector	6.1	4.6	14.0
Other Public Sector	0.8	1.5	2.0
TOTAL £m	18948	33125	75800

Source: Financial Statistics

The number of societies has steadily decreased throughout the century, from over 2000 in 1900 to 227 at the end of 1982 (Table 4.2). The rate of decline has been increasing in the last two decades. Indeed, in the last five years the number has fallen by almost one-third. However, measured in any other terms (e.g. assets, amount advanced or the number of share accounts and borrowers) the size of the industry has been growing rapidly, the rate of growth rarely even decelerating (Table 4.2).

Table 4.2: The Changing Structure of the Building Society Movement

	No. of Societies	No. of Borrowers	Amount Advanced	No. of Share Accounts	Total Assets
		'000s	£m	'000s	£m
1900	2286	–	9	585	60
1930	1026	720	89	1,449	371
1960	726	2349	560	3,910	3,166
1970	481	3655	1,954	10,265	10,819
1980	273	5383	9,503	30,636	53,793
1981	253	5490	12,005	33,388	61,815
1982	227	5645	15,036	36,607	73,033

Source: BSA Bulletin

Concentration in the industry has increased even more rapidly. In 1957 the five-firm concentration ratio (CR_5) measured in terms of assets was just under 0.44 and that for the top two firms was 0.27. By 1970 the top five firms controlled over half the assets of the industry and the top two almost one-third. By 1982 the asset based CR_5 stood at 0.55 and CR_2 at 0.35.[7] Thus the dominant position of the top five and particularly the top two societies continues to grow. The top five are still the same societies as they were in the 1950s and within this dominant group relative positions have remained stable, with a single change in the order, between numbers 4 and 5 in 1971.

The next group of five societies hold about 15 per cent of total assets, as do the next group of ten. Here there has been growing merger activity in the last years resulting in some changes in order as well as in increasing concentration. Now the top twenty societies, making up less than 10 per cent of registered societies, old nearly 90 per cent of the assets. At the other extreme the bottom 30 per cent account for less than 0.1 per cent of the assets. If the industry is properly defined in terms of registered societies and the concentration ratio is a reasonable measure of market power it would appear that the industry is fairly heavily concentrated, that the market power of its largest members is growing and that the hierarchy of members is relatively stable.

On other concentration measures market power appears, although growing, to be more limited. An estimate of the Herfindahl index for instance ($\sum_{i=1}^{n} s_i^2$ where s_i = share of total assets held by society i, and n = number of societies) gives a concentration measure of about 0.085, as opposed to about 0.075 ten years ago. This summary measure equals 1 if the industry is a monopoly and tends to zero if made up of a large number of very small firms. Market power is affected by both the total number of firms and their relative size. On this measure one would perhaps argue that the structure tends far more towards competition than implied by the concentration ratio.

Interpretation of this measure is, however, crucially dependent upon the assumption that the societies act independently. For instance, if the top two societies were regarded as acting together the Herfindahl index would rise to 0.15 and if the top five were seen to act as one it would be above 0.3. This value is more in line with that for the CR_5 whose interpretation similarly implies that the top firms act together. A relevant question is therefore whether in the absence of a cartel the structure of the industry would still tend to induce collusion among the largest societies.

A further factor affecting the structure and operation of the industry is the ease and extent of entry and exit. While the movement has been growing continuously the number of societies has been falling rapidly. In the main this decline has been effected by the merging of societies of all sizes, rather than by dissolution. In most such mergers at least one party has been small (i.e. holding less than 0.5 per cent of the movement's assets). However, in the last decade there have been five mergers involving only larger societies, two of these in the last year. The vast majority of mergers that take place are between fully operational societies. Only in a handful of cases have societies shown overt signs of failure as a result of mismanagement, fraud or sudden localised economic problems. Wherever such difficulties have arisen other societies have stepped in rapidly to take over their responsibilities.

The Chief Registrar of Friendly Societies also plays a role in identifying potential difficulties and may facilitate the transfer of operations of such societies. The number of dissolutions has been small — eleven since 1980 — and these usually affect only dormant societies.

Perhaps oddly, in such a rapidly growing industry, entry has been even more limited. Since 1980 there has been only one — the Ecology Building Society. There is of course, a formal entry barrier in that a society must be registered with the Chief Registrar of Friendly Societies and meet certain legal requirements. However there is no reason why this barrier should prove insuperable. The lack of entry suggests a number of other possible hypotheses,

Table 4.3: Net Advances by Institution

	1978	1979	1980	1981	1982
Building Societies					
£m	5115	5271	5722	6331	7855
% Change (year on year)	+25	+3	+9	+11	+24
% Total Advances	92	80	77	66	57
Banking Sector					
£m	275	597	593	2447	4927
% Change	+127	+117	−1	+313	+101
% Total	5	9	8	25	36
Local Authorities & other public sector					
£m	−26	367	708	600	866
% Change	–	–	+91	−15	+44
% Total		5	9	6	6
Insurance Companies etc.					
£m	166	357	376	239	161
% Change	+39	+115	+5	−36	−33
% Total	3	5	5	3	1
Total Lending	5530	6592	7399	9617	13809
Increase in Total Lending (%)	+27	+19	+12	+28	+44
Building Society recommended Mortgage Rate (end year)	11.75	15.00	14.00	15.00	10.00

Source: Financial Statistics

including that existing organisations have an absolute cost advantage, that they undertake entry-deterring practices and that entry into the provision of house purchase finance is now easier and cheaper via other forms of institution.

Until 1979 it was reasonable to describe the housing finance industry in terms of building society behaviour. In the last three or four years the picture has changed. When funds became tight in 1979 the commercial banks entered the market, providing mortgages at rates and conditions competitive with societies. At this time they stated that they were committed to a continuing long-term role in the housing market. In practice the situation turned out to be far less straightforward.

In 1979 there was a clear gap in demand left by societies which was mainly filled by the banks who doubled their absolute involvement (Table 4.3).[8] In 1980 societies were able to increase their lending and banks apparently withdrew, as had been the experience in the past. However, in 1981 and 1982 when building societies were increasing their own lending quite strongly the banks expanded extremely rapidly, until at their highest point they were meeting over 30 per cent of total demand. Late in 1982 the position changed again. Although demand for housing finance remained strong, banks started to restrict mortgage availability, reducing their lending from an average £350m per month to something of the order of £100m to £150m per month by mid 1983. If this position were to continue their net advances would drop back to well under 15 per cent of the total market.

Thus the mortgage market has been characterised by overall expansion, generally obtained through the internal growth of building societies. Larger societies have grown more rapidly than smaller and this, together with increasing merger activity, has led to a decline in the number of societies and increasing concentration. However the potential for entry by other institutions has always existed and there has been significant actual entry in the last few years.

The position in the savings market is rather different. Here building societies compete with other institutions, particularly the banks and national savings, for personal sector funds. They compete both in price and non-price terms, differentiating their product by size of deposit, ease of withdrawal, numbers of branches, their commitment to providing mortgages to savers and in many other ways. They have had two significant advantages over other financial institutions, particularly the banks. First, societies pay tax on interest paid to savers at the composite tax rate, which takes account of the fact that a proportion of savers are not taxpayers, and then pay interest free of basic rate tax. In comparison to other institutions they are therefore able to attract more funds from taxpayers for a given pre-tax interest rate, as long as non-taxpayers find this interest rate attractive.[9] The benefit to societies has declined over the last 20 years as the proportion of the population not paying tax has been reduced and the range of savings available for such groups has increased. At the beginning of 1970 the composite tax rate was 34 per cent below the basic rate. Now it is only 16 per cent below. Secondly, building society deposits have not been counted as part of the money supply. Societies have therefore been free of monetary controls if not of government intervention. In particular they were unaffected by the Supplementary Special Deposits scheme (the 'corset') which constrained bank lending during much of the 1970s (Bank of England, 1982).

Table 4.4: Personal Sector Liquid Assets

<table>
<tr><th></th><th>End 1970
%</th><th>End 1975
%</th><th>End 1980
%</th><th>End 1982
%</th></tr>
<tr><td>Building Societies</td><td>34.5</td><td>42.4</td><td>46.1</td><td>47.5</td></tr>
<tr><td>Banking Sector</td><td>34.6</td><td>36.5</td><td>34.9</td><td rowspan="2">36.8</td></tr>
<tr><td>Savings Banks</td><td>6.1</td><td>5.3</td><td>7.1</td></tr>
<tr><td>National Savings</td><td>22.8</td><td>15.0</td><td>11.4</td><td>15.4</td></tr>
<tr><td>Other</td><td>2.1</td><td>0.7</td><td>0.6</td><td>0.3</td></tr>
<tr><td>Total £m</td><td>29,085</td><td>52,977</td><td>107,370</td><td>140,527</td></tr>
</table>

Source: Financial Statistics

Given this framework the building societies had little trouble throughout the 1970s in increasing their holdings either absolutely or relative to other personal savings institutions (Table 4.4).

However since 1979 the position has become more competitive (Whitehead, 1981). Many controls on bank lending have been removed. The government has decided to raise more money via national savings schemes and a wide range of new savings opportunities for small savers has been introduced. These factors have all increased the level of competition, pushing up real interest rates, as well as significantly increasing the importance of non-price competition, particularly advertising.

Thus in the savings market building societies have acted mainly as a cartel in competition with other institutions, some monolithic, some operating together and some strictly competitive with one another, within a framework of controls specified by government. There is evidence of a certain amount of segmentation of the market between institutions but also of growing responsiveness to interest rate changes and of a generally more competitive environment.

The Relevant Oligopoly Models

Four main questions arise from the description of the behaviour of the housing finance market and particularly of the building society movement so far:

Why have the societies felt the need for a cartel and particularly for the recommended rate system?
How has the cartel managed to survive so long?
Does the cartel have a major effect on the way the housing finance market operates?
Is the cartel likely to continue?

In attempting to answer these questions, general theories of oligopoly and competition are obviously not completely apposite, if only because they start from the assumption of profit maximisation. However, some of their implications are clearly relevant to the rather different form of cartel operated by the BSA.

The simplest model of oligopoly behaviour suggests that in order to maximise profit firms will attempt to operate as one, setting price and quantity so as to obtain all possible monopoly profit. This objective is only easily attained in extremely restrictive circumstances. If the product is homogenous and costs are the same for all firms each firm will take an equal share of the market and will wish to set the same price and quantity. Chamberlain (1929) argued that under these conditions, where the number of sellers is small, oligopolists will automatically realise their interdependence and operate to maximise joint profit without the need for formal agreement. However, even under these conditions an agreement might be desirable in an uncertain world because firms would then be unsure of how others might react to change and response might be slow. Secondly, as the number of firms increases, individual firms would be more prepared to ignore their own effect on price. In this case, without agreement, firms would expand output until price fell to the competitive level.

If firms face different cost structures, if the product is differentiated or existing market shares are unequal for other reasons it is more difficult to obtain profit-maximising price and output levels independently. If firms produce under different costs conditions but initially have similar market shares, they will have conflicting views as to the most desirable price. If the good is homogenous all firms must sell at the same price but generally those with lower costs will want a lower price with commensurately higher total output. In this case a joint profit-maximising price can only be obtained if market shares are specified on the basis of cost information. At the least this will require an information agreement and will often need a much higher level of collusion, including the reallocation of profits between participants. Otherwise the lowest price is likely to prevail, resulting in reduced profits, and an incentive for higher cost producers to retaliate by reducing price further in the hope of coercing the low cost producer towards a more acceptable position. In these circumstances price may be driven down to its competitive level. If cost differences are very large there may be no joint profit-maximising position which includes production by the highest cost suppliers. In these circumstances merger may be the most desirable solution from the point of view of the industry, as competition to force the firm out of business will result in loss of profits, while a profit sharing agreement where some firms produce no output is unlikely to be acceptable.

Analogous difficulties arise where cost structures are similar but market shares differ as a result e.g. of product differentiation, historical ties or capacity differences. In general, if marginal costs within the relevant range are rising the firm with the smallest market share will prefer the lowest price. If, on the other hand, marginal cost is falling those with the smallest share will want the highest price. Only where marginal costs are constant is there no conflict between different sized firms. This position is more likely to occur where firms make decisions in relation to long-run rather than short-run factors.

The effects of differences in costs and market shares may sometimes offset one another, reducing the problems of determining a mutually acceptable price — for instance where small firms have lower capitalisation and therefore higher marginal costs. However, if disparities which are not exactly symmetric remain, individual firms will still want different market prices and output levels. Collusion, and in particular formal agreements, may then help to increase total profit.

Further difficulties arise when market factors change, either because adjustments have to be made in response to these changes in demand or cost or because there is perceived to be a benefit from attempting to modify the demand curve. Again independent responses which take account only of that firm's expectations are likely to create tensions which move the industry away from its profit-maximising position.

Under this type of model building societies might be expected to benefit from a cartel simply because of their numbers and the variability in their sizes. Differences in objectives and in costs and demand conditions would imply greater benefits from a cartel if it were able to improve the flow of information, modify external factors and build up a team spirit. However, the low level of concentration measured by the Herfindahl index, which takes account both of relative size and the absolute number of firms, suggests that the industry would find it difficult to operate an effective agreement unless market conditions were particularly favourable or the benefits of a cartel overwhelmingly obvious.

Simple game theoretical models of oligopoly (Scherer, 1970) lead to similar conclusions in that they suggest that there will often be differences between the jointly desirable action and the apparent benefits of independent decisions. In these conditions factors which help member firms to recognise and evaluate the costs of competition and to monitor others' competitive behaviour would improve the chance of a stable agreement. However such agreements would be extremely difficult to enforce without effective monitoring and penalties for non-compliance unless again market conditions favour cooperation.

Another class of oligopoly model which might be of relevance to building society behaviour is that of the dominant firm (Stigler, 1965). This predicts that the dominant firm, or a smaller group of firms acting as one, will maximise short-run profits using as its relevant demand curve market demand less that provided by fringe firms. Fringe firms will act as price takers and will be able to flourish under the dominant firm's 'umbrella' even if they face higher costs. In the long-run continued entry and expansion by fringe firms would erode profitability unless there were barriers to entry, such as continuing cost advantages to the dominant firm or group, or unless the dominant group is able to institute anti-competitive strategies. If the relevant group can be readily identified, the concentration ratio defined for that number of firms would be a reasonable measure of market power. Changes in the ratio would reflect the effect on the dominant group of allowing freedom of action to the fringe firms.

In these conditions a cartel could have two distinct and important roles. The sub-cartel that made up the dominant group would be necessary to obtain agreement on the optimal price and output for that group given market demand and fringe firm activity. The overall cartel would then provide information to the fringe firms about the dominant group's decisions and, probably more importantly in practice, define the limits of fringe firm behaviour acceptable to the dominant group.

More general models of oligopoly behaviour identify attributes of firms and markets that would make collusion easier (Yamey, 1975). These include many of the factors discussed above such as the number and relative size of firms in the industry, the similarity of cost and demand conditions, the stability of the environment (including both the extent of random variability and of structural change), the potential for external competition and the existence of barriers to entry. In addition they concentrate on two factors; the extent to which the industry is made up of old established firms with similar objectives and wide knowledge of each other's behaviour and of the degree of interdependence between their decisions; and the extent of transparency in the market which allows an easy flow of information and simple monitoring of competitors' behaviour.

In the next section we examine the extent to which these models can be used to help explain the existence and stability of the building society cartel as well as the extent to which its existence may modify the operation of the housing market.

Building Society Behaviour and Market Conditions

The attributes of building societies and the market which are likely to be important in determining the extent of collusion and the effectiveness of a cartel include:

the objectives of societies,
the homogeneity of the product and the transparency of the market,
societies' cost conditions,
the number of societies and their relative size, and
entry barriers and external competition.

Building Society Objectives

Building societies most obviously differ from the analysis above because they do not maximise profit. Indeed the regulatory framework requires them to be mutual organisations making no profit for distribution to shareholders. They are however required to hold minimum reserves specified on a (reducing) sliding scale as a proportion of assets. Thus as they grow they must make surpluses to add to reserves. The rationale for these requirements is prudential — to cover losses on mortgages and other investments (Boléat, 1982, pp. 57–8). In actuality societies hold considerably more reserves than are legally required reflecting a 'recurrent judgement about the effects of ratios on the confidence of investors' (Department of Environment 1977, Technical Volume 2, p. 104). As such the holding of reserves may be regarded more as a constraint than an objective.

What the societies' objectives actually are is far less clear. Formally their only role is to make advances to members yet the fact that they have normally operated at interest rates which result in unsatisfied demand implies that they do not simply wish to maximise the quantity of advances or the growth of assets (but see Hadjimatheou, 1976). Behavioural models probably provide a better explanation (Gough, 1982) because of the clear separation between 'ownership' — the investing members who regard themselves as depositors rather than owners and take little part in the running of societies — and control as exercised by the managers employed by the societies. In these circumstances managers may still try to maximise the true surplus, taking for themselves as much as they can through salaries and other monetary benefits. Alternatively they may take some utility in the form of costs and non-pecuniary benefits (Yamey, 1972; Hindley, 1969), many of which are thought to be positively related to growth (Williamson, 1970). Satisficing models which predict that managers will attempt to meet specified targets rather than maximise surplus or utility have also been thought to be relevant (Davies, 1981).

The lack of a strong profit motive could be expected to result in wide variations in behaviour, with managers seeking many different types of utility. However, the movement is characterised by extreme risk aversion (Ghosh, 1974) arising from their belief that investors' confidence comes from 'the sheer standing of building societies as financial institutions' (Department of Environment, 1977, p. 104). Managers therefore fear that the failure of even one society to meet accepted standards would adversely affect all other societies' capacity to achieve their own objectives. In particular a significant proportion of total savings is thought to be attracted by savers' positive attitudes to the movement as a whole rather than to the popularity of any single institution. Under these conditions managers are likely to be predisposed to accept constraints that apply to all members alike and clearly help to enhance security. They are the more likely to agree because members realise that most societies operate with relatively unsophisticated financial management skills.

This view of the interdependence between all members of the movement, however large or small, provides a very strong incentive for cooperative behaviour. In this environment the BSA plays an important part in giving the movement an identity, helping to achieve consistent aims, clarifying to members the benefits from joint action, specifying limits to individual behaviour and minimising the costs to the movement when particular societies do run into trouble. Such a role has undoubted benefits to the movement quite separate from those from rate setting and would be likely to continue even if the recommended rate system were abandoned. Thus although in principle building societies might be expected to have rather diverse aims unconstrained by the need to provide dividends to their members, in practice the strong interdependence between their activities leads them to act together.

The Building Society Product

The mortgage product marketed by societies has in the past been almost completely homogenous mainly because for the majority of consumers one mortgage has seemed as good as another and the security of societies has been unquestioned. The continuing existence of queues has provided little incentive to compete through product differentiation and societies have agreed on the relative suitability of households and dwellings. Legal requirements concerning security and the form of mortgage instruments further limit differentiation. Discussion within the Association has probably been a major factor in determining the extent of agreement on lending policy while the recommended rate system has allowed the continuation of excess demand. Evidence from other countries, notably the United States and Australia (Tuccillo *et al*, 1981; Tucker 1981; Yates, 1981) suggests that were there to be greater competition a wider range of mortgage instruments and of terms and conditions would emerge. Thus it can be argued that homogeneity of product is not inherent but a result of the conservative attitudes of societies and the operation of the cartel.

The product on the savings side has similarly been homogenous until the last few years when term shares and other special schemes were introduced in response to external competition. This has almost certainly limited the extent of inter-society competition and helped to hold down the average interest rate paid for funds. Thus again the cartel has modified members' behaviour in line with joint objectives perhaps at the expense of savers. How long such an agreement could last in the face of strong external competition has yet to be tested.

The cartel's role as a forum for discussion and the provision of information undoubtedly increases the transparency of both mortgage and savings markets, making it easier for societies to monitor one another and decreasing the incentive to individual initiatives. Yet it is not clear that this should be enough to force compliance, given the lack of any overt penalty, unless the benefits are very great or the environment particularly favourable.

Thus the general acceptance of the recommended rate system and of the interdependence of societies has effectively limited inter-society competition within a generally uncompetitive environment. However, the conditions do not seem to exist for this level of agreement to survive in a more strongly competitive world. In the end continued collusion would depend on the larger societies' estimates of whether they themselves can gain or lose by breaking away.

Cost Conditions

The models of oligopoly suggest that similarity of cost structures helps to produce consistent decisions in the absence of collusion. Society costs are made up of interest payments, tax on interest and profit, and management expenses. In 1980 these accounted for respectively 70 per cent, 21 per cent and 8 per cent of total expenditure. As the cartel generally determines interest rates and the government the tax rate the vast majority of these costs are roughly proportionate to the level of activity and will otherwise not vary between societies. Management expenses may vary because of computerisation, allowing the possibility of economies of scale (Boléat, 1982), branching and advertising, which both increase costs and the level of activity (Boléat, 1981).

Overall one would therefore expect to find fairly similar cost structures with perhaps a tendency for large societies to face lower avoidable costs unless management slack increases with size. This is consistent with the estimate made by Cooper (1980) which showed some economies of scale at the lower end of the size spectrum and limited evidence of increasing costs among the largest societies. This would suggest that middle range and larger societies would want slightly lower prices than those desired by smaller societies. Thus the cartel, through the recommended rate system, helps remove much of the pressure that might arise from potentially heterogenous cost structures. In addition because long-run average costs appear to be nearly constant except at the bottom end of the market (below £10m assets) there are likely to be few problems arising from the disparity in market shares. Cost and demand conditions would therefore generally seem to assist collusion.

The Number of Firms

Although many of the conditions for easy collusion exist, with or without formal agreement, one might perhaps still argue that the number of firms was too large to constitute a successful collusive oligopoly. Although the CR_5 at 0.55 is high the next fifteen firms account for a further 35 per cent of assets, quite enough to upset a price leadership arrangement not thought to be in the interests of individual members. Nor does the Herfindahl index at 0.085 imply strong oligopoly power. Again, therefore, ready acceptance of interdependence of objectives and a favourable environment would appear to be necessary for the long-running success of any agreement.

Even then the ready acceptance of large scale non-compliance (in terms of number of societies) must be explained. The most obvious explanation is that the fringe firms who do not comply are not seen as a threat to the dominant group because of their limited capacity to expand and particularly their higher costs. Certainly even though they do not comply with the recommended rate system smaller societies have grown less rapidly than have larger institutions. Many of those who pay more for their funds do not charge more for their mortgages, suggesting both that they find it harder than average to attract funds and that they face a lower demand for mortgages.[10] One reason for this would appear to be that branching is a necessary condition of relative growth (Boléat, 1981; Davies, 1981) but entails significant set-up costs. Most small societies are made up of one office or a few branches in the same locality. Further, Cooper (1980) suggests that costs are higher for single branch societies. In addition they may well have to achieve relatively higher surpluses to prove to savers that they are as secure as larger, better known, societies.

If this is the case larger societies can readily tolerate non-compliance with the recommended rate as long as smaller societies are prudently managed and the risk of failure is limited. The cartel's role in ensuring standards and minimising the costs to the movement of problems faced by individual societies is therefore of particular importance.

The attributes of building societies so far discussed all suggest that there is a strong community of interest among societies and little pressure arising from cost and demand conditions or from within the movement to compete. It also suggests that the recommended rate system is by no means the most important element in the operation of the cartel. However, there is evidence to suggest significant management slack in the system both because of the lack of a shareholder constraint and because rates have been set to achieve continuing excess demand. Significant long-term entry into the market could be expected to change this situation and put at least some elements of the building society agreement under pressure.

Entry Barriers and External Competition

There are no obvious barriers to entry to the provision of mortgages and indeed many other organisations are in the market (see Table 4.1). However, before 1979 such competition as there was hardly impinged on building societies. This suggests that there were strong constraints on others' desire or ability to enter the mortgage market.

Undoubtedly government controls over the banking sector

limited their capacity to expand (Bank of England, 1982). Other types of institution do not seem to have regarded the risk-adjusted rate of return obtainable as desirable (Caves and Yamey, 1971).[11] Since 1979 the banks have been in a position to compete but are now beginning to set a limit to their involvement. A number of reasons for this can be put forward. First, the very high levels of lending in 1981 and 1982 may have been undertaken to increase the banks' mortgage holdings to the desired long-term proportion of their portfolios and now that position has been reached lending has been reduced to the long-term average required. Second, other lending opportunities have improved, so mortgage lending is no longer relatively so desirable. Third, absolute interest rates have now fallen to a level where banks, given their relative inefficiency in collecting small scale funds and administering mortgages, are no longer able easily to compete with building societies, because societies have themselves moved towards market interest rates.

The question in the long-term is whether building societies have a continuing relative advantage. Being non-profit organisations they have the potential to compete on price terms against other oligopolies, if they can control their management slack. The composite tax rate gives them some benefit on the savings side but this is being eroded. Their main argument is that, specialising in the collection of small savings and the provision of mortgages, they are able to operate at lower cost. If this is the case building societies will continue to flourish (unless they attempt to diversify into areas where they are not so effective). The detailed evidence on which to assess their claims to relative cost effectiveness is not however available (Hill and Gough, 1982).

Conclusions

The building society cartel is unusual because it has held prices down rather than increasing them. This is not inherently desirable as it excludes from housing finance consumers who are prepared to pay. Further it has allowed societies to operate 'in the interest of the least efficient societies who are being cushioned against economic forces' (Stow, 1978). It has also meant that the product available and society cost structures have been relatively homogenous.

The recommended rate system is only one element in the

activities of the BSA. The whole range of activities is aimed at producing a strong cooperative movement in which societies recognise that the overall growth of the movement helps their own objectives more than would inter-society competition, at least in the longer run.

Increasing competition especially from the banks appears to have put elements of this agreement in jeopardy. Continuing strong competition could be expected to improve the efficiency of the building societies and to lead to a wider range of terms and conditions for both mortgagors and savers. It would probably lead to a rapid increase in mergers both to improve the capacity of individual societies to compete and to assimilate societies which could not survive in such an environment. The recommended rate system would be replaced by overt inter-society competition for mortgages as well as savings. Yet even in these circumstances there would be major benefits to the societies in keeping some level of agreement on the terms and conditions offered to savers and in particular in ensuring the secure operation of all societies. Many of the elements of the cartel would probably remain.[12]

Notes

1. Anyone who invests in a building society share account is automatically a member of that society. Membership also includes non-investing borrowers.
2. Rule 2 of the Association sets out its objectives in detail. See Boléat (1979) p. 12.
3. These studies include Price (1958), Cleary (1965), and Ashworth (1980). See also Building Societies Association (1978) chapter 2.
4. The Council consists of thirty-five members, fifteen elected nationally, ten nominated by the ten largest societies and ten by the regional associations.
5. Between 1974 and 1979 rates were set after discussions with the Department of Environment with this purpose particularly in mind.
6. This paper was written in 1982. In October 1983, after the decision of the Abbey National to withdraw from the agreement, the BSA replaced the recommended rate system with advised rates together with an information agreement. Since that time there have been some slight differences in the rates set by the largest societies, mainly in relation to base mortgage rates. However the extent of collusion remains high.
7. Total assets appear to be a reasonable measure of concentration as capital/labour ratios and the extent of integration are not strongly correlated with industry size (Hill and Gough, 1980).
8. The other significant change observable in Table 4.3 is the increase in local authority and other public sector lending since 1980. This however, still plays a strictly residual role, arising in the main from the Housing Act 1980 which gave most public sector tenants the right both to buy and to a public sector mortgage if unable to obtain one from a building society.

9. Since April 1985 this benefit has been further eroded as banks now also pay a composite rate.

10. This stronger constraint was interpreted by Gough and Taylor (1979) as implying that smaller societies were more efficient. However it does not follow that larger firms are unable to produce at lower cost (Yamey, 1972). See BSA (1982b) for a general discussion of the interpretation of building society performance indicators.

11. Indeed insurance companies seem to have found it more desirable to link up with building societies in the provision of mortgage insurance, rather than to compete directly.

12. Indeed this seems to be a reasonable reflection of the position in late 1985.

References

Ashworth, H. (1980) *The Building Society Story*, London, Franey and Co.

Bank of England (1981) 'The Supplementary Special Deposits Scheme' *Bank of England Quarterly Bulletin*, March

Boléat, M. (1979) *The Building Societies Association*, London, Building Societies Association

Boléat, M. (1981) *Building Society Branching*, London, Building Societies Association

Boléat, M. (1982) *The Building Society Industry*, London, George Allen and Unwin

Building Societies Association (1978) *Evidence Submitted by the BSA to the Committee to Review the Functioning of Financial Institutions*, London, The Association

Building Societies Association (1979) *Mortgage Finance in the 1980s* (The Stow Report) The Association

Building Societies Association (1982a) 'The Determination of Building Society Interest Rates' *BSA Bulletin* No. 29, January

Building Societies Association (1982b) 'Building Society Performance Indicators' *BSA Bulletin* No. 32, October

Caves, R. E. and Yamey, B. S. (1971) 'Risk and Corporate Rates of Return: Comment', *Quarterly Journal of Economics, LXXXV*, 513–7

Chamberlin, E. H. (1929) 'Duopoly: Value where Sellers are Few', *Quarterly Journal of Economics, XLIV*, 63–100

Cleary, E. J. (1965) *The Building Societies Movement*, London, Elek Books

Committee to Review the Functioning of Financial Institutions (The Wilson Committee) *Report* (1980) Cmnd 7937, London, HMSO

Cooper, J. C. B. (1980) 'Economies of Scale in the UK Building Society Industry', *The Investment Analyst*, January

Davies, G. (1981) *Building Societies and their Branches — Regional Economic Survey*, London, Franey and Co.

Department of Environment (1977) *Housing Policy — A Consultative Document* Cmnd 6851 and Technical Volumes, London, HMSO

Ghosh, D. A. (1974) *The Economics of Building Societies*, Farnborough, Hants, Saxon House

Gough, T. J. and Taylor, T. W. (1979) *The Building Society Price Cartel*, Hobart Paper No. 85, London, Institute of Economic Affairs

Gough, T. J. (1982) *The Economics of Building Societies*, London, Macmillan

Hadjimatheou, G. (1976) *Housing and Mortgage Markets*, Farnborough, Hants., Saxon House

Hill, S. and Gough, T. J. (1980) 'Concentration and Efficiency in the Building Society Industry' UWIST Discussion Paper in Economics, Finance and Politics, No. 1/80, February
Hindley, B. (1969) 'Capitalism and the Corporation', *Economica, XXXVI*, 426–39
Maclennan, D. (1982) *Housing Economics*, London, Longman
Mayes, D. (1979) *The Property Boom*, Oxford, Robertson
Price, S. J. (1958) *Building Societies: Their Origin and History*, London, Elek Books
Scherer, F. M. (1970) *Industrial Pricing: Theory and Evidence*, Chicago, Rand McNally and Co
Stigler, G. A. (1965) 'The Dominant Firm and the Inverted Umbrella' *Journal of Law and Economics, VIII* (Oct.), 167–73
Stow, R. (1978) 'Building Societies' *Glasgow Herald*, January
Tuccillo, J. (1981) *Housing and Investment in an Inflationary World*, Washington, DC, Urban Institute Press
Tucker, S. M. (1981) *Quantitative Comparisons of the Costs of Housing Finance and Subsidy Schemes*, Melbourne, CSIRO
Whitehead, C. M. E. (1981) 'Housing Finance: A Changing Market', *Public Money, 1*, No. 1, 39–42
Williamson, O. E. (1970) *Corporate Control and Business Behaviour*, Englewood Cliffs, NJ, Prentice-Hall
Yamey, B. S. (1972) 'Do Monopoly and Near Monopoly Matter' in M. H. Peston and B. C. Corry (eds.) *Essays in Honour of Lord Robbins*, London, Weidenfeld and Nicolson
Yamey, B. S. (1975) 'Some Problems in Oligopoly' in M. Ariga (ed.) *International Conference in International Economics and Competitive Policy Papers and Reports*, Tokyo
Yates, J. (1981) 'Deregulation of Interest Rates for Housing?' Paper presented at Winter School of New South Wales branch of Economic Society of Australia and New Zealand

PART THREE

AUCTION MARKETS

5 COMPETITIVE BIDDING AND THE PRICE MECHANISM

L. Roy Webb and Piet de Jong
Griffith University

1. Introduction

In this paper we discuss some of the implications of sealed bidding, or tendering, for the theory of price. The present version of the paper has had an unusually long gestation period, and the reader, particularly the reader in whose honour the present volume has been prepared, is entitled to some explanation.

Professor Yamey first saw, and was instrumental in developing, many of the propositions made in this paper when he acted as PhD supervisor to the first-named author in 1960–62 (Webb, 1962). Since then the literature on competitive bidding has grown rapidly, as is evident from the bibliography prepared by Stark and Rothkopf (1979).[1] The rapid progress of the literature was such as to persuade the first-named author (and some referees of earlier versions!) of the present paper that more work needed to be done before publication would be appropriate. Accordingly, there appeared Webb (1964), de Jong and Webb (1973) and de Jong and Webb (1975).

Two considerations have led to the decision to offer this version of the paper in honour of its original foster parent. The first is that, in spite of the growth of the literature to which we have referred, the problems raised by tendering still receive little attention in textbooks on price theory. This may be because much of the literature has employed game theory and is highly mathematical by average textbook standards. Or it may be a consequence of the emphasis in bidding theory on operations research rather than economic analysis. Whatever the explanation, it remains a puzzling fact that microeconomic texts largely ignore a method of price formation which accounts for a substantial proportion of sales in the areas of, for example, heavy engineering, building and construction, government procurement, 'own' brands in retail markets and some commodity markets. The present paper attempts to build a bridge between conventional microeconomic theory and some of the work by operations researchers on competitive bidding. The approach adopted is non-strategic and is in the tradition of the theory of the firm associated with Cournot, Marshall and Chamberlin. The diagrams used make the analysis accessible to students with a background in basic economics and statistics.

The second reason for offering the paper is to suggest an alternative and more general interpretation of competitive bidding models. This interpretation rests on the proposition that competitive sealed bidding for contracts has much in common with the process, which is characteristic of a great deal of economic activity, whereby sellers 'bid' for shares of product markets (and profits) by nominating prices for goods of specified quality.

In the absence of industrial espionage, these prices (on which investment and production plans are based) frequently remain confidential, or 'sealed', until goods are ready for sale. Thus, many of the uncertainties and responses to uncertainty which characterise competitive bidding for contracts are present in the process of competitive bidding for market shares of sales of manufactured and other commodities. Price 'bids' may be represented as the result of adding to estimated unit operating costs of production (and distribution where appropriate) a margin to provide a return on capital.[2] The estimation of operating costs for a given rate of capacity utilisation and for a given technology, and the choice of a capital charge per unit of output by which to amortise capital outlay, are of course part of the process of estimating long-run marginal cost (Turvey, 1969). The end result of the process is an estimate of the price (embracing an estimate of marginal cost) which the firm is prepared to 'try out' in the market and on the basis of which it proceeds with its investment and production plans. It is this element of testing the market with a price bid which is more effectively modelled, we believe, using the competitive bidding approach rather than the conventional pricing models. The reader is left to keep this alternative interpretation in mind as the discussion of competitive bidding proceeds. The notion of competing for a share of the market for a particular product may be substituted for the notion of competing for a share of a set of contracts, but otherwise the existing notation is sufficient to carry the alternative interpretation.

2. Competitive Tendering and the Dutch Auction

The distinctive problem arising from competitive sealed tendering is a consequence of its secrecy. Under this system the prospective buyer invites tenders from sellers in respect of a commodity with given specifications. These tenders must usually be submitted in writing prior to an advertised date. Collusion aside, each tenderer must prepare to bid in ignorance of the bids of rivals, so that each tenderer is uncertain of success. On the basis of experience of previous competitions for contracts with similar specifications, each tenderer may be able to estimate the likely levels of rival bids and make a probability judgement about the chances of winning a given competition, but certainty about the outcome is in the nature of the case unattainable.

The bidding conditions created by the secret tendering system are analogous to those created at an auction by the Dutch bidding procedure. At a Dutch auction the auctioneer (acting for the seller) offers successively lower prices in connection with a particular lot. Unlike the bidder at a conventional progressive auction, the bidder at a Dutch auction has only one chance; the first bid is the winning bid. The longer a bidder restrains himself from bidding, the more likely it is that some other bidder will produce the winning bid. On the other hand, the further a seller's offer-price falls below a bidder's subjective valuation of the lot, the greater the bidder's surplus in the event of his bid being the first bid. Each actual bid at a Dutch auction therefore represents a trade-off of the benefits and costs of postponement of the bid (Vickrey, 1961).

For the firm engaged in secret tendering there is a similar conflict. The buyer takes the place of the seller at a Dutch auction as the sponsor of the bidding competition. Each tender is a single-chance bid, so that the determination of its size poses the same kind of problem as that facing a bidder at a Dutch auction. The higher the bid the greater is the tenderer's potential profit, but the greater also is the risk that another tenderer will produce the winning bid. The initial task is thus to discuss ways in which a tenderer might optimise his behaviour in the context of this conflict. The basic approach used in this paper is adapted from the pioneering work of Sasieni, Yaspan and Friedman (1959, pp. 172–4).

Throughout the following analysis it will be assumed that

tenders consist of a fixed price rather than an offer to supply at cost plus a stated profit margin, that each tenderer seeks to maximise his expected profits, that the lowest tenderer for a contract is assumed to win that contract (that is, non-price factors, which in reality may be important elements in the overall assessment of a tender, are ignored), that there is no collusion between tenderers, that each firm ignores the effect, if any, of its own policies on the future behaviour of rivals, and that there are no government taxes or subsidies.

3. The Analysis of Bidding for a Single Contract

Assume that there are a number of tenderers competing for a specified contract. Different states of knowledge on the part of the tenderer will be examined and it will be found, not unexpectedly, that the optimal tendering policy for a given firm needs to be adjusted according to the state of the tenderer's knowledge. This state of knowledge will be characterised by a subjective probability distribution.

Let us concentrate our attention on one tenderer. In respect of a particular contract the firm makes a cost estimate c, say, and a corresponding bid to the value b. The higher the bid the higher will be the realised profit margin if the contract is won, and the lower the chance of this occurring. In setting the value for the bid the firm must reconcile these two conflicting ends. In doing so it will have to make some subjective judgement about the likelihood or probability of the lowest rival bid taking certain values. Let us designate the unknown lowest rival bid as the random variable X having probability density function g(x). The density reflects the judgement of the current tenderer as to the lowest of rival bids. A density which is 'spread out' is indicative of a large element of uncertainty as to the lowest opposing bid. By contrast, a density concentrated on a narrow interval is associated with a high degree of certainty. To summarise the density g(x) we shall consider the mean μ, the standard deviation σ and the mean deviation ρ defined as

$$\rho = \int_0^\infty x-\mu/g(x)\,dx \qquad (1)$$

The mean μ is in the current tenderer's subjective evaluation the most likely value of the lowest bid from amongst its rivals. Both σ

and ρ indicate the degree of scatter about the mean and are thus measures of ignorance on the part of the current tenderer regarding the lowest bid.

How should a tenderer proceed to maximise its expected profits? Clearly the tenderer would like to make a bid just fractionally less than the realised value of X provided this exceeds the cost c. If it can do this it will win the contract at the highest profit margin consistent with the given behaviour of its rivals. The achievement of such results would imply that the tenderer was in possession of 'inside' information, and is of course inconsistent with the formulation of the tendering problem as one essentially involving some measure of ignorance of rival bids.

Given a bid to the value x by the tenderer the expected profit from this bid is

$$(x-c)P(X>x) + 0.P(X<x) = (x-c)\int_x^\infty g(z)dz \tag{2}$$

where it is assumed that the cost outcome given the contract is won is independent of X. Maximising the expected profit $(x-c)P(X>x)$ with respect to x leads to the first order condition for the optimal bid, b

$$0 = G(b) + (b-c)G'(b) = G(b) - (b-c)g(b) \tag{3}$$

where $G(x) = P(X>x)$ is the integral in the right hand side of (2), and $G'(x) = -g(x)$ is the derivative of $G(x)$. Hence

$$b = c + G(b)/g(b) \tag{4}$$

which is not less than c. The optimal bid is thus the cost c plus a margin $G(b)/g(b) = -G(b)/G'(b)$. The expected profit corresponding to the maximum is given by $G^2(b)/g(b)$ which is simply the margin $G(b)/g(b)$ multiplied by the probability $G(b)$ of winning the contract.

The maximising solution b and its corresponding expected profit may be illustrated in a diagram. In Figure 5.1 the values x of tenderers' bids are measured along the horizontal axis, while probabilities y of winning the contract are plotted on the vertical axis. The various combinations of bid x and probability y which yield constant expected profit $(x-c)y$ are joined by equal-expected-profit curves. These constant expected profit curves form rectangular hyperbolas with respect to the axes $x=c$ and $y=0$.

Figure 5.1: Equilibrium For a Given Contract

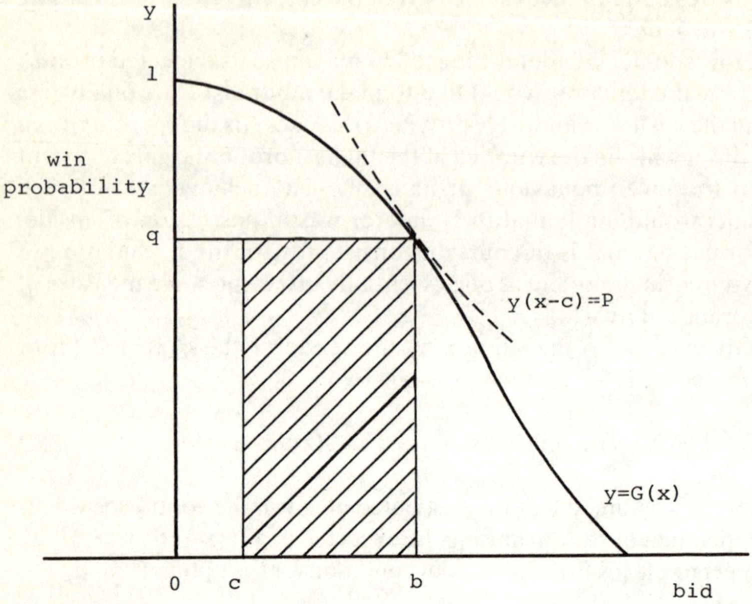

Consider the point (b,q) on the diagram. At this point q=G(b) and q=p/(b−c). Hence p=(b−c)G(b). Moreover at this point the slopes of the two indicated curves are equal and consequently we have p=(b−c)g(b). Combining these two expressions for p yields b=c+G(b)/g(b) and hence the point (b,q) is that corresponding to the maximising bid. Evidently q is the resulting probability of success at the optimising bid whereas the resulting maximum expected profit corresponds to the shaded area bounded by the lines x=c, x=b and y=q. Since rectangular hyperbolas all have an elasticity of minus one we can characterise the optimum solution in familiar terms as follows: increase the profit margin x−c until the proportionate increase in the profit margin is equal to the proportionate decrease in the probability of success.

To further explore the maximising solution we consider both the Normal and Uniform distribution. The former, like most distributions, does not admit a closed solution for the optimal bid in terms of the parameters of the density and c. The latter does admit such a representation. Indeed if the density is uniform on the interval (u,v) then

$$G(x) = (v-x)/(v-u), \qquad g(x) = 1/(v-u) \qquad u<x<v$$

and the optimising solution takes the following form:

$$b = (v+c)/2, \qquad G(b) = (v-c)/[2(v-u)]$$

provided $u < c < v$. Interestingly, the optimum bid in this situation depends on the mean and variance of the density only through the right end-point v. Straightforward computations show that $\mu=(u+v)/2$, $\rho=(v-u)/4$ and hence $b=\mu/2+\rho+c/2$ and that the expected profit corresponding to this bid is $(\mu+2\rho-c)^2/(16\rho)$. Contracts are thus not necessarily awarded to those with the lowest costs but rather to those who have (a) relatively low (and possibly unrealistic) cost estimates, (b) relatively low (and possibly pessimistic) estimates of the opposing bids and (c) relatively firm ideas as to the lowest opposing bid.

Generalising these last three features of the optimising bid, we can show that regardless of the actual density both the optimising bid and the maximum expected profit are homogeneous functions of degree one in the parameters μ, ρ (or σ) and c. To establish this let X have mean μ and mean deviation ρ and generally let $b(\mu, \rho, c)$ be the optimising bid corresponding to these parameters and cost c. For positive λ the random variable λX has mean $\lambda\mu$ and mean deviation $\lambda\rho$ and the optimising bid $b(\lambda\mu, \lambda\rho, \lambda c)$ is that x which maximises

$$(x-\lambda c)P(\lambda X>x) = \lambda(x/\lambda-c)P(X>x/\lambda).$$

But the right hand side is maximised by $x/\lambda = b(\mu, \rho, c)$ and hence $b(\lambda\mu, \lambda\rho, \lambda c) = \lambda b(\mu, \rho, c)$ with an identical result for the actual maximum. Accordingly it suffices to consider solutions only as functions of say μ/c and ρ/c.

Table 5.1 illustrates the optimal bid and the associated probability of winning for a variety of μ/c and ρ/c combinations when the underlying distribution is Normal.[3] It may be shown that for the Normal distribution $\rho=0.798\sigma$. The table indicates that, like the Uniform situation, the optimal bid and expected profit increases with the mean μ. This holds true for any distribution: a proof and details are provided in Appendix 5.A. On the other hand, again like the Uniform setup, expected profit both declines and increases as a function of the 'spread' of the density. We return to this phenomenon in Section 4.

Table 5.1: Optimal Markups and Win Probabilities[a]

μ/c	ρ/c 0.05	0.09	0.13	0.17	0.21	0.25	0.29
0.60	0.00	0.00	0.00	0.01	0.03	0.05	0.07
	0.00	0.00	0.00	0.01	0.02	0.04	0.05
0.80	0.00	0.01	0.03	0.05	0.08	0.10	0.13
	0.00	0.01	0.04	0.07	0.09	0.11	0.13
1.00	0.03	0.06	0.09	0.12	0.15	0.17	0.20
	0.24	0.24	0.24	0.24	0.24	0.24	0.24
1.20	0.15	0.16	0.18	0.21	0.23	0.26	0.29
	0.86	0.67	0.56	0.48	0.44	0.41	0.38
1.40	0.30	0.29	0.30	0.31	0.34	0.36	0.38
	0.97	0.89	0.78	0.69	0.62	0.57	0.52
1.60	0.48	0.45	0.44	0.44	0.45	0.47	0.49
	0.99	0.96	0.90	0.83	0.76	0.70	0.65
1.80	0.67	0.62	0.59	0.58	0.58	0.59	0.61
	1.00	0.98	0.95	0.90	0.85	0.80	0.75

Note: a. Top entry in each cell is markup, bottom entry is win probability.

4. Analysis of a Group of Contracts

The tools and techniques of the previous section can be adapted to derive equilibrium conditions when a group of contracts is up for tender. We assume that a tenderer submits bids for each of a group of contracts by adding a given (absolute) markup to each cost estimate. The situation we have in mind is where an individual maximisation (for each contract) along the lines of Section 2 is not practical or feasible and the tenderer simply decides to submit bids equal to estimates of costs plus a fixed profit margin with the markup calculated to maximise profits. A set of contracts is amenable to the analysis below to the extent that the strategy of adding a constant margin to all contracts is a realistic policy.

To determine the optimal profit addition, the tenderer will have

Figure 5.2: Equilibrium for a Group of Contracts

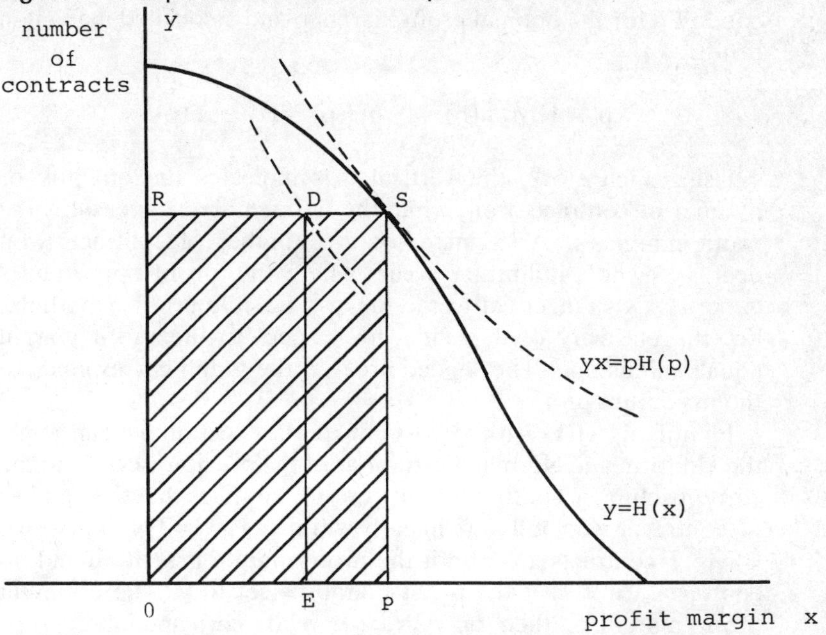

to make some judgements regarding the number of contracts that can be captured at different profit margins. The basis underlying such judgement could be an empirical frequency distribution indicating the scatter of profit margins experienced in the context of a comparable set of contracts. Such experience may embody both that of the current tenderer or that of competitors since the winning profit margins (or some idea of them) are common knowledge to all tenderers. We shall denote the frequency distribution as h(x) where x is the profit margin.

A particular contract is won if the profit margin plus estimated costs on the contract is less than any of the competitors' bids. As x increases fewer contracts are won but those that are won will generate higher profits. The aim is thus to maximise

$$x \int_0^\infty h(z)dz = xH(x) \tag{5}$$

where H(x) is the integral in the left hand side and hence $H'(x) = -h(x)$ which is exactly the relation connecting G and g of the last section. In other words H(x) is the 'demand' for contracts that the current competitor experiences when it sets its profit margin to x. Maximising (5) with respect to x leads to the following condition for the optimal profit margin p and associated maximum profit:

$$p = H(p)/h(p), \qquad pH(p) = H^2(p)/h(p).$$

Using Figure 5.2, the vertical axis indicates the quantity or number of contracts won, while the horizontal axis measures the profit margin x. As x increases the number of contracts won decreases and equilibrium occurs where the 'profit opportunity' curve H(x) is tangential to the highest possible profit hyperbola, i.e. the elasticity of demand with respect to the profit margin equals minus one. The shaded area on the graph corresponds to the maximum profit.

Identifying H(x) with G(c+x) of the last section we can apply the Uniform and Normal illustrations of the previous section to the current setup. A Uniform density on (u,v) implies that the number of contracts won falls off linearly with x: $H(x)=T(v-x)/(v-u)$, where T contracts are won if the profit margin is set to u and no contracts are won if the profit margin is set to v. The optimum profit margin is then $p=v/2=\mu/2+\rho$ with corresponding profit $Tv/[2(v-u)]=T(\mu+2\rho)^2/(16\rho)$.

To illustrate the Normal density we again first note that for all densities the optimum profit margin p and the associated maximum profit is homogenous of degree one in the parameters μ and ρ. Accordingly it is sufficient to consider the optimum margin and proportion of contracts won only as a function of say μ/ρ. Table 5.2 presents some results. As μ increases for fixed ρ, i.e. the 'demand for contracts' increases, the optimal margin increases. This again is analogous to the Uniform density and can be shown to be true for any density: details are in Appendix 5.A. Con-

Table 5.2: Optimal Margins and Proportion of Contracts Won[a]

				μ/ρ				
−2.50	−1.00	−0.50	0.00	0.50	1.00	2.00	4.00	8.00
0.07	0.35	0.51	0.69	0.90	1.13	1.65	2.91	6.09
0.01	0.09	0.16	0.24	0.34	0.45	0.64	0.86	0.97

Note: a. Top entry is optimal margin, bottom entry is proportion of contracts won.

versely, as ρ increases for fixed μ the optimal margin both increases and decreases. The ramifications of this are considered in the next Section.

5. Tendering and Predictive Ability

The two models of the previous Sections assume that the tenderer is in possession of what might be called 'parametric' knowledge, i.e. knowledge as to the location and dispersion of the function g(x) or h(x), but no information as to, for example in the first case, the actual value of the opposition's lowest bid, or in the second case, the particular maximum profit margins that may be used to capture specific contracts. Knowledge, or more particularly the relative lack of it, is a basic hallmark of the tendering problem; where knowledge is perfect buyers will not be interested in the tendering mechanism at all (the very act of calling for tenders is a confession of ignorance about each potential seller's price), while a seller will not waste time and money submitting a tender if he already knows that some other seller is willing to offer a lower price. An important question thus centres around the precise influence of the state of knowledge on both bids and profits.

In the model of Section 2 the first kind of knowledge that may be distinguished is so called 'inside' knowledge as to the lowest opponent's bid which may for example have been gained as a result of espionage. In this case the tenderer sets his bid just fractionally lower than the revealed minimum, provided this covers costs. Prior to the tenderer gaining this inside knowledge he conjectures that the most likely value of the lowest opposing bid is μ and that to be the winner of the contract he has to set his bid marginally below μ. The profit which he expects to make from the contract, prior to embarking on gathering the inside information is thus $\mu - c$. An integration by parts shows that

$$\mu = \int_0^\infty G(x)dx \qquad (6)$$

where, as before, $G(x)=P(X>x)$. In other words the expected profit under 'inside' information corresponds to the whole area underneath the G(x) curve in Figure 5.1 to the right of the vertical $x=c$. This clearly dominates the maximum expected profit indicated by the shaded area (the optimum solution in the absence of inside information) and hence the expected 'value' of inside information is non-negative. This value is small if the curve G(x) follows the line segments y−q and y−0 over the ranges $c<x<b$ and $b<x$ respectively. This implies that g(x) is negligible in the relevant range apart from a small interval around $x=b$. Since inside knowledge implies the ability to predict the lowest rival bid, it is not surprising that the reward for this knowledge should increase as the scope for its exercise increases, that is the dispersion of g(x) increases.

For the 'group of contracts' model of Section 3, inside knowledge corresponds to the ability to pair each contract off with its maximum possible profit margin rather than apply a fixed profit margin to all the contracts in the group. Such complete knowledge again increases profits. In Figure 5.2 the whole area beneath the curve H(x) to the right of the y axis corresponds to the profit obtainable from a set of contracts by a tenderer with complete knowledge. In the limiting case, where the variance associated with h(x) is zero, parametric knowledge is equivalent to complete knowledge, and hence complete knowledge marks an extreme boundary to the parametric situation. When the variance is not zero it is not surprising to find that a variable policy taking account of all information is more profitable than a constant markup policy applied to all contracts and where such markup is calculated from only a summary of the information that is potentially available.

In a natural fashion the mean deviation or variance associated with g(x) or h(x) measures the ignorance on the part of the tenderer and hence it is of interest to observe the reaction of the maximising solutions to changes in ρ. Taking the model of Section 3 and the Uniform density we have seen that the optimising solution leads to profit of $T(\mu+2\rho)^2/(16\rho)$. Differentiating this with respect to ρ and equating to zero leads to the conclusion that profits are maximum for given μ when $\rho=\mu/2$. This means that we cannot be certain about the effect of a change in the uncertainty of profit margins on profits unless we know the initial value of ρ. This same phenomenon is present in Tables 5.1 and 5.2. For example in Table 5.1 an increase in ρ/c is accompanied by an increase in the optimal margin and an increase in expected profit whenever μ/c does not exceed 1. If μ/c does exceed unity then the optimal markup both declines and increases. Similarly considering Table 5.2 and fixing μ at 10 say, ρ at levels 5, 10 and 20 leads to profits proportional to 5.30, 5.09 and 6.12 respectively, i.e. increasing ρ leads to firstly a fall, followed by a rise in profits.

Figure 5.3: Changing the Level of Uncertainty

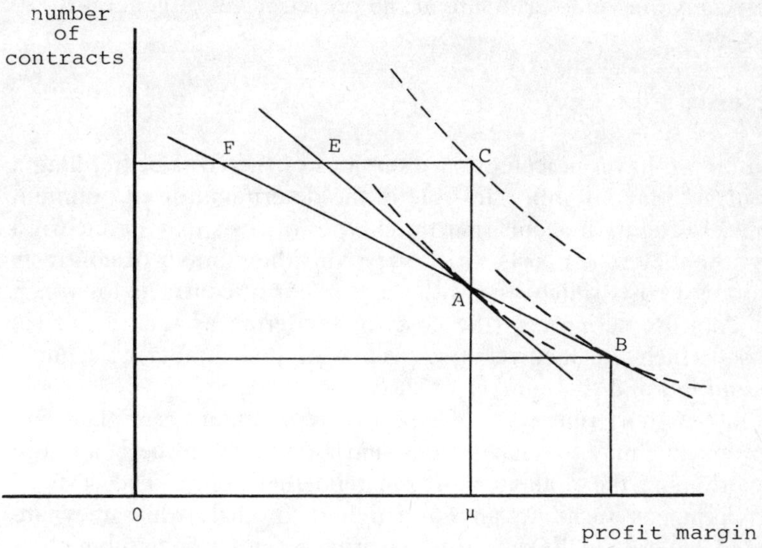

Figure 5.3 gives a diagrammatic representation of the effects of a change in the parameter ρ where for simplicity we have taken the uniform density as an example. With $\rho=0$ and hence no uncertainty in profit margins the optimal margin is μ and the resulting profit is that indicated by the hyperbola passing through the point C. As ρ increases in such a way as to keep the mean fixed, suppose the line of tangency pivots on the point A (and hence, by formula (6) the mean indeed stays constant). An integration by parts shows that

$$\rho = 2 \int_0^{\mu} [1-G(x)]dx = 2 \int_{\mu}^{\infty} G(x)dx$$

and hence when the point of tangency is at A the value of ρ is proportional to the area of the triangle AEC. From the diagram it is clear that for ρ less than this area the optimal margin is less than μ while the profit is less than that in the certain situation represented by the hyperbola passing through C. Now increasing ρ beyond the area AEC to the area of triangle AFC evidently leads to higher optimal margins and higher profits. Whereas the mean effect is unequivocal in the sense that a change in μ leads, *ceteris paribus*, to a change in profits in the same direction, the uncertainty effect may have positive or negative impact according as ρ or σ moves towards or away from a critical value. A combination of the two effects is thus indeterminate at the present level of generality.

6. Fixed Costs

So far we have indicated that estimates of the costs of fulfilling a contract play an important role in the determination of optimum bids. In reality it seems that three types of costs may be incurred by a tenderer: (a) costs which vary with the number of contracts won; (b) costs which vary with the number of contracts for which tenders are submitted (the costs of tendering as such); and (c) costs which are incurred irrespective of the number of tenders submitted and the number of successful tenders.

In the short run, costs of type (c), representing, say plant and equipment, may be unavoidable, and may therefore be ignored in determining the optimal short-run tendering policy. The costs of tendering as such are an unusual item in that, while they are avoidable even in the short run (the firm does not have to submit bids in order merely to remain in existence) they are fixed relative to the number of contracts won. Thus these costs must be treated as overhead expenses in the short run. While the tenderer may be able to estimate the cost of preparing a tender for each contract, it cannot know in advance of submitting its bids those particular contracts for which its bids will be successful (unless the tenderer has complete knowledge). Hence it cannot know how to distribute its tendering costs over the group of contracts for which it is successful until it knows the identity of such contracts; but then it is too late.

Tendering costs, however, along with other overhead costs may be treated in the following way. In Figure 5.2, for example, we have assumed that the axes represent the zero-profit rectangular hyperbola. This is true so long as we exclude all costs except those of type (a). If there are other costs it will be necessary to re-label the rectangular hyperbolas so that the zero-profit curve appears as one of the hyperbolas contained within the diagram. Let it be assumed that there are fixed costs represented by area ORDE. In the short run profit will be ORSp. In the long run, with all costs avoidable, the tenderer will still choose p as the optimal profit margin, but will regard profit as being only EDSp. In the long run the hyperbola passing through D is the zero profit hyperbola.

7. The Equilibrium of the Tendering Group

In the preceding sections we have considered methods of profit maximisation for an individual tenderer on the assumption that the distribution of minimum rival bids or profit margins, g(x) or h(x), is given. We must now consider the implications of assuming that all firms in the group adopt the profit maximisation procedure we have described. However, no attempt will be made to deal with the problem of oligopolistic interdependence; we continue to assume that firms ignore such impact as their policies may have on rivals. Oligopoly in the present context seems to open up the same range of multitudinous assumptions and conclusions as we find in other studies of the problem, leading to the familiar proposition that explicit or implicit collusion among businessmen is likely to be a popular response to the experience of interdependence.

In the theory of perfect competition price is a datum for the individual firm but is an explicandum of the theory of equilibrium for the industry as a whole. Similarly, in the theory of competitive tendering the g(x) or h(x) density may not be treated as a datum when we are seeking to define equilibrium concepts for a group of tenderers. In fact we shall find that changes in the form and parameters of the density are a manifestation of disequilibrium in much the same way as are changes in unit price in the static theory of perfect competition. Other things being equal, a stable density is a condition of group equilibrium since, where there are changes in the distribution, there will be revisions by tenderers of their calculations of optimal margins, possible revisions by buyers of the number and specifications of the contracts for which they invite tenders and, hence, further changes in the underlying distribution. In this section we shall spell out this kind of sequence in more detail, showing that while an equilibrium situation is feasible, it does not appear to be a goal towards which the tendering group necessarily moves.

We shall adopt a form of period analysis in order to suggest what might happen over time in the tendering group. For concreteness we use the 'group of contracts' model of Section 3, although it will be apparent that the same considerations apply to the model of Section 2. In the current period t, the tenderer prepares an h(x) distribution on the basis of past experience. The record of his experience in period t becomes the basis for the tenderer's revision of the distribution for period t+1. We thus assume in effect that tenderers base their revisions solely on their experience with respect to similar contracts in the preceding period. In reality of course revisions may be influenced by factors not connected with this past experience at all.

In period t each tenderer determines an optimal margin to apply to contracts in that period. Each will, on the basis of these profit margins expect to win a particular share of the total number of contracts open for competition in period t. These separate expectations are consistent only in the apparently accidental circumstance where all the individual expected numbers add to the total number of contracts up for tender in period t. Accordingly, even assuming that the number and variety of contracts open for competition remain constant from period to period, the tenderers are unlikely all to be correct in their expectations. If a tenderer's realised share of contracts differs from his expected share, then there will be revisions in h(x). In addition to such sources of revision we can identify other causes such as changes in the behaviour of rival tenderers, and changes from one period to another in the set of contracts for which buyers invite tenders. All these changes will lead to a frustration of expectations and to revisions of their tendering policies by tenderers, since the current experience becomes the basis for the revision of h(x).

Reactions by buyers from period to period are worth a further comment. There seem to be two sources of change in the nunber and variety of contracts for which tenders are invited. First, there may be changes in the wealth and/or tastes of the buyers; these changes are of the same type as those which, in conventional price theory, affect the position and shape of the demand curve. We shall ignore such changes. Second, buyers may alter the number and nature of the contracts for which they invite tenders because of their experience in the previous period. The h(x) distribution resulting from a given set of competitions may be such as to cause buyers to revise their 'offers-to-buy'. For example the winning bids in the previous period may be lower than those anticipated by buyers, and in the current period they may increase the number of contracts for which they invite tenders, or perhaps increase the amount of work or materials involved in each contract. An unexpectedly high set of winning bids may have the opposite effect. These changes, again by analogy with conventional price theory, are similar to those which involve movements along a given demand curve. In terms of the kind of responses described in the 'cobweb' theorem, we are suggesting that buyers adjust their 'offers-to-buy' on the basis of their experience of the 'supply price' associated with the previous offers-to-buy. In a tendering industry the 'supply price' is typically a distribution of winning bids for a heterogenous collection of goods rather than a single price for a unit of an homogenous and divisible commodity.

The h(x) distribution may therefore vary over time on account of both demand side and supply side changes. As h(x) varies then each tenderer's calculations of the optimal profit margin will be revised, introducing further changes in a subsequent h(x). The tendering group may be defined to be in a state of equilibrium when h(x) is unchanging from period to period. Each tenderer will then use the same h(x) in calculating his profit margins in each period. Thus equilibrium in a tendering industry may be regarded as involving concepts similar to those characteristic of equilibrium in market models of the perfectly competitive or monopolistically competitive kind: the output of the industry, in the sense of the number and variety of contracts fulfilled, is constant; there is no tendency for firms to enter or leave the industry since profits are constant for each firm over time (new tenderers having been attracted to the tendering competitions so long as super-normal profits appeared, on an *ex ante* basis, to be obtainable); and 'price' is stable in the sense that the winning bids for contracts having similar specifications are the same over time.

However it is unlikely that such an equilibrium will be reached, even given the specific assumptions we have made about the expectations and the one-period lags separating events and the reactions to those events. To make essential points suppose that μ_t and ρ_t are the mean and mean deviation of a particular tenderer's h(x) distribution in period t and let m_t and r_t be the corresponding sample quantities determined from the observed distribution of profit margins in period t. A mathematical formulation of the revision mechanism described above might be

$$\mu_{t+1} = \mu_t + a(m_t - \mu_t) = (1-a)\mu_t + am_t$$

$$\rho_{t+1} = \rho_t + e(r_t - \rho_t) = (1-e)\rho_t + er_t$$

where a and e, both between 0 and -1 are coefficients reflecting the credibility that is attached to the most recent information. For example, a or e near zero indicates that the most recent experience is heavily discounted.

Given the above formulation, suppose that the observed m_t and r_t approach μ_t and ρ_t respectively, these being the parameters forming the basis of the current tenderer's h(x) in the current period. Evidently since m_t and r_t are the same for all tenderers this implies that all opinions regarding the distribution of profit margins are converging on the same values. As a result each tenderer's expected share and optimal profit margin approaches the same values. Again we point to the fact that it is unlikely that all these expected shares are consistent. Frustrated expectations will lead to revisions on the part of some or all tenderers and hence a movement away from the path converging to equilibrium.

In the case where a sequence of identical single contracts comes up over time the above results can be made even more explicit. In this case it is reasonable to suppose $m_t = x_t$ and $r_t = |x_t - \mu_t|$. Now if x_t approaches some constant value i.e. the observed winning profit margin approaches constancy, then r_t must approach zero. Hence a constant μ_t appears to be consistent only with increasing certainty on the part of all the competitors. The analysis of Section 2 has shown that increasing certainty is associated with an increasing perceived probability of success. However at most one competitor will win the contract and hence all but one of the increasing expectations will be frustrated. This will lead to revised calculations and ultimately a movement away from the path towards equilibrium. Thus the most that can be expected even under constant demand conditions appears to be a statistical equilibrium where bids, the number of competitors and shares of contracts are constantly fluctuating with a statistical regularity. Alternatively an increase in certainty is consistent with a decrease in the profit margin, period by period, by the incremental amounts necessary to undercut the margin of the previous period. At the limit of this process each contract will be won (with zero profit) by the least-cost tenderer, who will by that time be the sole bidder for the contract, higher-cost tenderers having found that they would have to use negative profit margins to win the contract. This result is necessarily attained only under conditions which are themselves antithetical to the tendering system i.e., under conditions of complete knowledge.

It was suggested in the introduction that the analysis of bidding behaviour provided in this paper might be applicable to markets in addition to those which use explicit bidding or tendering procedures. Microeconomic textbooks frequently proceed to discuss market models such as perfect competition or monopolistic competitions on the assumption of perfect knowledge (by each firm and household of all the data relevant to its decisions) and without detailed discussion of the methods by which prices are assumed to be set. If uncertainty is introduced and, as suggested in the introduction, prices set by firms are construed as bids (for market shares) to be tried out and adjusted in the light of experience, the relevance of the analysis provided in this paper may extend well beyond the group of industries where bidding procedures are explicit. An implication of the analysis, in terms of the alternative interpretation, is that the competitive market processes may have equilibrium characteristics of the 'statistical' kind which emerge in competitive bidding for contracts, or else no well-defined equilibrium characteristics at all. Such a result would cause no surprise or alarm to certain students and/or proponents of the market as an allocative device, but would surprise readers of many undergraduate microeconomic textbooks.

Appendix 5.A

We wish to determine the behaviour of the optimal margin and profit under changes in the mean of the density. For concreteness, consider the model of Section 3. Referring to Figure 5.2 it is clear that the uniform rightward translation of the profit opportunity curve H(x) must lead to higher profits and higher optimal margins. Such a uniform translation corresponds to an increase in the mean. We now make this argument precise. Denote by H(x) the profit opportunity curve corresponding to mean μ, and $H_\delta(x)$ that after the mean is increased by a small amount δ. Subscript all other quantities similarly e.g. p_δ is the optimal margin associated with $H_\delta(x)$.

We have

$$\begin{aligned} 0 &= H(p) - ph(p) \\ &= H_\delta(p+\delta) - ph_\delta(p+\delta) \\ &= H_\delta(p+\delta) - (p+\delta h_\delta(p+\delta) + \delta h(p). \end{aligned}$$

Hence if $h(p) \neq 0$ then $p+\delta$ cannot be the optimising margin associated with the mean $\mu+\delta$. In fact if p_δ is this margin then from the second order conditions for a maximum

$$H_\delta(x) - xh_\delta(x) > 0$$

whenever x is marginally less than p_δ with the inequality reversing for x marginally exceeding p. Noting that h(x) is positive we conclude that $p + \delta > p$ if and only if δ is positive. Dividing both sides by δ and rearrangement leads to the conclusion that $(p_\delta - p)/\delta < 1$ and hence that the optimal profit margin fluctuates less than the mean.

Turning to the behaviour of profit under changes in the mean it is shown that the maximum profit is a non-decreasing function of δ. Given a margin x the profit is given by $xH_\delta(x)$. Holding x at an arbitrary but fixed level and considering this expression as a function of δ, then this expression is non-decreasing in δ. Now this is true for arbitrary x and hence is true for the optimising margin p associated with $\delta = 0$. But $pH_\delta(p) < p_\delta H_\delta(p_\delta)$, and this establishes the result.

Notes

1. A paper by Riley and Samuelson (1981) on optimal auctions has come to our notice after this paper was substantially finalised. Riley and Samuelson's paper considers the position of a seller of a good or service, faced by a fixed number of buyers. Transposed to our context of a buyer faced by a set of potential sellers, Riley and Samuelson's model supposes each bidder is confronted with a price or value below which the contract is unprofitable. These values are assumed to constitute independent draws from some common distribution, known to all participants. Each bidder then formulates a strategy or function of the value. The article gives consideration to such things as equilibrium strategies (i.e. where the adoption of the same strategy by all but one participant, makes it appropriate for the final participant to adopt the strategy as well), the expected cost to the buyer, and alternative auction rules.

In contrast to Riley and Samuelson's model, the model explored in this paper is less formalistic and more akin to those of orthodox micro-economics: each bidder formulates a personal expectation of the winning bid, and strategies consist of maximising expected profit given these personal views. Our notions of equilibrium are non-strategic and no specialised assumptions are made about zero profit price bids.

2. The authors do not intend the above statement to indicate that they have taken sides in the full-cost *versus* marginalism debate — rather they believe that for much of manufacturing industry the two approaches boil down to one. But this is not the place to elaborate this point.

3. Computations were carried out using a root-seeking algorithm applied to (3).

References

de Jong, P. and Webb, L. R. (1973), 'Tendering and the Theory of Price', Research Paper No. 3, Department of Economics, University of Melbourne

de Jong, P. and Webb, L. R. (1975), 'Tendering and the Theory of Price', Economic Statistics Papers No. 11, Department of Economic Statistics, University of Sydney

Riley, J. G. and Samuelson, W. F. (1981), 'Optimal Auction', *The American Economic Review, 71*

Sasieni, M., Yaspan, A. and Friedman, L. (1959), *Operations Research: Methods and Problems*, New York: John Wiley and Sons

Stark, R. M. and Rothkopf, M. H. (1979), 'Competitive Bidding: A Comprehensive Bibliography'; *Operations Research, 27*, 364–90

Turvey, R. (1969), 'Marginal Cost', *Economic Journal, 79*, 282–99

Vickrey, W. (1961), 'Counterspeculation, Auctions and Competitive Sealed Tenders', *The Journal of Finance, 16*

Webb, L. R. (1962), 'Some applications of Frequency Distributions in the Theory of Price', PhD Dissertation, London School of Economics

Webb, L. R. (1964), 'Tendering and the Theory of Price', Paper delivered to Section G, Australian and New Zealand Association for the Advancement of Science (Canberra)

PART FOUR

FIRM BEHAVIOUR

6 ECONOMETRIC ASPECTS OF FIRM GROWTH BEHAVIOUR*

S. C. Peck
Electric Power Research Institute

Preamble

I attended Basil Yamey's graduate industrial organisation class at the London School of Economics in 1966–7. Basil covered the existing empirical studies of industrial organisation in great detail. The careful attention he focused on such studies conveyed two points. First, empirical studies can provide considerable insight about important aspects of the workings of firms and markets. Second, empirical studies should always be evaluated carefully to determine if their insights are valid.

In writing this paper, I remembered what I had been taught. Basil's first point was that empirical studies can be important in providing insights about firms and markets. In the paper I deal with Gibrat's Law of Proportionate Effect (LPE) as applied to firm behaviour within a market. The LPE is a hypothesis that the distribution of a firm's growth rate is independent of initial firm size. If the LPE is true, its implication is that market concentration will have a continual tendency to increase. Such an insight would be important in understanding the determinants of concentration and in designing appropriate public policy to deal with issues of industrial structure.

Basil's second point was that studies should always be evaluated carefully to determine if their insights are valid. I believe that this has not been done with existing studies of the LPE. A major problem with these studies is that they have not been based on any formal theory of firm growth. In this paper I develop a reasonable theory of firm growth which incorporates lumpiness of investment and a consequent sequencing of investments by firms in a market. The theory is used to show that even though firm growth behav-

* This work was partially completed while the author was an Assistant Professor at University of California, Berkeley. It was partly supported by a grant from the Sloan Foundation. I am grateful to Alice Amsden, Darius Gaskins, Richard Gilbert and Scott Harvey for helpful discussions. All errors are my own.

iour may be quite inconsistent with the LPE, an unwary analyst may be misled into accepting the LPE when it is in fact not valid. I hope that this paper will cast doubt on all major studies of the LPE for firms within markets and will cause a re-analysis of the data using more refined empirical approaches.

1. Introduction

There have been numerous studies of the relationship between the distribution of firm growth rate and firm size. Typical of these are the studies of Hart and Prais (1956), Hymer and Pashigian (1962), and Mansfield (1962). Hart and Prais analysed those companies engaged in mining, manufacturing or distribution quoted on the London Stock Exchange. They split the period 1885–1950 into five subperiods of length 12 to 16 years. Their central conclusion was that Gibrat's Law of Proportionate Effect (henceforth LPE) was valid in the majority of subperiods. The LPE states that the probability distribution of firm growth rate is independent of firm size. The major, but by no means only, technique whereby they investigated the growth process of firms was by a cross-sectional regression of the logarithm of firm size at the end of the period on the logarithm of firm size at the beginning. If the slope coefficient of this regression was close to unity, they did not reject the null hypothesis that the LPE was valid. The study of Hymer and Pashigian took the largest firms in ten 2-digit US industries and computed the growth rate of each firm from 1946 to 1955. For each industry they sorted the firms into quartiles by initial size and computed the average and standard deviation of growth rate within each quartile. They found that the mean growth rate was unrelated to the size of firm whereas the standard deviation of the distribution of growth rates was inversely related to the size of firm. Other tests, including disaggregation into 3-digit industries, did not cause them to reject their initial conclusion. Mansfield, remarking on the fact that previous studies had used only large firms, tested the LPE with data from ten industry time-period cross-sections. He found that if the LPE was interpreted as applying to all firms, it was rejected primarily because the probability of death was higher for small firms. If the LPE was interpreted as applying to all surviving firms, the slope coefficient of the regression of the logarithm of terminal size on the logarithm of initial size was less than unity in nine out of ten cases; hence the LPE was rejected. If the LPE was interpreted as applying to all firms larger than minimum optimal scale, the slope coefficient was less than unity in only seven of ten cases and never significantly so. He also found that the variance of growth rates tended to decline with firm size in a large number of cross-sections.

My interpretation of these studies is that there has been a gradual shifting away from the strong version of the LPE espoused by Hart and Prais through the study of Hymer and Pashigian which disputed the claim that the variance of firm growth rates was independent of firm size to the Mansfield study which disputed the claim that the mean growth rate was independent of firm size.[1] This change of interpretation has also been shown in a second set of studies which take their evidence primarily from the distribution of firm sizes. A well-known paper in this genre is that of Simon and Bonini (1958). They show that the Yule distribution can be generated by assuming (a) that the distribution of percentage changes in firm size, over a year, of the firms in a given size class is the same for all size classes; (b) new firms are born into the smallest size class at a relatively constant rate. They also show that the Yule distribution in its upper tail approximates the Pareto distribution. In their empirical work they demonstrate that the Yule distribution provides a good fit to various data samples. A recent paper by Vining (1976), however, claims that the distributions of firm sizes observed in practice has too many middle-sized firms to be fitted well by the Pareto distribution and that this could be an indication of a negative correlation of firm growth rate and size.

In the majority of studies the relationship between the LPE and an underlying theory of the firm is not analysed in great detail. For instance, Simon and Bonini (1958, p. 609) provide justification for the LPE as follows: '. . . if as we have postulated there exist approximately constant returns to scale (above a critical minimum size of firm) it is natural to expect the firms in each size-class to have the same chance on the average of increasing or decreasing in size in proportion to their current size.' Likewise, Vining, in reporting recent studies which have found a negative relationship between firm size and rate of growth, says that this is consistent with the firms being subject to decreasing returns to scale. The study of Hymer and Pashigian was the earliest to relate in a detailed manner the empirical results to an underlying theory of the firm, but they also assumed that average growth rate would be independent of firm size if there were constant returns to scale.[2] An attempt to model formally the relationship between a firm's growth rate and the size was made by Sherman (1971). He set up a model of an industry in which entry was barred, price competition was ineffective, firms' sales were proportional to their capacities, and there were constant returns to scale. A prediction of this model was that the gain from capacity expansion (and hence actual investment) declined as a firm's share of total market capacity was larger.

In Section 2 of this paper I present a different formal model of firm-industry interaction and firm growth behaviour; in the model the firms produce under constant returns to scale. The assumptions of the model are such that a firm's investment can affect the price charged for the industry's output and a prediction of the model is that a small firm will have a higher percentage growth rate than a large firm. Thus both Sherman's model and my own show that constant returns to scale do not necessarily imply independence of firm growth rate and size. Although my model predicts a strong negative relationship between firm growth rate and firm size, I argue in Section 3 that the model can produce data which seem to be consistent with the results of the studies of firm growth behaviour reported above. In particular, the observed data generated by my model will frequently show that there is no relationship between average firm growth rate and firm size and that the variance of firm growth rates is heteroscedastic. In Section 4 I provide a demonstration of these results by means of a simulation experiment in which the model is used to generate data which is then analysed by regression analysis. The results of the 60 simulations which I carry out confirm my hypothesis that if the LPE is not true, regression analysis will show a weak version of it (the version allowing heteroscedasticity) to be true in a sometimes large number of cases. Thus the usual methods of regression analysis do not constitute a powerful statistical test of the LPE. Section 5 concludes the paper.

2. A Model of Firm Investment Behaviour

The model is characterised by the following set of assumptions.

A1: There are n firms in the industry. These firms are arrayed in a sequence; the *ith* firm in the sequence has capacity k_i.

A2: Each firm in the industry has an output rate equal to its installed capacity.
A3: Each firm in the industry can produce output at constant average cost c until its capacity is reached.
A4: The demand for the output of the industry is given by the following equation where p is the price, Q is the quantity sold, and g is the exponential growth rate:

$$p = a - be^{-gt}Q.$$

A5: Firms invest in the sequence in which they are arrayed. If the last firm to invest was the (i − 1)*th*, the i*th* firm must invest when the market price reaches p_m ($p_m > c$) or the (i + 1)*th* firm will invest in its place. The first firm invests after the n*th* firm, thus starting the sequence again. The size of the i*th* firm's investment is denoted y_i.
A6: Subsequent to the (i + 1)*th* firm's investment, the i*th* firm anticipates that the price will remain at some average level p_a, where $c < p_a < p_m$.
A7: The price p_m is sufficiently low that new entry is not attracted into the industry.
A8: There is a positive rate of interest r.

These assumptions characterise an industry, the demand for whose output is growing over time. It has been argued that in such an industry, there may be chaos because there is no mechanism at work to nominate those firms which should invest (Scherer, 1973, pp. 318–20). G. B. Richardson has argued that the absence of a nominating mechanism may cause underinvestment. Scherer, in reporting Richardson's work, has argued that it might just as well cause overinvestment. In this paper I assume that firms adopt a sequencing rule to avoid the chaos.[3] If the last firm to have invested is the (i − 1)*th* firm, then the i*th* firm must invest when the price reaches p_m. The investment y_i, which I assume to be made at time zero, will cause industry capacity to increase from K to K + y_i and the price will fall below the average cost of production c. In the course of time as the demand curve shifts to the right, the price will rise until p_m is once again reached. Let this occur at time t′. At this time the (i + 1)*th* firm will invest. For ease of modelling I assume that firm i believes that the price will remain at the average p_a subsequent to the investment of firm (i + 1). For the same reason I assume that firm i optimises only with respect to its current investment, thus neglecting all investments which it will make in the future.

It is evident that firm i faces an optimisation problem. The larger the investment made, the larger will be the postinvestment firm size $(k_i + y_i)$ and hence the larger will be the opportunity of the firm to suffer gains or losses. But the larger the investment, the more the price will fall below average cost of production (c) immediately following an investment and the longer it will take for price to rise again until c is attained once more. Let the objective of firm i be to maximise the present value of profits from time zero to infinity.

$$PV_i(0,\infty) = \int_0^{t'} e^{-rt}(p - c)(k_i + y_i)\,dt + \int_{t'}^{\infty} e^{-rt}(p_a - c)(k_i + y_i)\,dt \quad (1)$$

Now, according to assumptions A2 and A4, the price path p subsequent to the *ith* firm's investment may be written

$$p = a - be^{-gt}(K + y_i), \quad (2)$$

where K is industry capacity just prior to the investment of firm i. Industry capacity K can be expressed in terms of parameters of the demand function and p_m, since at time $t = 0$, when $p = p_m$, industry demand Q was equal to K; thus

$$p_m = a - bK \Rightarrow K = \frac{(a - p_m)}{b} \quad (3)$$

Thus, substituting (3) into (2), we find

$$p = a - e^{-gt}(a - p_m + by_i) \quad (4)$$

Substituting (4) into (1) and carrying out the integrations, we find

$$PV_i(0,\infty) = (k_i + y_i)\left\{\frac{1 - e^{-rt'}}{r}(a - c) - \frac{1 - e^{-(r+g)t'}}{r + g}(a - p_m + by_i) + \frac{e^{-rt'}}{r}(p_a - c)\right\} \quad (5)$$

Now, t′ is the time at which the (i + 1)*th* firm invests. It can be computed easily because it is the time at which price once again reaches p_m, while industry capacity equals $K + y_i$.

$$p_m = a - be^{-gt'} (K + y_i) \tag{6}$$

Substituting into (6) for K from (3) and solving for t′ yields

$$t' = -\frac{1}{g}\log\left\{\frac{a - p_m}{a - p_m + b_{y_i}}\right\} \tag{7}$$

Finally, collecting terms in equation (5) and substituting from equation (7) yields[4]

$$PV_i\,(0,\infty) = (k_i + y_i)\left\{\frac{a - c}{r} - \frac{a - p_m + by_i}{r + g}\right.$$
$$\left.\left[\frac{a - p_m}{a + p_m + b_{y_i}}\right]^{r/g} \times \frac{r(p_m - p_a) + g(a - p_a)}{r(r + g)}\right\} \tag{8}$$

From expression (8) it is obvious that the optimal firm investment denoted y_i^* depends on the parameters a, b, c, p_m, p_a, r, g, k_i. Comparative static properties of y_i^* were investigated by numerical methods. The global maximum y_i^* was found for an initial set of parameters; then one parameter was changed and the maximum was found again. The initial set of parameters used was $a = 9.25$, $b = 4/100$, $c = 5$, $p_m = 5.25$, $p_a = 5.125$, $r = 0.10$, $g = 0.06$, $k = 10$. It was found that $\partial y_i^*/\partial a > 0$ for $6.25 \leqslant a \leqslant 13.25$, $\partial y_i^*/\partial b < 0$ for $2/100 \leqslant b \leqslant 16/100$, $\partial y_i^*/\partial p_m > 0$ for $5.125 \leqslant p_m \leqslant 5.75$, $\partial y_i^*/\partial r < 0$ for $0.06 \leqslant r \leqslant 0.12$; $\partial y_i^*/\partial g > 0$ for $0.04 \leqslant g \leqslant 0.12$ and $\partial y_i^*/\partial k_i < 0$ for $5 \leqslant k_i \leqslant 40$. The relationship between y_i^* and k_i for different values of b is shown in Figure 6.1.

The comparative static properties of the model make intuitive sense. When a, the intercept of the demand function, is large, the market is large and y_i^* is large. When b, the demand function's slope at time zero, is small, the market is large and y_i^* is large. When p_m, the price at which investment takes place, is large, investment is relatively profitable and y_i^* is large. When the interest rate r is high, the immediate losses are weighted more heavily than the future benefits of a large investment and hence y_i^* is small. In a rapidly growing market, y_i^* is large. Finally, the larger a firm is, the smaller is its optimal investment. This is presumably because the

Figure 6.1: Plot of y_i^* against k_i

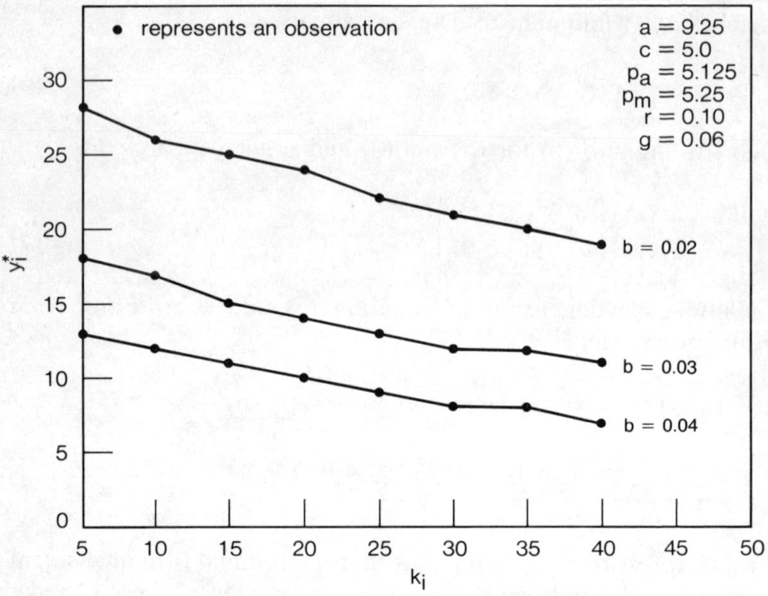

future gains to a new investment are proportional to the investment size, but the immediate losses are borne by the firm's entire capacity.[5] The last relationship between optimal investment and firm size is particularly interesting in its implications for LPE. Obviously, if optimal investment size is negatively related to firm size, then, *a fortiori*, optimal growth rate (y_i^*/k_i) will be negatively related to firm size.

A further interesting result from the comparative statics is that one cannot predict that optimal investment size and market size will always be positively related. This is because market size is not a true parameter of the model but only a function of the true parameters. Recall equation (3) which expresses K in terms of a, b, p_m. From equation (3), $\partial K/\partial a > 0$, $\partial K/\partial b < 0$, $\partial K/\partial p_m < 0$. In addition, as reported above, $\partial y_i^*/\partial a > 0$, $\partial y_i^*/\partial b < 0$, $\partial y_i^*/\partial p_m > 0$. Thus, if market size changes due to a change in parameter a, $\partial y_i^*/\partial K = \partial y_i^*/\partial a / \partial k/\partial a > 0$. If market size changes due to a change in parameter b,

$\partial y_i^*/\partial K = \partial y_i^*/\partial b / \partial k/\partial b > 0$. But if market size changes due to a change in parameter p_m, $\partial y_i^*/\partial K = \partial y_i^*/\partial p_m < 0$. Thus $\partial y_i^*/\partial K$ does not have a unique sign.

3. Econometric Problems

In this section I argue for the following proposition. The model above generates data which are clearly inconsistent with the LPE; nevertheless, an econometrician studying the process of firm growth in such an industry may be misled into believing that firm average growth rate is unrelated to firm size.

Let us first recall how a study of the relationship between firm growth rate and firm size is usually made. Consider Mansfield's (1962) study of capacity growth in the steel, petroleum, and rubber tyre industries. In his study of the rubber tyre industry, for instance, he split the period 1937–1952 into two approximately eight-year subperiods, 1937–45 and 1945–52, and he investigated the relationship between average growth rate and firm size in two ways for each of these two cross-sections. First, he classified firms by their initial size $S_i(t)$, computed the frequency distribution of $S_i(t + \Delta)/S_i(t)$ within each size class and used a χ^2 test to determine whether the frequency distributions were the same in each class. ($S_i(t + \Delta)$ is the size of firm i at the end of the period; firms that died during the period were assumed to have a terminal size of zero). Second, for all surviving firms, he computed regression (9) and tested whether the coefficient δ was equal to unity (log refers to the natural logarithm):

$$\log S_i (t + \Delta) = \gamma + \delta \log S_i (t) + \tilde{u}_i (t, \Delta) \qquad (9)$$

I provide arguments below that the investigation of firm growth behaviour by a linear regression can give very misleading results. The same arguments apply also to the investigation of firm growth rates by averaging, so I do not give them.[6]

Suppose now that the data are generated by the firm investment model and a linear regression (10) is used to investigate the relationship between growth rate and firm size:

$$\log \frac{S_i(t + \Delta)}{S_i(t)} = \alpha + \beta \log S_i(t) + \tilde{u}_i (t,\Delta) \qquad (10)$$

I prefer to make the argument in terms of regression (10) rather than (9) because the independent variable can be interpreted as the Δ-period firm growth rate and because $\beta = \hat{\delta} - 1$ and $\hat{y}\hat{\beta} = \hat{\delta} - 1$ where $\hat{\beta}$ and $\hat{\delta}$ are ordinary least squares estimates.[7]

Figure 6.2: Plot of $\text{Log}\left(\frac{k_i + y_i^*}{k_i}\right)$ against Log k_i

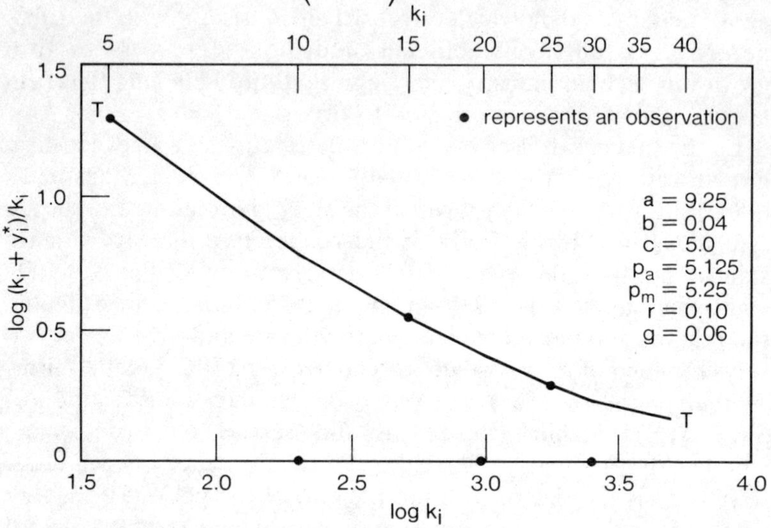

Since the data are generated by the firm investment model, the relationship between $\log (k_i + y_i^*)/k_i$ and $\log k_i$ is shown in Figure 6.2 which is drawn so as to be consistent with Figure 6.1 with b = 0.04. Assume that a, c, p_a, p_m, r, g are constant so that the function TT does not shift. Suppose that there are six firms in the industry of sizes 5, 10, 15, 20, 25, 30 units. Also suppose initially that the function TT shifts to the right very slowly because of decreases in b induced by market growth. Now consider a time period $(t, t + \Delta)$ sufficiently short that only three of the firms reach their turn to invest. Let these firms be of initial sizes 5, 15, 25. Then the observations corresponding to these firms will lie on the function TT as shown, and three observations corresponding to the three firms which did not invest (of initial sizes 10, 20, 30 units) will lie on the horizontal axis as shown. Obviously, the least squares line fitted to these data will have a slope which is less than the slope of the true relationship TT. Because of this downward bias, an econometrician is less likely to reject the null hypothesis that the slope β equals zero. Also, although there is in this model no random error term, the fact that some firms invest and some do not will give rise to non-zero residuals. Furthermore, the residuals about the fitted line appear to come from an heteroscedastic population. This is a result reported by a large number of investigators such as Hymer and Pashigian (1962), Mansfield (1962) and Singh and Whittington (1975). It is also likely that the slope of the fitted regression will be very unstable. Consider, for instance, a situation in which the firms of initial size 5, 10, 15 invest and those of 20, 25, 30 do not. Then the fitted line will have a steeper downward slope than that of TT. Or, consider a situation in which the firms of initial size 20, 25, 30 invest and those of 5, 10, 15 do not. Then the fitted line will slope upwards relative to TT.

Superficially, it would appear that these difficulties can be avoided by choosing a regression period $(t, t + \Delta)$ sufficiently long that all of the firms have time to invest. This, however, neglects the fact that the demand curve is continually shifting to the right (as represented by a falling value of b) and that the function TT must be replaced by a family of functions T_1T_1, T_2T_2,. . . . Again the slope of a regression such as (10) may bear little resemblance to the downward slope of the function T_iT_i. Two examples suffice to illustrate this. In Figure 6.3 the firms invest in order of ascending initial size. In this case the fitted regression line (when all firms invest) will approximate FF which is flatter than the true relationship. Conversely, if the firms invest in order of descending initial size, the fitted regression line will be steeper than the true relationship.

In the section on econometric problems, four hypotheses have been developed. If the observation period is short relative to the market cycle time, the negative relationship between firm growth rate and firm initial size (1) will be obscured on average, (2) will be very unstable, and (3) will usually appear to have heteroscedastic errors. If the observation period is approximately equal to the market cycle time (4) the relationship between firm growth rate and firm size will still be unstable.

The hypotheses were developed in some cases by assuming a particular sequencing of firm investments. But, of course, the sequencing is not given *a priori* and results may differ for alternative sequences. In the next section of the paper, the validity of the four hypotheses is investigated further in a simulation experiment in which 60 random sequences of investment are generated and various regressions are computed.

Figure 6.3: The Generation of Data when All Firms Invest

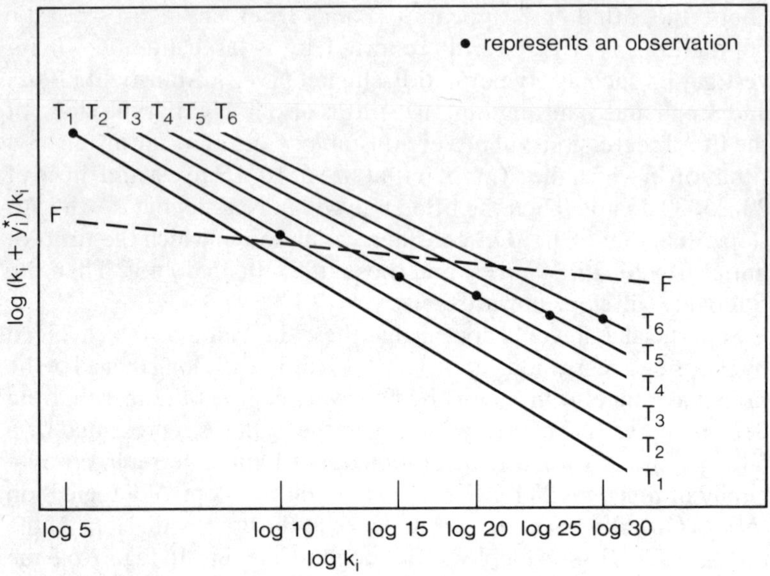

4. Simulation Experiments

In the previous section I developed several hypotheses concerning the data which would be generated by the firm investment model. In order to provide some evidence that these hypotheses were valid, I carried out a simulation experiment. The steps in the simulation experiment were as follows. (Figure 6.4 shows the steps in the simulation experiment in a compact way.)

(1) For a sample of nine firms I chose a set of firm sizes which was approximately lognormally distributed. The set of firm sizes denoted $\{k_j^0\}$ was $\{5,6,8,10,12,15,18,23,32\}$. The index j runs from 1 to 9.

(2) I generated a random order in which the firms would invest. Each of the integers 1, 2, . . ., 9 had an equal chance of appearing in a given location in a list of length 9. As an example, the first order denoted $\{i_j\}$was $\{9,4,7,6,2,5,3,8,1\}$.

(3) I then used the order $\{i_j\}$ to arrange the firm sizes $\{k_j^0\}$ into

the sequence in which they would invest. The latter sequence is denoted $\{k_j\}$. It was formed by setting $ki_j = k_j^0$, j = 1,2, . . .,9. For example, for j = 1, $ki_1 = k_1^0$, or $k_9 = 5$; thus the firm of size 5 would invest ninth. The entire first sequence was {32,12,18,6,15,10,8, 23,5}.

(4) For the sequence $\{k_j\}$ I computed the optimal set of investments $\{y_j^*\}$ as follows. I set a = 9.25, b = 4/130, c = 5, p_a = 5.125, p_m = 5.25, r = 0.10, g = 0.06. The firm of initial size 32 invested first; its optimal investment conditional on the parameters above was found to be 12 units. The time until p_m was attained again and, hence, until the second investment, was computed to be 1.47 periods and the value of b was updated as b = 4/130 exp $\{-1.47g\}$. The firm of initial size 12 invested second; its optimal investment conditional on the parameters above and the updated value of b was 17 units and the time of the third investment was computed to be 3.36 periods. The value of b was updated as b = 4/130 exp $\{-3.36g\}$ and the optimal investment was found for the firm of size 18. This was done for all nine firms and the optimal investment and time of the next investment are shown in Table 6.1. The time for all firms to invest is known as the market cycle time and is 15.38 periods in this case.

Table 6.1: Optimal Investments for the First Simulation

Initial firm size	Optimal investment	Time of next investment
32	12	1.47
12	17	3.36
18	18	5.14
6	24	7.26
15	25	9.22
10	30	11.29
8	35	13.43
23	36	15.37
5	46	17.57

(5) I now carried out five sets of three regressions. The first set of regressions assumed an observation period of (0,4), the second of (0,8), the third of (0,12), the fourth of (0,16), and the fifth, an observation period sufficiently long so that all nine firms had invested; in this case it was (0,15.38). The first set of regressions for (0,4) included the investments made by the firms of initial sizes 32, 12, 18 but set the investments of the other firms to zero. The

set of regressions for (0,8) included the investments made by firms of initial sizes 32, 12, 18, 6, 15, but set the investments of the other firms equal to zero. In this run the fourth and fifth sets of regressions were the same.

The three regressions carried out were as follows. The first investigated by ordinary least squares the relationship between initial firm size and firm growth rate:

$$\log \frac{S_{ij}(\Delta)}{S_i(0)} = \alpha_j(\Delta) + \beta_j(\Delta) \log S_i(0) + \tilde{u}_{ij}(\Delta), \; i = 1, 2, \ldots, 9. \quad (11)$$

$S_{ij}(\Delta)$ is the size of the *ith* firm at time Δ in simulation j. $S_i(0)$ is the initial size of the *ith* firm. $S_i(0)$ is the same in all simulations. The second regression investigated whether the error term was heteroscedastic by taking the absolute value of the residual and regressing it against $\log S_i(0)$:

$$|\hat{u}_{ij}(\Delta)| = \Theta_j(\Delta) + \phi_j(\Delta) \log S_i(0) + \tilde{v}_{ij}(\Delta), \; i = 1,2, \ldots,9, \quad (12)$$

The third regression obtained generalised least squares estimates of $\alpha_j(\Delta)$ and $B_j(\Delta)$ by using the least squares estimates $\hat{\Theta}_j(\Delta)$ and $\hat{\phi}_j(\Delta)$ from equation (12) as follows: (for i = 1,2, . . .9)

$$\{\log S_{ij}(\Delta)/S_i(0)\} / \{\hat{\Theta}_j(\Delta) + \hat{\phi}_j(\Delta) \log S_i(0)\} =$$
$$d_j(\Delta)/\{\hat{\Theta}_j(\Delta) + \hat{\phi}_j(\Delta) \log S_i(0)\} +$$
$$\beta_j(\Delta) \log S_i(0)/\{\hat{\Theta}_j(\Delta) + \hat{\phi}_j(\Delta) \log S_i(0)\} + \tilde{w}_{ij}(\Delta)$$

For each of the three regressions the multiple correlation coefficient R^2 was computed.[8]

(6) I now went through steps (2) to (5) again, hence generating another set of regression coefficients for a different sequence of firm investments. Altogether this process was repeated 59 times giving rise to 60 sets of regression coefficients.

(7) Means and standard deviations of the regression coefficients were now computed in a natural way to provide summary statistics of their distributions. For instance, the average (AV) and standard deviation (SD) of the ordinary least squares slope coefficient in equation (11) for the (0,4) observation period were

$$AV\{\hat{\beta}(4)\} = \frac{1}{60} \sum_{j=i}^{60} \hat{\beta}_j(4),$$

Figure 6.4: The Seven Steps in the Simulation Experiment

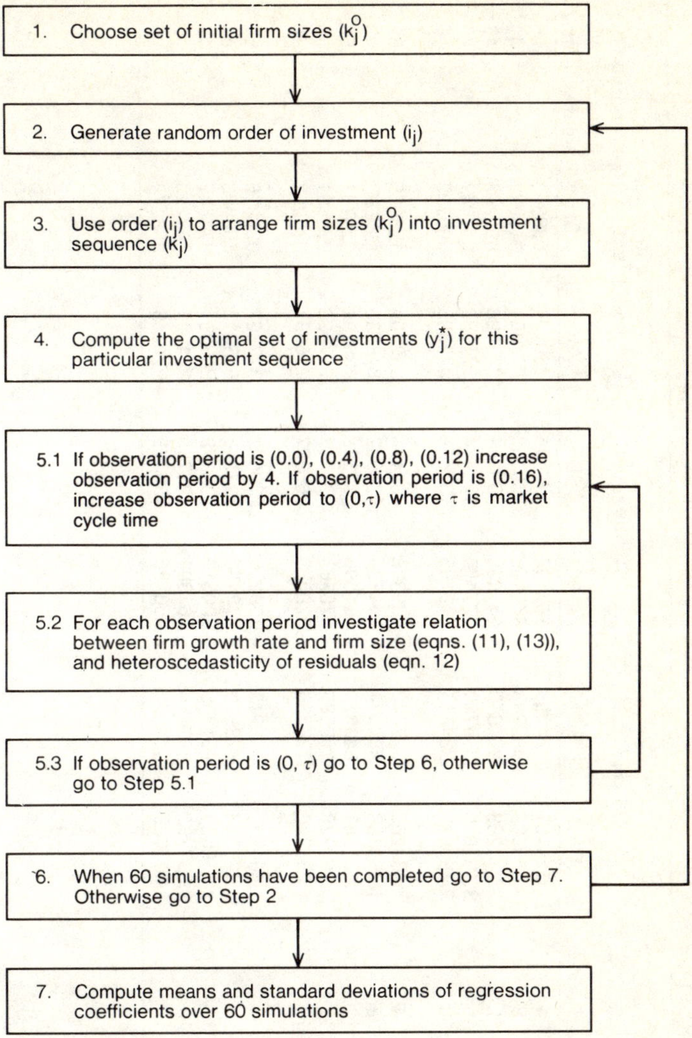

$$SD\{\hat{\beta}(4)\} = \surd(\frac{1}{60} \sum_{j=i}^{60} [\hat{\beta}_j(4) - AV\{\hat{\beta}(4)\}]^2)^{\frac{1}{2}}$$

The summary statistics are provided in Table 6.2.

Let us now consider the previously developed hypotheses in the

Table 6.2: Summary Statistics for the Simulation Experiment

Regression	Period	Intercept AV	Intercept SD	Slope AV	Slope SD	Correlation coefficient AV	Correlation coefficient SD	Proportion of times/slope/is smaller than .25
Ordinary	4	.715107	.754059	–.167108	.277516	.386604	.098869	.55
least squares	8	1.449583	.962788	–.360133	.360130	.577487	.113621	.42
(11)	12	2.217283	.964949	–.547836	.359371	.779096	.092803	.17
	16	3.137870	.318789	–.777475	.125464	.971589	.007047	0
	≅18	3.130610	.334614	–.773785	.132835	.972385	.006299	0
Investigation of	4	.839268	.527040	–.189338	.182408	.822009	.128025	.58
heteroscedasticity	8	1.054189	.389074	–.241835	.138002	.876235	.0862215	.43
(12)	12	.821641	.649870	–.181096	.237178	.738281	.123743	.53
	16	.250928	.185386	–.026363	.072447	.767026	.071801	1.0
	≅18	.255740	.175336	–.029058	.066987	.766097	.072252	1.0
Generalised	4	.560592	.653712	–.109225	.239662	.377367	.058976	.53
least squares	8	1.495713	.878570	–.378488	.327946	.633912	.100598	.43
(13)	12	2.355069	.901365	–.600619	.338378	.886391	.074647	.17
	16	3.097792	.340416	–.761304	.133719	.974271	.008229	0
	≅18	3.096309	.344174	–.760165	.136479	.974249	.008179	0

light of the evidence summarised in Table 6.2. First, it was claimed that when the regression period was short, the slope of a regression line such as (11) is probably biased up. In order to evaluate this claim it is necessary to know the 'true' downward slope of equation (11). This was computed as follows. Optimal investments were computed for firms of sizes {5,6,8,10,12,15,18,23,32} assuming parameter values a = 9.25, b = 4/130, c = 5, p_a = 5.125, p_m = 5.25, r = 0.10, g = 0.06. The value of b was not updated after each investment. Then, regression (11) was computed for a period Δ sufficiently long so that all firms invested. The estimated relationship had a slope of −.64504. This was the slope of the *ceteris paribus* relationship between firm size and growth rate at the beginning of an investment cycle. To find the *ceteris paribus* relationship at the end of the investment cycle the same procedure was carried out except b was set equal to 0.012, its value after approximately 16 periods. In this case the estimated relationship had a slope of −.83467. Now, from Table 6.2, we see that the average slope of the least squares line for a four-year regression period was −.167108 and even though the coefficient had a large standard deviation, 0.277516, it is possible to reject at the 1 per cent level the hypothesis that the slope equals −.64504.[9] The average slope of the least squares line for the 8-period regression is −.360133. Again, this is far greater in magnitude and significantly greater at the 1 per cent level than the slope of −.64504. Even the 12-period slope is significantly greater at the 2.5 per cent level than −.64504.

It was also claimed above that when the observation period (t,t + Δ) was short, the least squares coefficients would be very unstable. Table 6.2 shows this to be so. For instance, for the 8-period regression the standard deviation of $\hat{\beta}_j(8)$ is .360130. This instability may also be observed in Figure 6.5 which presents histograms of $\hat{\beta}_j(\Delta)$ for Δ = 4,8,12. Interestingly enough, the instability only falls off when Δ = 16 and all the firms have invested in almost every simulation.

The instability of the slope coefficient together with its upward bias will lead an unwary econometrician into frequently accepting the null hypothesis that there is no relationship between average firm growth rate and initial size. This can be inferred from Figure 6.5 by observing how frequently $\hat{\beta}_j(\Delta)$ is close to zero. In addition, Table 6.2 shows how often $-0.25 \leqslant \hat{\beta}_j(\Delta) \leqslant +0.25$, where I defined 0.25 to be 'close' to zero. It may be seen that $\hat{\beta}_j(4)$ lies

Figure 6.5: Histograms of $\hat{\beta}_j$

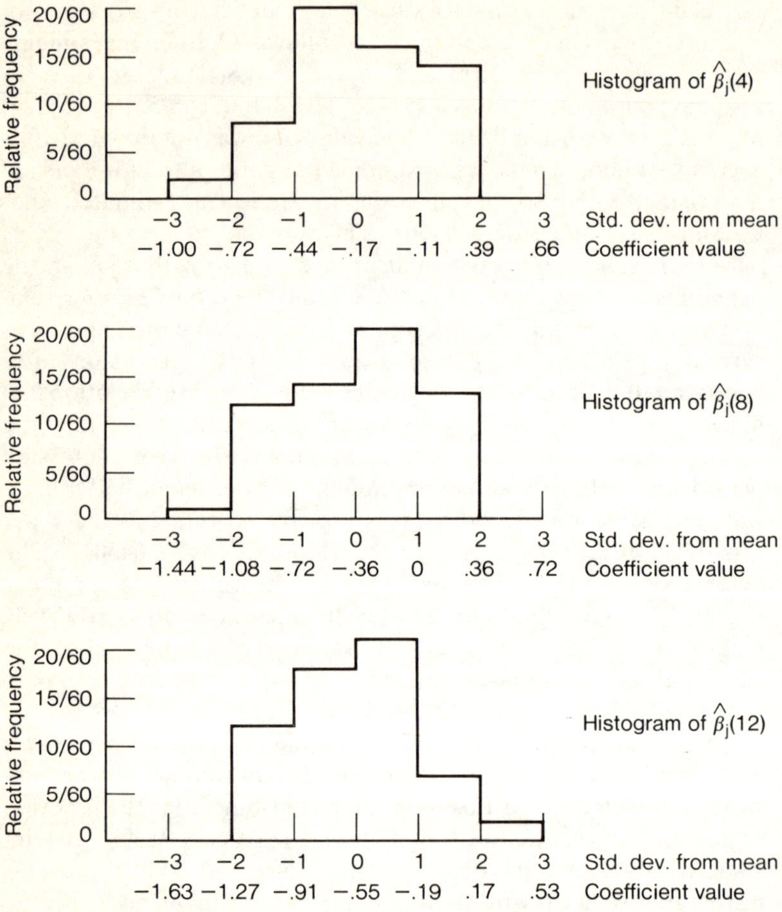

within these limits 55 per cent of the time, while $B_j(8)$ lies within the limits 42 per cent of the time.

It was also claimed above that when the observation period (t,t + Δ) was short, the errors will seem to have been generated from a heteroscedastic population. Table 6.2 confirms that this is the case. For instance, $\hat{\phi}_j(8)$ has a mean of 1.054189 and $\hat{\phi}_j(8)$ has a mean of $-$ 0.241835. This implies that, on average, a firm of size 32 appears to have an error term with a standard deviation only one-third as large as a firm of size 5. Also, the null hypothesis that the average of $\phi_j(8)$ equals zero can be rejected at the 1 per cent level. Finally, the residuals appear to display heteroscedasticity for $\Delta = 4,8,12$; the heteroscedasticity vanishes only for $\Delta = 16$ when all the firms in almost all the simulations have invested.

It was hypothesised for a long observation period that the relationship between firm growth rate and firm size would still be unstable due to the fact that a different investment order generates a different regression line. Table 6.2 suggests that this hypothesis is valid. If we look at the regression in which all firms invested, we find that the average value of the slope is $-.773785$ and the standard deviation is 0.132835. The standard deviation is still relatively large. It is interesting to note that the 60 estimates of the slope are bracketed between an estimate of .35409 obtained by allowing the firms to invest in the sequence $\{5,6, \ldots, 23,32\}$ and an estimate -1.10934 obtained by letting the firms invest in the sequence $\{32,23, \ldots, 6,5\}$. Note finally that for a long observation period, although there is a lot of instability in the slope of the regression line, all regression lines seem to fit very well as demonstrated by the mean and standard deviation of R^2.

5. Conclusion

A firm investment model was set up which made the intuitively appealing predictions that the percentage growth rate of a firm was (a) inversely related to firm size and (b) positively related to market size (neglecting complications caused by changes in p_m). The model in Appendix 6.A shows that these results were not due to the particular idiosyncrasies of the firm investment model used. The simulation experiments showed that when the observation period was less than or equal to three-fourths of the market cycle time, the fitted relation between firm growth rate and initial size was biased so that on average it lay between its true value and zero; it was also shown that the least squares line was very unstable and that the residuals displayed heteroscedasticity. Even when the observation period coincided with the market cycle time, the least squares line was unstable due to different least squares lines being generated by different firm investment sequences. It is shown in Appendix 6.B that these problems are not resolved by the choice of an observation period longer than the market cycle time. In fact, it is possible that a very long observation period exacerbates certain aspects of the instability.

I am not committed to the particular model of firm investment behaviour presented in the text. In fact, I believe that a more realistic model would incorporate features which would reduce but not eliminate the difference between the proportional growth rates of large and small firms. However, I believe that any model with the reasonable properties that a firm's proportional growth rate was inversely related to firm initial size and directly related to market size would generate data which would give rise to the same sorts of difficulties that were discussed in this paper.

The next stage of this investigation will be an attempt to estimate the *ceteris paribus* relationship between firm growth rate and initial size for a body of real data. Since the market cycle time plays such an important role in the correct specification of the model, an important element of the empirical procedure will be to estimate the market cycle time.

Appendix 6.A: Econometric Problems When the Observation Period is Longer than the Market Cycle Time

The simulation experiments did not address the question of what would happen if the observation period were longer than the market cycle time. My hypotheses are as follows. Suppose that the true relation between terminal firm size and initial firm size is given by equation (1) and suppose initially that this function does not shift due to market growth:

$$\log (k_i + y_i^*) = \varepsilon + \upsilon \log k_i \tag{1}$$

If the observation period lies between one and two times the market cycle time, then some firms will invest twice. If z_i^* is the optimal size of the second investment, then for a firm which invests twice

$$\log (k_i + y_i^* + z_i^*) = \varepsilon + \upsilon \log (k_i + y_i^*) = \varepsilon(1 + \upsilon) + \upsilon^2 \log k_i \tag{2}$$

Figure 6A.1 shows the relationships between initial size and terminal size for firms which invest once (11) and for firms which invest twice (22). Suppose that there are six firms in the market of sizes 5, 10, 15, 20, 25, 30 and that the observation period is such that three firms invest once and three firms invest twice. Let the firms which invest twice be of sizes 5, 15, 25. Then the regression line will have a slope intermediate between υ and υ^2 and the residuals will appear to be heteroscedastic. In addition, the regression line will be unstable. For instance, if the small firms (5,10,15)

Figure 6A.1: Initial and Terminal Size Relationship

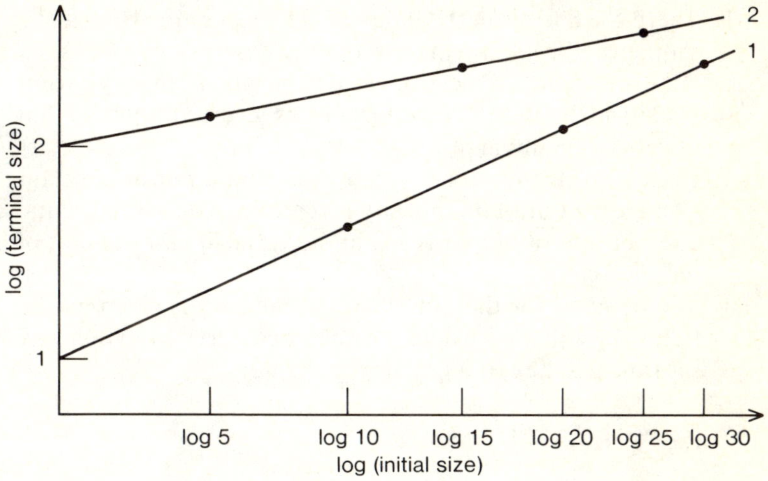

invest once and the large firms (20,25,30) invest twice, the regression line will have a slope steeper than υ; and if the small firms invest twice and the large firms invest once, the regression will have a slope less steep than υ^2.

Finally, recall that function (1) shifts upward due to market growth. This means that an additional source of instability is added to the regression line because its position depends on the order in which the firms invest, as was demonstrated in Figure 6.3 in the paper.

Appendix 6B: An Alternative Model of Firm Investment

The model employed in the paper assumed that when the *ith* firm invested, it operated immediately at capacity and thus imposed a burden on all the firms in the industry by depressing the price. In this appendix a model is presented in which the *ith* firm carries the entire burden of its new investment. The model presented here displays qualitatively the same comparative static properties as the model in the main body of the paper. Thus we can be confident that the simulation results were not a property of the idiosyncrasies of a particular model.

The model is characterised by the following set of assumptions.

a1: There are n firms in the industry. The firms are arrayed in a sequence; the *ith* firm in the sequence has capacity k_i.

a2: All firms in the industry operate at installed capacity except firm i which invested last. Firm i sets its own output so that the price remains at p_m.

a3: Each firm in the industry can produce output at constant average cost until its capacity is reached. The capital rental cost per unit of output is c_f and the variable cost per unit of output is c_v.

a4: The demand for the output of the industry is given by the following equation where p is the price, Q(t) is the quantity sold and g is the exponential growth rate:

$$p = a - be^{-gt}Q(t).$$

a5: Firms invest in the sequence in which they are arrayed. If the last firm to invest was the $(i - 1)$*th*, the *ith* firm must invest when firm $(i - 1)$ is operating at full capacity or the $(i + 1)$*th* firm will invest in its place. Thus the price is prevented from rising above p_m.

a6: The *ith* firm anticipates that the price will remain at p_m subsequent to the $(i + 1)$*th* firm's investment where $p_m \geqslant c_v + c_f$.

a7: The price p_m is sufficiently low so that new entry is not induced into the industry.

a8: There is a positive rate of interest r.

Assumption a4 specifies the demand function as

$$p = a - be^{-gt}Q(t) \tag{1}$$

By assumption $p = p_m$, so demand $Q(t)$ is given by

$$Q(t) = \frac{a - p_m}{b} e^{gt} = Q(0)e^{gt} \tag{2}$$

Let b be chosen such that firm i invests at $t = 0$; then the present value of profits is

$$PV_i(0,\infty) = \int_0^\infty e^{-rt}(p_m q_i - c_v q_i - c_f(k_i + y_i))\,dt, \tag{3}$$

where

$$\begin{aligned} q_i &= k_i + (Q(t) - Q(0)), & 0 \leq t \leq t' \\ q_i &= k_i + y_i, & t > t' \end{aligned} \tag{4}$$

t' is the time at which firm $(i + 1)$ invests. t' is expressed in terms of y_i as follows:

$$y_i = Q(0)(e^{gt'} - 1) \tag{5}$$

Since $Q(0) = (a - p_m)/b$, it follows from equation (5) that

$$t' = \frac{1}{g} \log \frac{(a - p_m + by_i)}{a - p_m} \tag{6}$$

Substituting for q_i in expression (3),

$$PV_i(0,\infty) = \int_0^{t'} e^{-rt}((p_m - c_v)(k_i + Q(0)(e^{gt} - 1)) -$$

$$c_f(k_i + y_i))\,dt + \int_{t'}^\infty e^{-rt}(p_m - c_v - c_f)(k_i + y_i)\,dt \tag{7}$$

Carrying out the integrations in (7) and substituting for t' yields

$$\begin{aligned} PV_i(0, \infty) = {} & (1 - \Theta^{-r/g}) \{(p_m - c_v)(k_i - (a - p_m)/b) - \\ & - c_f(k_i + y_i)\}/r + (1 - \Theta^{-(r-g)/g})(p_m - c_v)(a - p_m)/b(r - g) \\ & + \Theta^{-r/g}(p_m - c_v - c_f)(k_i + y_i)/r \end{aligned}$$

Where $\Theta = (a - p_m + by_i)/(a - p_m)$

Several comparative static properties of the optimal solution y_i^* were investigated. Again, the method of analysis was computer search for the optimum y_i^* conditional on an initial set of parameters. One parameter was then changed and the optimum found again. The initial set of parameters used was $a = 9.25$, $b = 4/100$, $c_v = 2$, $c_f = 3$, $p_m = 5.25$, $r = 0.10$, $g = 0.06$, $k_i = 10$. It was found that $\partial y_i^*/\partial k_i = 0$ for $5 \leqslant k_i \leqslant 40$,[10] $\partial y_i^*/\partial a > 0$ for $6.25 \leqslant a \leqslant 13.25$, $\partial y_i^*/\partial b < 0$ for $2/100 \leqslant b \leqslant 5/100$ and $\partial y_i^*/\partial p_m > 0$ for $5.125 \leqslant p_m \leqslant 5.75$.

The only qualitative difference between the model in the text and this model was that in the former case $\partial y_i^*/\partial k_i < 0$, whereas in this case $\partial y_i^*/\partial k_i = 0$. This would not make much difference to the simulations because in both cases the percentage growth rate is inversely related to initial firm size.

Notes

1. The interested reader should also refer to the papers of Jacquemin and de-Lichtbuer (1973) and of Singh and Whittington (1975). The study of Singh and Whittington seems to dispute my interpretation above. They find for 1948–60 the mean growth rate is (weakly) positively related to initial firm size within 19 of 21 2- digit UK industries. However, their study suffers from two flaws: (a) their 2-digit industries are frequently highly aggregated, (b) they count mergers as growth. Point (b) is especially important because according to Samuels (1965), mergers caused greater proportionate growth of large firms than small firms over the period 1951–1960.

2. A very simple price theoretic model of firm growth which would be consistent with LPE is as follows. Suppose that the excess rate of profit in an industry with constant returns is π, and suppose that on average each firm invests a fraction α of its excess profits in additional plants. Then the profits of a firm of capacity k are πk dollars, the investment in new plants is $\alpha\pi k$ dollars, and the percentage growth rate is $\alpha\pi$ which is independent of firm size.

3. Such a rule has been shown to be optimal under certain conditions in a recent paper by Gilbert and Harris (1980).

4. The steps are as follows:

$$PV_i(0,\infty) = (k_i + y_i)\left\{\frac{1 - \Theta^{r/g}}{r}(a - c) - \frac{1 - \Theta^{(r+g)/g}}{r + g}(a - p_m + by_i) + \frac{\Theta^{r/g}}{r}(p_a - c)\right.$$

where $\quad \Theta = \dfrac{a - p_m}{a - p_m + by_i}\dfrac{\delta y_i}{\delta k_i} =$

Collecting terms, $PV_i(0,\infty) =$

$$(ki + yi)\left\{\frac{a - c}{r} - \frac{a - p_m + by_i}{r + g} + \Theta^{r/g}\,\frac{- a - c}{r} + \frac{a - p_m + by_i}{r + g} \times \Theta + \frac{p_a - c}{r}\right\}$$

Substituting for Θ and simplifying within the last bracket yields

$$PV_i(0,\infty) = (k_i + y_i)\left\{\frac{a-c}{r} - \frac{a-p_m+by_i}{r+g} + \Theta^{r/g}\left(\frac{p_a-a}{r} + \frac{a-p_m}{r+g}\right)\right\}$$

And further simplification within the last bracket yields equation (8).

5. Since the intuition underlying this result is not obvious, it may be helpful to provide the comparative statics. Expression (8) may be written

$$PV_i(0,\infty) = (k_i + y_i)f(y_i)$$

The first- and second-order conditions for a maximum yield

$$(k_i + y_i)f'(y_i) + f(y_i) = 0,$$
$$(k_i + y_i)f''(y_i) + 2f'(y_i) < 0.$$

If we make the reasonable assumptions that in the neighbourhood of the optimum, $PV_i(0,\infty) > 0$ and $(k_i + y_i) > 0$, it follows that $f(y_i) > 0$. Then from the first-order condition it follows that $f'(y_i) < 0$. Now, finding the total differential of the first-order condition yields

$$\frac{\partial y_i}{\partial k_i} = \frac{-f'(y_i)}{((k_i + y_i)f''(y_i) + 2f'(y_i))} < 0$$

6. An empirical study of the LPE will also be confused by other factors. The theory derived above refers to a firm's behaviour in a single market. Real firms however operate in many markets which may differ by product line or by geographical region. For instance, in an empirical study of the LPE in the US oil refining industry (Peck and Harvey (1979)) it was demonstrated that there is a bias towards acceptance of the LPE when the LPE is not valid if (a) asphalt plants are included inappropriately in the same market as full range refineries or if (b) refineries on the US West Coast are considered inappropriately to be in the same market as those on the US East Coast.

7. Denote $\log S_i(t + \Delta)$ by Y_i and $\log S_i(t)$ by X_i. Then,

$$\hat{\beta} = \frac{\Sigma(Y_i - X_i)(X_i - \bar{X})}{\Sigma_i(X_i - \bar{X})^2} = \frac{\Sigma Y_i(X_i - \bar{X})}{\Sigma(X_i - \bar{X})^2} - \frac{\Sigma X_i(X_i - \bar{X})}{\Sigma(X_i - \bar{X})^2}$$
$$= \hat{\delta} - 1.$$

8. Let a general representation of each of the regression equations (11), (12), (13) be

$$Y = X\beta + u,$$

$Y = (9 \times 1)$, X is (9×2), β is (2×1), u is (9×1). The R^2 was computed as $1 - (\hat{u}'\hat{u}/Y'Y)$ rather than the usual $1 - (\hat{u}'\hat{u}/y'y)$, where y is the vector of deviations of Y about its sample mean. The former definition was used because it makes more sense in a regression without a constant term such as (13).

9. To carry out a t-test it is necessary to transform the estimated standard deviation by multiplying it by $(60/59)^{1/2}$. The t-statistic then becomes

$$t = (-.167108 + .64504) \div (.277516 \times \frac{\sqrt{60}}{\sqrt{59}} \times \frac{1}{\sqrt{60}}) = 13.2.$$

10. In fact, it can be shown quite easily from expression (8) that y_i^* is independent of k_i.

References

Gilbert, R. and Harris, J. (1980) 'Notes on Investment in Oligopolistic Markets', University of California, Berkeley, Working Paper

Hart, P. E. and Prais, S. J. (1956) 'The analysis of business concentration: a statistical approach,' *Journal of the Royal Statistical Society, A, 19*, 150–81

Hymer, S and Pashigian, P. (1962) 'Firm size and rate of growth,' *Journal of Political Economy*, 556–69

Jacquemin, A. P. and Cardon de Lichtbuer, M. (1973) 'Size structure, stability, and performance of the largest British and EEC firms,' *European Economic Review, 4*, 393–408

Mansfield, E., (1962) 'Entry, exit, and the growth of firms,' *American Economic Review, 52*, 1962, 1023–51

Peck, S. C. and Harvey, S. (1979) 'Factors Leading to Structural Change in the U.S. Oil Refining Industry in the Postwar Period' in R. Pindyck (ed.), *Advances in the Economics of Energy and Resources*, Vol 1, JAI Press

Samuels, J. M., (1965) 'Size and the growth of firms,' *Review of Economic Studies*, April, pp. 105–12

Scherer, F. (1973) M., *Industrial Market Structure and Economic Performance*, Chicago, Rand McNally

Sherman, R., (1971) 'Entry barriers and the growth of firms,' *Southern Economic Journal*, October, pp. 238–47

Simon, H. A. and Bonini, C. (1958) 'The size distribution of business firms,' *American Economic Review, 48*, 607–17

Singh, A. and Whittington, G. (1975) 'The size and growth of firms,' *Review of Economic Studies, 42*, 15–26

Vining, D. P., (1976) 'Autocorrelated growth rates and the Pareto Law, a further analysis,' *Journal of Political Economy, 84*, 369–80

7 MONOPOLY, ENTRY AND PREDATORY PRICING: THE HOFFMAN-LA ROCHE CASE*

Paul K. Gorecki
Economic Council of Canada

1. Introduction

In a judgement released on February 5, 1980 Hoffman-La Roche Ltd. (hereinafter referred to as Roche) was found guilty[1] in that, between 25 June 1970 and 30 June 1971,

> . . . in the City of Toronto, in the Province of Ontario and elsewhere in Canada, [it] did engage in a policy of selling articles, to wit: a mild tranquilizer known as Valium containing diazepam as the chemically active ingredient to hospitals in Canada at unreasonably low prices, having the effect or tendency of substantially lessening competition in the sale to hospitals of mild tranquilizers containing diazepam as the chemically active ingredient, or of eliminating competitors selling or attempting to sell to hospitals in Canada, mild tranquilizers containing diazepam as the chemically active ingredient, or designed to have the effect of substantially lessening such competition or eliminating such competitors, and did thereby commit an indictable offence contrary to section 34(1)(c) of the Combines Investigation Act, R. S. 1970, Chapter c-23, as amended (Linden, J., *R. vs Hoffman-La Roche Ltd.*, (1980) 28 O. R. (2d) 164 at 217–218 hereinafter referred to as Linden, J.).

The Roche case has all the hallmarks of the use of predatory pricing to maintain a monopoly (initially established by patent

---

* This paper draws extensively upon the documentary and oral evidence submitted at trial in *R. vs Hoffman-La Roche Ltd.* in the Supreme Court of Ontario. I should like to thank the Bureau of Competition Policy of the Federal Department of Consumer and Corporate Affairs for allowing me access to this material in preparing this paper. L. G. Buchanan and S. D. Whittaker provided useful comments on an earlier version. Any errors are the responsibility of the author alone, while the views expressed do not necessarily reflect those of the Economic Council of Canada.

protection afforded diazepam) by preventing the successful entry of a new entrant, Frank W. Horner Ltd. (hereinafter referred to as Horner). Valium, Roche's brand of diazepam, was sold below cost, indeed given away free, for a sufficiently long period of time (a year) for it to be more than a temporary expedient to meet, indeed beat, the lower prices of Horner — up to 43 per cent below those of Roche prior to the entry of Horner in May 1970. The cost in forgone sales of Valium was estimated by Roche at $2.6 million. The parent firm in Basle, Switzerland was kept fully informed of the policies of its Canadian subsidiary. The intent of Roche was to eliminate Horner from the diazepam market. In his judgement Linden, J., remarked, 'Consequently, I am convinced beyond a reasonable doubt on all the evidence before me that officials of Roche had the design of eliminating competitors. . . .' (p. 212). Somewhat later in his judgement, the following passage appeared, 'It is one thing to compete with others and try to reduce their impact on the market. It is quite another thing to try to force one's competitors completely out of the market with a massive giveaway program on this scale' (p. 213). Officials of both Horner and Roche agreed the size of the giveaway was unprecedented (p. 180). The predatory pricing forced the new entrant to withdraw from the hospital market for the period of the giveaway. On July 2, 1970 Horner wrote a letter to hospital pharmacists which read, in part, as follows, 'While we have succeeded in effecting a lowering of diazepam prices, we feel we are not now in a position to offer it free to hospitals . . . we will not be able to meet this competition.' (as cited in Linden, J., p. 179). Finally, it should be noted that diazepam was by far the most important of Roche's many products, accounting for half of its total pharmaceutical sales.[2]

The Roche case provides a rare *prima facie* example of predatory pricing, adding to the small stock, some of which were analysed by B. S. Yamey (1972). Hence the opportunity arises to test the rule established by McGee — that predatory pricing is an extremely rare phenomenon because it involves certain losses today against uncertain gains in the future, while, at the same time, there are cheaper alternatives such as merger or collusion. McGee's conclusion was based on a careful and exhaustive study of the available evidence in the case concerning Standard Oil (NJ), which had long been held to have used predatory pricing to achieve or maintain its monopoly in the late nineteenth and early twentieth century. McGee's findings, published in his now famous 1958 article in the *Journal of Law and Economics*, exploded this popular view by showing that predatory pricing had not been used and that instead Standard had achieved and maintained its monopoly position by merger and acquisition. Subsequent to McGee's original contribution there were a number of additional detailed case studies of predatory pricing such as those on the American Sugar Refinery monopoly (Zerbe, 1969) and the gunpowder trust (Elzinga, 1970), both of which reached conclusions similar to those of McGee. In reviewing these and other studies McGee (1980) found little reason to change or alter his conclusions of 22 years previously.

This paper addresses the question of whether the Roche case is an exception to the McGee rule. Attention is paid not only to the diazepam market but also to another related market, chlordiazepoxide, which is vital to any appreciation of the Roche case. The background to the problem of new entry threatening Roche's monopoly of diazepam is sketched in Section 2. Predatory pricing and other solutions to the threat of new entry are described, discussed and evaluated in Section 3. The final section addresses the question of whether Roche's predatory pricing is the exception which proves the McGee rule.

2. Roche's Problem

In the 1960s, Roche, one of the world's leading pharmaceutical firms, had two major drugs which accounted for the vast majority of its sales and profits. In his trial testimony Roche's secretary-treasurer in Canada, Mr. Nowotny, considered the two products 'winners', which a drug firm may produce only once in every decade or two. One stock analyst called the two drugs, 'the most profitable products now produced by the pharmaceutical industry'.[3] Roche sales in Canada alone reached millions of dollars for both drugs: chlordiazepoxide $2.9 million in 1963, peaking at $4.9 million in 1966, then declining somewhat to $4.4 million in 1969; the corresponding figures for diazepam were $0.3 million, $3.2 million and $8.4 million, respectively.

Chlordiazepoxide, for which Roche's brand name is Librium, was introduced in the Canadian market in 1960 and by 1963 accounted for slightly in excess of 50 per cent of Roche's pharmaceutical sales, falling to just under a quarter in 1969. Diazepam, for which Roche's brand name is Valium, was introduced on the Canadian market in 1963 and climbed steadily in significance until it accounted for a few percentage points less than half of Roche's sales in 1969. The change in relative significance of the two drugs in Roche's sales reflects the fact that while both were mild tranquillizers, treating anxiety and tension, diazepam had the added advantage of also acting as a muscle relaxant, thus enabling it to reach a wider market. Hence the two drugs were substitutes in some respects, while in others diazepam satisfied demands that chlordiazepoxide could not. The patents relating to both drugs are Roche's exclusive property with expiry dates in Canada of 1980 for chlordiazepoxide and 1985 for diazepam.[4] Both drugs can only be obtained with a physician's prescription presented to a registered pharmacist to dispense to the patient.

Competition between drug firms has traditionally taken the form of research and development aimed at the discovery of new drugs which offer advantages over existing treatments: reduced side effects; easier administration to the patient; or lower cost than alternative surgical techniques. For example, chlordiazepoxide and diazepam do not encounter the same overdose problems of barbiturates, which have led to poisonings and deaths. Promotion of the new drug to the medical profession is conducted through journals, samples, and visits by detail men to individual physicians. Particular attention is paid to the hospital market, which heavily influences the physician's prescribing habits in private practice. Because of this the hospital market is believed to be much more important than suggested by the 20 per cent of Valium and Librium sales for which it accounted.

The drug industry has traditionally been characterised by little price competition[5] because patent protection afforded new drugs forced rival firms to offer improved products rather than lower priced copies, restrictions exist on price disclosure at the retail level and the prescriber is not the person responsible for payment. Indeed, the physician may be unaware of prices since these do not form a prominent feature in the drug advertising literature. Nevertheless, in the 1960s, the hospital market became increasingly price competitive as hospital physicians were required to delegate the choice of brand of a given drug to purchasing committees, which used tendering systems in selecting brands, and hospitals formed buying groups for a wide variety of hospital supplies, including drugs.

The net result of this industry structure and the form of competition was, according to a series of government reports in the 1960s[6] that Canadian prices were considered high both in relation to production costs and to price levels in other advanced western industrial nations. It was believed that the 17-year patent protection afforded drugs was the major cause of this situation.

The patent protection afforded drugs in Canada contained certain provisions which allowed, theoretically at least, entry of competitors to take place while the patent was still extant. Of particular interest in the present context are the compulsory licensing provisions of the *Patent Act*.[7] Between 1923 and 1969 section 41(3) of this Act allowed licences to be issued by the Commissioner of Patents to *manufacture* drugs for which the patent was extant. The section stated that in fixing a royalty the Commissioner '. . . shall have regard to the desirability of making the . . . medicine available to the public at the lowest possible price consistent with giving to the inventor due reward for the research leading to the invention.' A 15 per cent royalty on the licensee's net selling price, when sold at arms length, of the bulk raw material was set by the Commissioner. The intent of the section was clear to those interpreting it — '. . . to bring about competition . . . "the specific public interest in free competition" was deemed to be more important than the maintenance of the patentee's monopoly rights . . .'[8]

Section 41(3) did not have a large overall impact on the drug industry in the 1950s and 1960s (with chlordiazepoxide being a prominent exception) because the Canadian market was too small to make manufacturing in Canada profitable. Indeed, 80 per cent of the bulk raw material was imported from a relatively small number of plants, which supplied the world-wide needs of the industry. Final dosage preparation, where production scale economies and capital requirements were relatively modest, was more likely to take place in Canada. Delays were experienced in being granted a licence. Furthermore, the structure and form of competition in the drug industry did not facilitate the success of lower priced brands of an existing well established patented brand.[9]

Circumstances changed in the 1970s. In particular, the June 1969 amendments to the *Patent Act* allowed licences to be issued for the *importation* as well as manufacture of the bulk raw material. And there were attempts by the federal and provincial governments to make physicians, pharmacists and, to a lesser extent, consumers, much more price sensitive. These structural changes resulting in new entrants importing the bulk raw material from countries such as Italy (which does not permit drugs to be protected), and competing in Canada with established drug firms on products for which the patent was still extant.[10] One of the first drugs which was subject to the June 1969 amendments was diazepam.

New entry occurred in the chlordiazepoxide and diazepam markets once sizeable sales volumes were attained. In the former case Elliot-Marion Ltd. (hereinafter referred to as E-M) entered with Protensin in April 1965, Nordic Biochemicals offered Nack in May 1966, Bell-Craig's Viaquil appeared in June 1967, followed by Horner with Solium in February 1968. By late 1969 there were nine brands competing with Roche's Librium. Horner, well established in the Canadian drug industry, was the first to enter the diazepam market with Vivol in early 1970. Roche's problem was how to deal with such new competitors, all of whom used lower prices to attract existing buyers, with particular emphasis on the hospital market.

3. Predatory Pricing and Other Tactics

Roche employed a variety of tactics against new entrants into the chlordiazepoxide and diazepam markets over the period 1965–70. The purpose of this section is not to describe these in great detail or even to list them all. Instead, an attempt is made to establish the place of predatory pricing in the overall strategy of Roche. In particular, Roche used three major tactics, one price and two non-price, in meeting competition in the chlordiazepoxide and diazepam markets. Each is briefly described with an evaluation of its success.

Roche stressed, in both the promotion conducted by its field staff and in printed material to physicians and hospital pharmacists, that it was the firm that conducted the R and D that led to the discovery of chlordiazepoxide and diazepam, that Roche had provided a reliable quality product and through its field staff and printed material had given advice and guidance to the health professions. In contrast, as one memorandum to all field staff put it, 'Point out that when they buy an imitation, they get what they *see* and that is all — there is nothing else!!'[11] At one point a letter was sent out to physicians signed by the President of Roche, J. S. Fralich, dated February 1968, which read, in part, as follows:

> The imitation philosophy was recently underlined by Dr. Alfred Gilman . . . when he wrote to US Senator Nelson: '. . . I consider the small generic drug company a completely parasite industry. . . .' Apart from the occasional counterfeiter the current duplications containing chlordiazepoxide are marketed under compulsory license by tradename. To our knowledge none of these imitators had to duplicate the enormous amount of work which is necessary in the compilation of a new drug application. Likewise, no clinical investigation activities of any consequence by these companies have come to our attention. (Exhibit 97)

However, it would appear that this tactic did not prevent hospitals from purchasing the brands competing with Librium. For example, the President of Roche in 1967 commented, 'Marketing department feels that there is no alternative method for competing for Government [i.e. hospital] business except on a price basis,'[12] while the minutes of the Sales Promotion Planning Group held on 21 February 1969, stated, 'Group reaffirms that the only basis which will maintain hospital unit sales [of chlordiazepoxide] will be related to prices competitive in the market place, regardless of any promotional or prestige activities.'[13] This reflects not only the price sensitivity of the hospital market but also the '. . . good reputation . . .' enjoyed by such firms as Horner and E-M.[14]

A second strategy of Roche in meeting competition from rival brands of chlordiazepoxide in the mid- and late 1960s was to encourage hospitals to switch to diazepam, where Roche had a monopoly until Horner entered with Vivol in early 1970. For example, in 1963 when Roche first became aware of possible competitors to Librium, the introduction of Valium was couched in the following terms, 'To distract the physician's attention from the promotional activity of Librium competitors . . . it is proposed to promote Valium as an improvement over Librium.'[15] Several years later, on 30 April 1968 officials of Roche comment '. . . we are actively pushing Valium in those hospitals where we have lost cdp business. Our efforts are reflected in the growth of Valium in the hospitals.'[16] From the available evidence it is not possible to estimate how successful this strategy was, but the information cited above shows that chlordiazepoxide's relative importance compared to diazepam did decline substantially, although given the advantages of diazepam some of this would have undoubtedly occurred in any event.

An important factor which enabled Roche to pursue this strategy was the classification of a drug as 'New' rather than 'Old' by regulatory authorities controlling drug introduction and sale.[17] An old drug is one where sufficient information has been collected on its use in the population at large for it to be considered safe and efficacious. A firm wishing to sell a drug accorded such a status only has to inform the regulatory authorities that it intends to market the drug. On the other hand, if a drug is on a new drug status, which means that some uncertainty or doubt still surrounds the use of the drug, then the firm wishing to market the drug must perform a number of tests to meet regulatory authorities' requirements. (Such tests are usually quite expensive, though not as great as those conducted by the originator prior to marketing the drug.) These tests thus raise a barrier to entry, particularly for the smaller potential entrants.

There is no set time period when the change in classification from new to old drug status occurs. The new entrant has the incentive to convince the regulatory authorities for an early switch while the originator has the opposite incentive. In the case at hand chlordiazepoxide was accorded old drug status in June 1967 when the third competitive brand entered, while for diazepam a similar change in status took place in the 1970s, with Horner entering while diazepam was classified as a new drug. Hence the new entrant had a lower cost of entry into the chlordiazepoxide market, for which sales did not start to fall until 1966, when a levelling off rather than a sudden drop occurred, than into the diazepam market. As a result many, indeed most, entrants may have decided to wait until the change in classification to old drug status occurred for diazepam before entering this market.

The final strategy followed by Roche in facing new competition was effectively to lower prices. This was mainly confined to the hospital market, the most obvious point of entry for new entrants: no large field staff was needed compared to the retail market where individual physicians in private practice had to be persuaded to switch brands — indeed apart from E-M, with a field staff of 35 and Horner, whose field staff matched Roche's, none of the entrants had a capability in this respect; and the hospital market was the most price sensitive section of the drug market — price being the major selling advantage that the new entrant advertised. The object of Roche was thus to exclude the new entrants from the hospital market' . . . and force them to develop the market in confrontations with individual physicians. This is a long, tedious and costly process . . .'.[18] Yet at the same time the hospital market was very important to Roche as a determinant of the prescribing habits of physicians in private practice. In Roche's 1969 annual budget submission to the parent in Basle the following passage appears:

> The area of greatest vulnerability to chlordiazepoxide formulations is in hospitals where the trend to purchase products by generic name is becoming more common practice due to pressure being exerted on hospital pharmacies by the administrative staffs of the hospitals together with Provincial governmental pressure. (Exhibit 141, Annual Budget, Pharmaceutical Division, 4 December 1969, pp. 38–9)

Hence the hospital market was of particular interest both to Roche and the new entrants.

Roche employed a variety of pricing strategies, short of predatory pricing, in confronting new entrants into the chlordiazepoxide and diazepam markets. Special offers were used, particularly when a new entrant was about to begin selling its competitive brand. These offers did not take the form of an explicit price cut but rather were of the form 'buy one tablet and get one, two or whatever free'. Such offers usually lasted for a limited period of time only and were made prior to the expected entry date of the new entrant, who would find demand satisfied for the product for some time, given the hospital market practice of ordering supplies for several months. For example, when E-M was expected to enter the chlordiazepoxide market in early 1965 at a discount of 19 per cent below Roche's price, Roche offered, for the period March 19 to April 30, 1965, 'Anniversary Deal Prices' which effectively undercut E-M's lowest price by 17 per cent. According to the Crown at trial deals of this nature, 'became a prototype of Roche's response to competition in Librium and Valium, and is often referred to as having been successful in blocking competition'.[19]

Another tactic was to offer quantity discounts on the total

purchase of *all* Roche products, not Librium or Valium taken separately.[20] Hence, although Librium may have been priced higher than competitive brands of chlordiazepoxide, the savings on Valium, due to combined quantity discounts, more than offset the price disadvantage on Librium. This tactic was likely to be particularly effective in the period when Roche had a monopoly for the sale of diazepam. No evidence is available on the success or otherwise of this tactic in preventing entry and retaining market share, but for Roche it had the advantage of keeping the price of Librium high in the hospitals and thus preserved some or all of its retail market. Furthermore the discount structure could easily be changed depending upon the extent of competition in various markets.

Librium, like Valium, can be sold in different dosage forms (capsules, tablets etc.) and strengths (5mg, 10mg, 25mg), some of which are more popular than others. For example, the most popular dosage form and strength was 10mg caps, a refinement on compressed 10mg tabs.[21] Roche between July 1968 and January 1970 used various deals on Librium whereby one dosage form and strength was given away 'free' where a hospital purchased a year's supply of the other dosage forms and strengths at regular (i.e., list) prices.[22] At first (i.e. July 1968–March 1969) the nearly obsolete 10mg compressed tablet was free with purchases of 5 and 25mg caps. Essentially Roche was '. . . using to best advantage a product that really had no demand . . .'[23] However, when the stocks of 10mg compressed tablets disappeared Roche, between April 1969 and January 1970, used 10mg capsules, which were in much greater demand, instead. The effect of this giveaway program, which appeared to run at the rate of three free with one purchased, was to keep Roche slightly below the price of the competition.[24] In a number of instances this tactic clearly allowed Roche to retain the chlordiazepoxide business and hence must be judged, at least in part, successful.[25]

In the course of the 10mg capsules giveaway in a number of instances it appeared that the three to one ratio was exceeded and that in particular deals losses may actually have been sustained.[26] Indeed, on three government contacts, each for a number of hospitals, Roche bid (September 1969, February 1970 and May 1970) only a nominal price.[27] However, while the judge agreed that some sales were made below cost he felt it was not a policy. In the case of the three contracts the judge accepted the explanation of Mr. Nowotny of Roche '. . . that the tenders were only made to test reactions . . .' (Linden, J., p. 203).

Most of the evidence presented so far has related to the use of various tactics by Roche to combat competition in the chlordiazepoxide market in the period 1965–70, prior to the predatory pricing Roche used in the diazepam market. Despite these tactics prices for Librium fell in the hospital but not the retail market and the overall market share of the chlordiazepoxide market held by Roche declined. For example, Roche's price to the hospitals for 10mg capsules fell from $38.25 per 1,000 on 100,000 lots in 1965 when E-M entered, to $34.50 in late 1966, to $28.00 per 1,000 in January 1967, to $18.40 per 1,000 in June 1967.[28] In terms of market share for combined hospital and retail markets of chlordiazepoxide, Librium accounted for 97.2 per cent in 1965, 94.6 in 1966, 90.2 in 1967, 85.0 in 1968, 79.4 in 1969 and 77.9 per cent in 1970, with the nearest competitor accounting for 4.9 per cent in 1968 and 11.4 per cent in 1970.[29] Despite the gradual decline in market share and price Roche considered the limited inroads made by licensee competition, particularly Horner's Solium and E-M's Protensin '. . . encourage us and indicate that our counter-promotional tactics have been effective'.[30]

It is against this background of competition and new entry in the chlordiazepoxide market that the predatory pricing described in the opening paragraph of this paper took place. Several issues need to be analysed: the success of predatory pricing and the motivation of what, at least according to McGee's views, was irrational for a profit maximising firm. In investigating these issues it should be possible to address McGee's claim that merger and collusion are more attractive alternatives to price cutting.

Roche's predatory pricing policy with respect to Valium was unsuccessful except for the period for which the drug was free to hospitals. However, even during this period Horner continued selling Vivol, apparently successfully, in the retail market.[31] As soon as Roche ceased to practise predatory pricing Horner re-entered the hospital market and new entrants appeared such that by June 1974 there were 17 brands of diazepam competing with Valium.[32] Prices of Valium declined. Although published prices remained the same Roche offered deals to hospitals which saw the price of Valium steadily decline from 1971 onwards — 'buy one get two free' in July-Dec. 1971 to 'buy one get four free' in July 1972 to Jan. 1974.[33] The price decline of diazepam was even more dramatic in some instances. In his judgement Linden, J. (p. 180) cites the following example concerning the Toronto General Hospital,

> . . . which bought Valium from Roche in the 1960s for $42.70 per 1,000 5mg, switched to buying from Horner from 1972–76 for $6.74 per 1,000 5mg, and now buys from ICN, a generic house, its EPAM for only $4.10 per 1,000 5mg, less than 10 per cent of the original Roche price.

Roche's share of the diazepam market (combined hospital and retail) declined steadily from 100 per cent in 1969 to 71.7 per cent in 1973. (Interestingly enough in 1973 Librium accounted for 74.5 per cent of the chlordiazepoxide market).[34] The above evidence also suggests that Roche would have been unlikely to recapture the forgone profits on the free Valium in the post-1971 period. However, results using stricter statistical procedures and data not presently available would be required to settle this particular question beyond doubt.

Roche's predatory pricing was doomed to failure from the start — changes in government policy allowed much easier entry into the hospital and retail markets, while, at the same time, lessening the significance of the influence of the hospital market over the retail market. Indeed, Mr. Nowotny subsequently admitted that the policy was a 'disaster' as well as an 'ill-conceived idea'.[35] The 1969 amendments to the *Patent Act*, noted above, allowed licences to be issued for the importation of diazepam and chlordiazepoxide (either in bulk raw material form or final dosage form), with a royalty fee of 4 per cent of the selling price of the licensee. Hence the bulk raw material and final dosage form did not have to be manufactured in Canada, as was the case prior to 1969. The net result was that the costs of entry were lowered. In the late 1960s and early 1970s governments introduced a number of programs which were aimed at making physicians aware of the relative prices of different brands of the same drug and their quality.[36] These programs were concerned principally with the retail market and hence reduced the significance of the hospital market in determining physicians' prescribing habits in private practice. Pharmacists changed the basis upon which a prescription was priced from a straight mark-up over cost to a flat dispensing fee for professional services plus the drug cost. Thus the incentive for dispensing a higher priced brand was lessened.

Roche was aware of the difference between the 1960s and early 1970s. The minutes of a meeting held in May 1970 contain the following passage,

> The basic difference in the case of the impending diazepam pormotional [sic] battle, as compared with the chlordiazepoxide promotional battle, will be the intervention of Provincial Governments at the level of the prescribing physician (especially Ontario) and at the level of the retail pharmacist (Ontario, Alberta and British Columbia).
>
> It was concluded that governments would attempt to influence prescribing habits of physicians and also attempt (even force) pharmacists to fill prescriptions with the least expensive product available.
>
> In view of the above points, the group was of the opinion that in the case of the 'battle of the diazepams', the prescription market for Valium will be in jeopardy, unless drastic action is taken promptly to influence physicians and pharmacists in a manner that will encourage them to reject interference with their professional rights to prescribe the product of their choice, in the case of the physician, and to dispense the product prescribed by the physician, in the case of the pharmacist. (Exhibit 158, minutes of Task Force on the Effects of Various Provincial Legislations on Operations and Determination of Policies Required, 25 May 1970, p. 3).

All these measures reduced the cost of entry and increased the potential return to the prospective entrant challenging Roche's dominant position.

If the above account is accepted as a reasonable interpretation of events, the issue still arises as to the reasons for Roche's behaviour, irrational though it may be. The state of mind among Roche officials must be recognised; they regarded the diazepam and chlordiazepoxide market as rightfully, indeed perhaps morally, theirs — Roche had discovered the two drugs, Roche owned the worldwide patents, Roche had promoted the drugs to hospitals and pharmacists. This state of mind is reflected in the documents — 'Stolen merchandise can always be sold at a lower price'; 'Such a move . . . will serve notice to all present and future parasites that we mean business,' new entrants were able to 'steal' what was 'rightfully theirs [i.e., Roche's]', Roche wanted to make

'E-M eat their blue capsules' in 1965 when Protensin was launched and, finally, on losing a hospital contract in 1966 to E-M, a Roche official wrote 'I share your concerns over this theft. . . .'[37] Such a state of mind may have hampered Roche officials in designing a rational plan of action. However, this does not explain why such drastic action took place in 1970, rather than 1965, when E-M entered with its brand of chlordiazepoxide.

The timing of the predatory pricing reflected the influence of a number of factors. One of the major tactics that Roche adopted in meeting competition in the chlordiazepoxide market was to use the monopoly in diazepam in the offering of various deals and in encouraging hospitals and physicians to use diazepam instead of chlordiazepoxide. A successful competitor in the diazepam market would seriously weaken such a strategy. The various government programs in the later 1960s and 1970s were targeted on the retail as well as hospital market and were likely to lead to significant competition in the lucrative retail market. These factors led Roche officials to a gamble that the giveaway policy would '. . . not only abort Horner's efforts, but serve as a warning to others who seem to be showing an interest in this [i.e., diazepam] product.'[38] The trial judge characterised Roche's reaction as follows:

> The compulsory licensing fee of 4% was felt by Roche to be inadequate and unfair. Roche feared that the Parcost program of Ontario and the other similar provincial programs would hurt its sales of Valium severely. It refused to give up without a fight.
>
> One can sympathize with Roche's fears and feelings at that time. They were in a panic. (Linden, J., pp. 206–7).

Predatory pricing, it would seem, was the culmination of a policy of incremental escalation by Roche to meet competition in the chlordiazepoxide and then diazepam market.

The alternatives to predatory pricing suggested by McGee — merger and collusion — were never considered, judging by the documentary and oral evidence submitted at the trial, by Roche. Instead Roche considered, but did *not* act upon, making an application for a compulsory licence on a major Horner product which could '. . . be used as scare tactics or as bargaining power. This information could be leaked out for subtle effect or used directly.'[39] Other major pharmaceutical firms were to be asked to apply for licences on different major Horner products. Another suggestion, also not acted upon, was the formation of a Roche branded generics firm which would sell drugs at low prices, provide no research and compete with firms such as Horner. If such a firm succeeded, Roche '. . . would gradually eliminate all small and generic houses . . .'[40] after which the firm could be closed.

The lack of any consideration by Roche of collusion with the new entrants, and to a lesser extent, merger, can be explained mainly in terms of their attitude toward their competitors. One does not usually cooperate with persons characterised as 'parasites' and 'thieves'. On economic grounds there are reasons for doubting the effectiveness of merger when, as occurred, especially after the 1969 amendments to the *Patent Act*, entry was easy. Acquisition might have led to a large supply of new entrants, with whom Roche would share some of its hitherto 'high' profits. (Under such conditions price reductions to meet or beat the competition might have been a better strategy).[41] More exhaustive study with data not presently available, would be required in order to evaluate fully whether merger or collusion would have been profitable alternatives. In any event Roche apparently never considered either.

4. Predatory Pricing: Rational or Irrational?

The major purpose of this paper has been to determine whether what is perhaps the most unambiguous example of predatory pricing documented to date is an exception to the rule formulated by J. S. McGee — that predatory pricing is an extremely rare phenomenon because it involves certain losses today against uncertain gains in the future while, at the same time, cheaper alternatives exist such as merger or collusion. McGee (1958, p. 142) felt predatory pricing was particularly unlikely to succeed where entry was easy,

> Obstacles to entry are necessary conditions for success [for monopolisation]. Entry is the nemesis of monopoly. It is foolish to monopolise an area or market into which entry is quick and easy . . . . In general monopolisation will not pay if there is no special qualification for entry, or no relatively long gestation

period for the facilities that must be committed for successful entry.

The conclusion of this paper is that Roche's behaviour is the exception that proves the McGee rule. Predatory pricing neither precluded the entry of Horner from the hospital market nor discouraged the entry of new competitors from the diazepam market. Furthermore, because Horner carried a wide range of drug products Roche could never hope to bankrupt this new competitor, who would always pose an entry threat once prices had been raised. Predatory pricing was an irrational act for a profit maximising firm.[42]

Notes

1. Subsequently the Crown appealed the sentence at trial ($50,000), while Roche cross-appealed the sentence and conviction. Both sets of appeals were dismissed by the Court of Appeal, Supreme Court of Ontario. (For details see *R. vs Hoffman-La Roche Ltd.*, (1982) 58 CPR (2d) pp. 1–44.) The case was not appealed, by either party, to the Supreme Court of Canada.

2. Exhibit 186, Corporate Marketing Group, 'Market Position of Librium and Valium,' 29 March, 1971, enclosure #2, p. 26. All figures cited below relating to relative significance and sales of chlordiazepoxide and diazepam are drawn from this source, as is the estimate of $2.6 million forgone sales cited earlier in this paragraph.

3. As cited in Ball (1971, p. 134).

4. These dates are taken from Pharmaceutical Manufacturers Association of Canada (1976, Appendix A, pp. 36–9). Note that the original patents for chlordiazepoxide expired in 1978, for diazepam, 1979. (Canada has a 17 year patent term). However, because there were additional patents in 1963 (for chlordiazepoxide) and 1968 (for diazepam) the expiry dates are those recorded in the text.

5. This does not mean, of course, that the drug firm can charge any price it likes. This is likely to vary with the therapeutic and other advantages the drug offers over existing treatments.

6. See Canada, Director of Investigation and Research (1961) Canada, Restrictive Trade Practices Commission (1963) Hall Commission (1964, 1965) and Harley Committee (1965).

7. For details see Gorecki (1981, Chapter II, pp. 25–47), which refers not only to compulsory licensing but the process-dependent form of drug patents.

8. Statement made by Jackett, J., of the Federal Court in *Hoffman-La Roche Ltd. v. L. D. Craig Ltd.*, 46 CPR 32 at 50.

9. Price was likely to be the only variable that the new entrant could employ to take away business from the established firm or patentee, who would usually have a good reputation for producing a reliable quality product. Roche remarked prior to the launch of Horner's Solium, that Horner's anticipated price reduction should be met, so that the 'very raison-d'être for duplication would be eliminated' (as cited in Linden, J., p. 173).

10. The various policy measures are outlined in Gorecki (1981, pp. 3–23, 36–47). The firms making applications for licences under the *Patent Act* are not usually the well established drug firms. See Gorecki (1981, pp. 75–77) for discussion of this characteristic of the licensees.

11. Exhibit 99, memo to entire Roche field staff from K. Bradshaw, titled 'Imitation Formulations of Chlordiazepoxide,' 2 April, 1968, p. 2, emphasis in original.

12. Exhibit 83, memo to Executive Group from J. S. Fralich, titled 'Librium Price Situation', 14 June , 1967, p. 2.

13. Exhibit 115, minutes of Hoffman-La Roche Ltd., Sales Promotion Planning Group, held on 21 Feb., 1969, p. 1.

14. Exhibit 186, p. 12. In this and other documents Roche distinguishes between Horner and E-M as compared to the smaller suppliers of chlordiazepozide which '. . . are not considered as reliable sources of supply,' (p. 12) by hospitals.

15. Exhibit 61, minutes of Executive Committee meeting, 8 February, 1963.

16. Exhibit 107, minutes of a Joint Marketing Group and a Sales Promotion Planning Group meeting, 30 April, 1968.

17. The discussion of Old and New Drug status in this and the next paragraph is taken from the Written Argument submitted by J. E. Sexton, QC and W. J. Manuel on behalf of the Attorney General of Canada in the Roche trial on 15 January, 1979, (pp. 53–7), the Written Argument submitted by G. F. Henderson, QC, C. Bynoe, QC, and R. G. McClenahan, QC on behalf of Hoffman-La Roche Ltd., in the Roche trial on 1 February, 1979, (pp. 8–12) and Gorecki (1981, pp. 61–8).

18. Exhibit 168, 'Sales and Promotional Report as at 30 June, 1970 (6 months)', no page number.

19. Written Brief submitted by AG, 15 January, 1979, (p. 29).

20. For details see Written Brief submitted by AG, 15 January, 1979, pp. 25–6.

21. See Written Brief submitted by Roche, 1 February, 1979, (pp. 3–5) and Linden J. (p. 174).

22. See Written Brief submitted by AG, 15 January, 1979, (pp. 41–9).

23. Written Brief submitted by AG, 15 January, 1979, (p. 42).

24. Written Brief submitted by AG, 15 January, 1979, (p. 46).

25. See, for example, Exhibits cited in Written Brief submitted by AG, 15 January, 1979, (pp. 46–7).

26. See Written Brief submitted by AG, 15 January, 1979, (pp. 47–9) and Linden, J., (pp. 174–5, 202).

27. See Written Brief submitted by AG, 15 January, 1979, (pp. 52–3) and Linden, J., (pp. 175–6, 203).

28. Price information is taken from Written Brief submitted by AG, 15 January, 1979, (pp. 27, 32) and Linden, J., (p. 173). Apparently Roche were able to maintain their prices in the retail market for much of the period under consideration. (See Written Brief submitted by AG, 15 January, 1979, pp. 23–4.)

29. Market share data are taken from Written Brief submitted by AG, 15 January, 1979, (p. 24).

30. Exhibit 141, Annual Budget, Pharmaceutical Division, 4 December, 1969, (p. 38).

31. Written Brief submitted by AG, 15 January, 1979, (p. 81) which cites the testimony of a Horner official at trial.

32. Written Brief submitted by Roche, 1 February, 1979, (p. 10).

33. Exhibit 188, 'Restrictive Government Practices Affecting Research-based Drug Industry', 31 January, 1974, Attachment III, no page number.

34. All market share figures are from Written Brief submitted by AG, 15 January, 1979, (p. 24).

35. Linden, J., (p. 211).

36. These programs are fully described and evaluated in Gorecki (1981). A number of documents make reference to these programs, particularly Ontario's PARCOST (prescriptions at reasonable cost). See, for example, Exhibit 141, (pp. 1–7), Exhibit 186, (pp. 1, 12), and passage cited in text.

37. These citations from the documentary evidence are taken from Linden, J., (pp. 173, 174, 206, 208) and Exhibit 76, memo from P. Prendergast to T. Gzebb, 7 October, 1966 (p. 1).

38. Exhibit 134, letter from J. S. Fralich, Montreal to E. Junod, Basle, 25 Sept., 1969, (p. 2).

39. Exhibit 136, Minutes of meeting held 27 September, 1969, p. 1.

40. Exhibit 189, Suggestions for Corporate Planning Meeting, Laurentians, 25–26 April, 1974 (pp. 3–4).

41. Where Roche faced competition on Valium injectables in 1974 a price reduction of 25 per cent was the favoured policy. (See Exhibit 192, 'Valium "Roche" Injectable Ampoules — 10mg/2ml Imminent Marketing Problems,' 19 July, 1974, Recommendations section, no page numbers).

42. It has been suggested that Roche may have, in following its pricing policy, aimed at retaining a target market share rather than maximising profits. The trial record is inconsistent with this viewpoint. Indeed, in the trial judgement Linden J. remarks,

> He [Mr. Nowotny] explained that one cannot hope to keep all competition out of the market. It just was not possible, in his view, in the context in which the drug industry operated. He insisted that Roche did not want to keep Horner out of the market, but only 'to protect as much of that market as [they] could'. When asked by Mr. Sexton [Crown Counsel] how much of the diazepam market he was willing to give up to Horner, Mr. Nowotny was unable to respond with a figure. (p. 207)

References

Ball, R. (1971), 'The Secret Life of Hoffman-La Roche,' *Fortune*, August, pp. 130–4, 162, 164, 166, 171

Canada. Director of Investigation & Research (1961) *Material Collected for Submission to the Restrictive Trade Practices Commission in the Course of an Inquiry Under Section 42 of the Combines Investigation Act Relating to the Manufacture, Distribution and Sale of Drugs*, (Ottawa: Mimeo). Reprinted as Appendix Q in Canada. Restrictive Trade Practices Commission (1963) *Report Concerning the Manufacture Distribution and Sale of Drugs*, Ottawa, Queen's Printer. All page references refer to the latter source

Canada. Restrictive Trade Practices Commission (1963) *Report Concerning the Manufacture Distribution and Sale of Drugs*, Ottawa, Queen's Printer

Canada. Royal Commission on Health Services (Hall Commission) (1964) *Report Vol. 1*, Ottawa, Queen's Printer

Canada. Royal Commission on Health Services (Hall Commission) (1965) *Report Vol. II*, Ottawa, Queen's Printer

Canada. Special Committee of the House of Commons on Drug Costs and Prices (Harley Committee) (1967) *Second (Final) Report*, Ottawa, Queen's Printer

Elzinga, K. G. (1970) 'Predatory Pricing: The Case of the Gunpowder Trust,' *Journal of Law and Economics, XIII*, (1) 223–40

Gorecki, P. (1981) *Regulating The Price of Prescription Drugs in Canada: Compulsory Licensing, Product Selection and Government Reimbursement Programmes*, Technical Report No. 8, Ottawa, Economic Council of Canada

McGee, J. S. (1958) 'Predatory Price Cutting: The Standard Oil (NJ) Case,' *Journal of Law and Economics, 1*, 137–69

McGee, J. S. (1980) 'Predatory Pricing Revisited,' *Journal of Law and Economics, XXIII*, (2) 289–330

Pharmaceutical Manufacturers Association of Canada (1976) *Economic Impact of Present Canadian Patent Law an the Pharmaceutical Industry*. Ottawa. PMAC

Yamey, B. S. (1972) 'Predatory Price Cutting: Notes and Comments.' *Journal of Law and Economics, XV*, (1), 129–42

Zerbe, R. (1969 'The American Sugar Refinery company, 1887–1914: The Study of a Monopoly,' *Journal of Law and Economics, XII*, (2), 339–75

PART FIVE

LAW AND ECONOMICS

8 MONOPOLISTIC COMPETITION AND SECOND BEST: SOME NEW CONCEPTUAL SCHEMES

Richard S. Markovits
University of Texas Law School

The past few years have witnessed a strong revival of interest in the various problems associated with monopolistic competition. However, all such work has employed a series of conceptual schemes that were elaborated before the importance of product and locational differentiation was fully appreciated. Thus, analyses of price competition in monopolistically competitive markets have continued to focus on the aggregate gap between price and marginal cost rather than on various subcomponents of that gap (for example, oligopolistic margins and overall competitive advantages);[1] studies of non-price competition in such markets have continued to assume that quality-or-variety-increasing (QV) investment competition can be analysed in the same way as price competition;[2] and allocative efficiency evaluations of various microeconomic policies have continued to ignore the impact of such policies on the set of product-distributive types that the economy offers for sale. Indeed, even those few analysts who have recognised this last issue have failed to distinguish the various kinds of QV investment misallocation that may occur or to note their relationship to imperfections in price competition.[3] Similarly, although attempts to respond to the challenge posed by the general theory of the second best continue to be made, all such efforts are based on general equilibrium models that ignore the various kinds of product type set errors (QV investment misallocations) that can take place in a monopolistically competitive world and cannot in any case generate practicable results in a world that abounds with competitive imperfections.

This paper delineates a series of descriptive concepts that are designed to deal with the phenomena of monopolistic competition and the interdependencies which second best theory has emphasised. More specifically, it develops four different sets of concepts that focus respectively on (1) various subcomponents of a firm's (P-MC) gap, (2) various factors that influence the intensity of quality-or-variety-increasing (QV) investment competition, (3) various types of QV investment misallocation, and (4) the various distortions that can lead firms to make allocatively inefficient decisions. The paper also provides a justification for these concepts by suggesting various reasons why they divide up the world in a more useful way than their conventional alternatives. In particular, the paper explains how this approach facilitates the identification and analysis of important new problems as well as the analysis of other problems that already have been defined.

1. The Components of a Firm's P-MC Gap

Price theorists have always focused on the aggregate gap between a firm's price and marginal cost (P-MC). However, in a monopolistically competitive world, it is essential to distinguish a number of components of the P-MC gap. This section distinguishes various components of this gap. In order to shorten and simplify the exposition, the discussion is limited to 'individualised pricing' situations in which sellers make separate price bids to each of their possible customers.[4] In particular, the commentary examines the gap between the individualised price actually charged by a best-placed supplier[5] X of some particular buyer Y and the seller's conventional marginal cost. Two major and four minor components of this gap are distinguished. The two major components of this P-MC gap are separated by what I call the 'highest non-oligopolistic price' (HNOP). This is the price that would maximise such a best-placed seller's profits in a perfectly informed world if he could not profit from engaging in oligopolistic pricing — i.e., if he could not rely on his rivals being deterred from undercutting by his ability to react to their counter-offers. In other words, the best-placed seller's highest non-oligopolistic price is the highest price he could charge without being profitably undercut by any rival if he could not react to such undercutting.

The gap between such a firm X's highest non-oligopolistic price and actual price (P-HNOP) is termed its 'oligopolistic margin' (OM). The best-placed supplier's (X's) oligopolistic margin (and oligopolistic pricing) is said to be 'contrived' when he has tried to deter undercutting by communicating his intention to sacrifice what would otherwise be his interests in order to punish his rivals' non-cooperation by retaliating and/or to reward their cooperation by reciprocating (i.e., by forgoing a profitable opportunity to undercut an OM the rival has charged). X's oligopolistic margin (and oligopolistic pricing) is said to be 'natural' when he can assume that his rivals will be deterred from undercutting by their realisation that his non-oligopolistic, profit-maximising response would make such undercutting unprofitable.

It is also useful to subdivide the gap between a best-placed seller's marginal cost and his highest non-oligopolistic price. In individualised pricing contexts, this gap consists of (1) the relevant seller's 'basic competitive advantage' (BCA) and (2) the contextual costs his closest rival would have to incur to beat his HNOP. The phrase 'basic competitive advantage' refers to the short-run position of a given seller in his dealings with a particular buyer whom he is best-placed to serve. More precisely, a best-placed seller's basic competitive advantage in his relations with his customer is said to equal the amount by which that buyer prefers the best-placed seller's product or distributive variant to the offering of that seller's closest rival plus the amount by which the short-run conventional marginal costs the best-placed seller has to incur to supply this buyer fall below those of his closest rival. The basic competitive advantage of the best-placed seller is thus equal to the sum of the best-placed seller's buyer preference advantage and his short-run marginal cost advantage.

The contextual component of a best-placed seller's (X's) P-MC gap reflects various costs his closest rival will have to incur because of the terms he would be required to charge to beat the best-placed seller's HNOP. Thus, since price discrimination will tend to encourage favoured customers to engage in arbitrage, disfavoured customers to intensify their bargaining, and in some legal regimes the government or eligible private parties to bring price discrimination suits, rivals who charge their own customers supra-marginal cost prices will have to incur various contextual marginal costs to charge X's customers the discriminatory, low, marginal cost prices they would have to charge to beat X's HNOP. The contextual component of X's HNOP can also be described as the sum of X's contextual marginal costs and his contextual cost advantage (CCA) over his closest rival. Best-placed sellers will normally enjoy such CCAs because their HNOPs will normally be less discriminatory than their closest rivals' matching offers. Hence, a best-placed seller's overall competitive advantage (OCA) will usually exceed his BCA by an amount equal to his CCA.

Before proceeding, it may be useful to suggest why this subdivision of the traditional P-MC gap is justified. First, theories that focus separately on each of these components will be able to generate far more accurate predictions of the impact of events or policies on P-MC than theories that deal directly with the aggregate P-MC gap. Such a scheme enables one to develop theories with more predictive power because the different components of the P-MC gap depend on distinct sets of variables which will not in general be highly correlated and which will not be affected in similar ways by the kinds of events or policies that government decision-makers are required to analyse.[6] Second, even if such an approach did not provide more accurate predictions of the effect of policies or events on the P-MC gap, the associated distinctions would be justified by the fact that the legal and policy (allocation efficiency) significance of a given change in the aggregate P-MC gap will depend on which component of that gap has been altered. Thus, since in some jurisdictions (such as the United States) contrived oligopolistic pricing is unlawful while competitive advantages and natural oligopolistic pricing are not,[7] the legality of an event that increases P-MC may depend on whether that change reflects an increase in competitive advantages or natural oligopolistic margins on the one hand or contrived OMs on the other. Similarly, since contrived oligopolistic pricing may be more misallocative than natural oligopolistic pricing (since contrived oligopolistic pricing is more costly to execute and more likely to generate undercutting and retaliation, whose short-run effects are misallocative), the overall desirability of prohibiting an event that will decrease P-MC may turn on whether the prohibition produces this effect by reducing contrived or natural OMs.[8] In short, my subdivision of the P-MC gap is justified by the legal and policy significance of the components isolated as well as by the capacity of the relevant distinctions to increase the accuracy of aggregate P-MC predictions.

2. QV Investment Competition and Its Components

Although competition theorists have realized that firms compete in other ways than by varying their prices, they have rarely developed competition theories that focus on quality and variety competition. In part, these theorists may have been misled by the fact that the intensity of *some* types of quality competition will respond to any event in much the same way as the intensity of price competition. Thus, since the intensity of price competition will probably respond to any given event in much the same way as the intensity of the kind of quality competition in which sellers increase the number of ounces of some product they offer at a given price, it probably would not be cost-effective to distinguish these two types of competition if one were concerned solely with the competitive impact of some event or policy (as opposed to its effect on allocative efficiency).[9] Unfortunately, however, the impact of any given event or policy on quality-or-variety-increasing investment competition will not in general be the same as its impact on price competition.

The following five facts are relevant in this connection. First, the effect of some acts (such as mergers) on the ability of the actors to introduce new product variants, distributive variants, or capacity may be quite different from their impact on the costs these parties must incur to produce their original product set: for example, a merger that creates such growth-related 'dynamic' efficiencies by combining one firm with excess managerial capacity in distribution with another with excess managerial capacity in production may create no static efficiencies or a merger that creates static efficiencies may create dynamic *in*efficiencies by making it profitable for the merger partners to allocate to the consolidation of the new enterprise managers who could otherwise have supervised the execution of new QV investments. Second, QV investment moves are less reversible than price or variable input moves. Third, QV investment moves affect a larger set of rivals than individualised pricing moves and a different set of rivals from across-the-board pricing or variable input moves. Fourth, and relatedly, one firm may constrain another's supra-competitive pricing more or less than it constrains the other's ability to restrict QV investment in the product space in question. And fifth and finally, although firms can make marginal changes in their prices, they cannot normally make marginal changes in their QV investments — i.e., QV investments are lumpy.

The relevance of the first of these facts should be obvious: since static efficiencies affect the profitability of competitive pricing moves while dynamic efficiencies affect the attractiveness of competitive QV investment moves, the fact that events may produce very different static and dynamic efficiencies implies that they may have very different impacts on price and QV investment competition. The next two facts are relevant because the attractiveness of any competitive move will depend not only on the profits it would yield if it did not induce any rival response but also on the costliness of the rival response it generates. Hence, even if all events have the same impact on the profits that price and QV investment moves would yield if they did not induce any rival response, their impact on price and QV investment competition will be different to the extent that the relative irreversibility of QV investment moves as well as the relative diffuseness of their competitive impact induce rivals to respond differently to them than to competitive pricing moves. More specifically, the related fact that any given rival may react differently to price moves and QV investment moves implies *inter alia* that horizontal mergers that eliminate an active competitor or conglomerate mergers that eliminate a well-placed potential competitor[10] may have different effects (1) on the losses the merged firm would sustain from its rivals' responses to its possible price or QV investment moves and concomitantly (2) on the intensity of price and QV investment competition. Finally, the lumpiness of QV investments is significant because it implies that the most attractive disequilibrating QV investment move a firm could make pre-event may be substantially unprofitable (though its most attractive pricing counterpart would presumably be only marginally unprofitable). Hence, even if an event has the same impact on (1) the profits that price and QV investment moves would yield in the absence of rival responses and (2) the losses the actor would realise as a result of his rivals' responses to each such type of move, it may have a different impact on the price and QV behaviour of those affected — i.e., even if an event changes the profitability of price moves and QV investment moves by the same amount, it may induce one such type of move and not the other (make one such move profitable and not the other). For all these reasons, then, anyone interested in increasing the accuracy of competitive impact predictions would find it extremely useful to distinguish between price competition and what I call QV investment competition. In fact, an event or policy that decreases price competition may increase competition overall by increasing QV investment competition or conversely.[12]

Moreover, the distinction between price and QV investment competition is also helpful for a number of purposes other than predicting the competitive impact of some event or policy. Most importantly, this distinction is crucial for the analysis of the allocative efficiency of any event or policy. Roughly speaking, this conclusion reflects the fact that increases in price competition will generally increase allocative efficiency (even in a worse-than-second-best world) while increases in QV investment competition will generally decrease allocative efficiency.[13] Policy analysts may also be interested in distinguishing QV investment competition from price competition because from various value perspectives the distributive consequences of increases in the former may be significantly different from those of increases in the latter: thus, if the beneficiaries of the increase in variety associated with an intensification of QV investment competition tend to be wealthier than the beneficiaries of the decrease in price associated with an increase in price competition, egalitarians or utilitarians may tend to be less pleased by the distributive consequences of policies that increase the former kind of competition than by the consequences of those that increase the latter.

For all these reasons, then, I have developed a special vocabulary that isolates the various factors that will influence the intensity of QV investment competition. In brief, my analysis distinguishes three such sets of factors.[14] The first set focuses on the various barriers to entry that would deter the QV investment of the firm that would be the best-placed potential entrant to the 'market'[15] in question at the entry-barring QV investment level. Thus the profit differential (π_D), risk (R), scale (S), and retaliation (L) barriers to entry all refer to factors that deter entry by reducing the supernormal rate of return the potential entrant anticipates realising post-entry below the rate the established firms realised pre-entry on their most profitable projects. More particularly, the profit-differential barrier to entry (π_D) reflects those factors that would reduce the new entrant's weighted average expected post-entry rate of return below the rate the established firms would expect to realise on their most profitable projects post-entry even if the threat of retaliation could be ignored. The risk barrier to entry (R) refers to those factors that increase the normal rate of return for the best-placed new entrant above its counterpart rate for the established firms on their most successful projects (e.g., product variants or outlets). The scale barrier to entry (S) measures the extent to which the best-placed potential entrant's entry will reduce everyone's rate of return. The retaliation barrier to entry (L) measures the extent to which the new entrant's expected rate of return over the full life of his investment is reduced by the possibility that his established rivals may retaliate against his entry. The second set of such factors focuses on the barriers to expansion that would deter the QV investment of the established firm that would be best-placed to execute a QV investment if QV investment in the relevant market had reached the level it would contain in equilibrium if entry were precluded. Once more, the π_D, R, S, and L* barriers to expansion (where the asterisk indicates the hypothetical, entry-precluded assumption) refer to factors that can account for the fact that this best-placed expander's expected, post-expansion, nominal super-normal rate of return will be lower than the rate the established firms would realise pre-expansion on their most profitable projects. The third set of such variables relates to the fact that the actual rate of return such a best-placed expander will anticipate realising on his expansion may differ from the nominal rate of return a conventionally kept set of books would indicate. Thus, to the extent that such an expander realises that his failure to expand would not induce anyone else to add to his market's QV investment level, his expansion's actual profitability will be reduced by the amount of profits his new project takes from his old (by taking sales away from his original products or outlets or by inducing his rivals to lower their prices) — i.e., the best-placed expander will face what I call a monopolistic investment disincentive M*.[16] M* is equal to the ratio of such avoidable damages to the size of the QV investment in question. It should be noted that when in the more general case an expander realises that his expansion will deter someone else from executing a QV investment that would be more damaging to his pre-existing capital than his own expansion, he will face a monopolistic incentive to expand. In any case, except where the best-placed potential entrant is far better placed than any other potential competitor and is unable to enter efficiently at more than a modest scale,[17] the intensity of QV investment competition (i.e., the rate of return the established firms will be able to realise in equilibrium on their most profitable QV investment projects) will equal the lower of $(\pi_D+R+S+L)_N$ and $(\pi_D+R+S+L*)_E+M*$, where N and E respectively stand for the relevant best-placed potential entrant and expander.[18]

3. The Various Types of QV Investment Misallocation

Until recently economists assumed that QV investment misallocation would arise only where public goods were involved. Admittedly, in the past few years, some attention has been given to the possibility that in a monopolistically competitive world consumer surplus might preclude the allocatively efficient introduction of additional product types even where public goods in the traditional sense were not involved.[19] However, everyone has overlooked the possibility that other Pareto imperfections (most importantly, imperfections in price competition) may distort investors' QV investment decisions. In my opinion, one cannot accurately predict the allocative efficiency of most policies without distinguishing such QV investment misallocation from the kind of top level misallocation on which economists have traditionally focused — viz., relative unit output (RUO) misallocation, which arises when the members of a given set of product-distributive types that are in production are produced in allocatively inefficient proportions. This opinion reflects a number of theoretical conclusions and empirical assumptions: (1) the conclusion that a given change in a variable that affects both RUO and QV investment misallocation (say P-MC in the industry in question) may decrease RUO misallocation and increase QV investment misallocation and vice versa;[20] (2) the conclusion that some variables that affect the amount of QV investment misallocation (the effective tax rate on business profits or the sales to QV investment ratio for new product variants) do not affect the amount of RUO misallocation and vice versa; (3) the conclusion that the ratio of QV investment misallocation to QV investment is much higher than its counterpart for RUO misallocation since the imperfections in competition that distort various QV investment decisions will be either compounding or less perfectly offsetting than their counterparts for RUO misallocation; and (4) the empirical judgement that a far higher percentage of our resources is allocated to QV investment uses than one might suppose. Put crudely, (1) and (2) imply that events or policies that decrease RUO misallocation may increase QV investment misallocation and conversely, while (3) and (4) imply that the impact of events or policies on QV investment misallocation will often be sufficiently large to affect critically their allocative efficiency.

So far, the argument has lumped together all the various kinds of misallocation that involve QV investments. In fact, it is useful to distinguish three kinds of QV investment misallocation. Roughly speaking, intra-industry QV investment misallocation is said to be present where the (transaction-costless) substitution of one product or distributive variant for another variant in the same product space would give its beneficiaries the equivalent of more dollars than it would take away from its victims.

Similarly, inter-industry QV investment misallocation is said to be present where resource allocation would have been superior in the above sense if some 'industries' had more QV investment (product variants, distributive variants, capacity or inventory) and others less than they have in the actual world. Finally, quantity-vs-QV investment misallocation is said to be present where resource allocation would have been superior if the economy had produced more physical units of a less diversified, less conveniently distributed, less quickly delivered set of products (or vice versa) — that is, if fewer (more) resources had been allocated to QV investment uses and more (fewer) to unit-output-increasing uses. In brief, it is beneficial to distinguish these various types of QV investment misallocation because a given event or policy may have different effects on each. More specifically, since different Pareto imperfections cause each type of QV investment misallocation and since imperfections that are off-setting in relation to one such type of misallocation may be compounding in relation to another,[21] a conceptual system that enables one to distinguish these three types of QV investment misallocation will substantially increase the accuracy of QV investment misallocation predictions.

4. A Distortion Analysis of Allocative Efficiency

Virtually all existing work makes one of two unsatisfactory responses to second best's demonstration that since two imperfections can offset each other, a situation in which there are more imperfections may be preferable to one in which there are fewer. Thus, researchers either have ignored this possibility and assumed that increases in competition and decreases in externalities will always lead to improvements in resource allocation or have developed general equilibrium models to determine the allocatively most efficient policy response to some imperfection in a world in which there are a small number of other imperfections which can be accurately and costlessly determined. Unfortunately, ignoring second best will often lead to errors that could have been avoided at non-prohibitive cost. And, although the general equilibrium approach can provide many useful insights, it cannot be made operational in a monopolistically competitive world in which Pareto imperfections abound and data are inevitably inaccurate and costly. What is needed, then, is a structure for doing not quite so general (or not quite so partial) equilibrium analysis for our worse-than-second-best world (in which data are inaccurate and costly).[22]

The approach I have developed uses the dollar measures normally associated with partial equilibrium analysis but focuses on the aggregate distortions (ΣD) affecting the marginal private decision-maker who is making the various decisions that determine whether and how much resource misallocation of each type results. More specifically, ΣD is defined to equal the difference between the private profitability of the decision-maker's choice ($P\pi$) and its allocative efficiency (LE): a positive ΣD therefore indicates that the private profitability of the relevant choice (e.g., to produce a last unit of some good x) has been artificially inflated by the relevant imperfections in the system. Obviously, where the various choices are marginal, the marginal decision will have been just barely profitable for its maker. Hence, in such cases, the definition of $\Sigma D = P\pi - LE$ implies that a marginal decision whose profitability has been artificially inflated (deflated) by ΣD will cause allocative inefficiency (efficiency) equal to ΣD (since $P\pi$ is zero). Thus, if ΣD for producer X's decision to produce his last unit of x is (+$5), that decision will have caused $5 in resource misallocation.

Basically, the distortion approach proceeds by determining (1) the probable effect of any given imperfection or policy on ΣD and (2) the probable effect of any change in the ΣD distribution on the extent of the relevant type of resource misallocation. The information it is designed to yield should improve policy analysis in two ways. First, by increasing our ability to assess the likelihood that more accurate estimates of particular imperfections will critically affect our analysis of some policy's allocative efficiency, it should increase the cost-effectiveness of various data collection decisions; second, by increasing our ability to determine the implications of various factual assumptions and findings for the allocative efficiency of particular policies, it should increase the accuracy of the allocative efficiency predictions policy analysts can provide to decision-makers.

For expository purposes, it is convenient to break down the distortion approach into four stages. In the first, one identifies the various kinds of resource misallocation that can be generated by each type of Pareto imperfection (e.g., respectively by externalities, imperfections in competition, taxes, human error and consumer surplus).[23]

In the second, one determines for each kind of resource misallocation the relationship between the various relevant Pareto imperfections of one type and the distortion that imperfections of that type would create for each private actor they affect if no other type of imperfection were present. For example, one determines the relationship between the distortion affecting the incentive of each producer who is deciding whether to make a marginal increase in his unit output and the various monopolies that would individually distort his incentives in a world in which there were no externalities, taxes, human errors, etc. In other words, one analyses the relationship between the distortion all relevant monopolies would create for a particular type of decision in an otherwise Pareto optimal world (the monopoly distortion — MD) and the distortion that would be created by each individual monopoly that would affect the relevant type of decision. When undertaking this type of analysis, it will often be useful to express ΣD as the difference between DU and DC where (1) DU stands for the distortion affecting the gains the relevant economic actor can achieve by using (hence D*U*) rather than costlessly destroying the output he produces with the resources in question (the distortion affecting the use of the relevant output or investment) and (2) DC equals the distortion affecting the *costs* (hence D*C*) he had to incur to obtain the constituent resources (the distortion affecting the cost of creating the relevant output or investment). It should be emphasised that this analysis must be executed for each kind of resource misallocation since imperfections of one type can offset each other in relation to one kind of misallocation and compound each other in relation to another kind of misallocation.

In the third stage, one analyses the relationship between the aggregate distortion affecting each individual choice (the distortion affecting producer X's unit output choice that resulted from the presence of all the various types of Pareto imperfections that influenced this decision) and the distortions that the presence of each separate type of imperfection would generate. This third stage itself involves the following steps. First, one distinguishes those kinds of resource allocation for which the total distortion ΣD is equal to the sum of the distortions each individual imperfection type will generate from those kinds of resource allocation for which ΣD does not equal the sum of the individual distortions so defined. In other words, one distinguishes the so-called additive case in which ΣD=MD+XD+ . . . (where MD stands for the monopoly distortion — the distortion that would result if the only type of imperfection were imperfections in competition — and XD stands for the externality distortion — the distortion that would result if the only type of imperfection were externalities) from various other non-additive cases in which ΣD is not even a function of MD, XD, etc. (but is a function instead of the individual monopoly and externality imperfections). Second, in the latter, non-additive cases, one determines the precise character of the relationship between ΣD and the relevant individual imperfections of the various types in question. Third and finally, in both the additive and the non-additive cases, one analyses the conditions that determine whether a policy that would produce a given change in some imperfection will reduce ΣD.[24]

In the fourth and last stage, one analyses the relationship between the total amount of each kind of resource misallocation and the sum of the ΣDs affecting the marginal choices of each private actor who makes such allocative choices. As it turns out, where some such choices are concerned (e.g., choices among known alternative production techniques for producing a given product), the total amount of associated misallocation depends solely on the sum of the relevant ΣDs across all marginal decision-makers. Where other kinds of resource allocation are concerned (relative unit output allocation and to a less certain extent inter-industry QV investment misallocation), the total amount of related misallocation depends on the variance of the distribution of such ΣDs as well as on its mean. In general, this difference reflects the fact that the elimination of a distortion that affects RUO choices can alter decisions that were originally intra-marginal as well as the marginal choices in question.

A summary might be useful at this point. The proposed distortion analysis of allocative efficiency employs four novel groups of concepts: (1) the basic notion of the aggregate distortion (ΣD) affecting the decision-makers who make marginal choices that relate to the various possible types of resource misallocation and the related notions of the distortion affecting the use (DU) and cost (DC) of the relevant resources to them; (2) the notion of the amount by which all examples of a particular type of Pareto imperfection would distort marginal choices relating to a given kind of resource allocation if no other types of Pareto imperfections were present (e.g., the externality distortion XD or the monopoly distortion MD); (3) the distinction between additive cases in which $\Sigma D = XD + MD$ . . . and non-additive cases in which ΣD is not even a function of XD and MD; and (4) the distinction between kinds of resource misallocation whose magnitudes are a function of the mean of the distribution of ΣDs affecting all relevant marginal decision-makers and kinds whose magnitudes are a function of the variance as well as the mean of such ΣD distributions. In brief, this set of concepts is designed to illuminate the factors that will determine the way in which changes in a particular type of imperfection will alter the amounts of all the various kinds of resource misallocation it affects.

I have already used more or less elaborate versions of this approach to analyse the allocative efficiency of a variety of antitrust policies,[25] of housing code enforcement policies,[26] of antipollution policies,[27] and of alternative tort law regimes.[28] The approach also has a number of clear implications for tax policies. Thus, it suggests the possible allocative efficiency of varying the effective tax rate in different portions of product space to overcome the tendency of more 'monopolistic' sectors to receive too much QV investment relative to less monopolistic sectors.[29] The approach also has clear implications for various investment-promoting tax policies: specifically, since the approach reveals that QV investments tend to be more profitable than efficient while cost-reducing investments (and related research expenditures) tend to be less profitable than efficient,[30] the allocative efficiency of pro-investment tax policies such as accelerated depreciation schemes depends critically on their being restricted to cost-reducing investments and research (for example, in their not being available to investors who wish to build additional distributive outlets, design additional product variants, or construct additional capacity in order to increase average speed of service through time).

Conclusion

Where systems of descriptive concepts are concerned, adjectives such as 'correct' and 'incorrect' are inapposite. The critical question is whether such systems are useful, whether they call attention to and facilitate the analysis of important questions. Accordingly, there are at least two different grounds on which one might reject the kind of conceptual systems this paper has delineated. First, one might argue that the extra phenomena they isolate or relationships they emphasise are empirically insignificant. Second, one might maintain that even if my distinctions do point to numerically important phenomena, models that incorporate them will not generate different legal or policy conclusions. Although some economists would make the first of these two types of objections, this paper has focused on the second. Thus, it argued that if, as I believe, oligopolistic margins and competitive advantages are both numerically significant, the distinction between them is important to recognise since (a) analyses that focus on either to the exclusion of the other may mispredict the sign or magnitude of the effect of any policy on P-MC and (b) the legal and policy significance of a given change in CAs may be critically different from their counterparts for an identical change in some types of OMs. Similarly, it contended that if, as I suppose, QV investment competition is an important phenomenon, it should be studied separately since (a) the same event may increase price competition and decrease QV investment or vice versa and (b) increases in QV investment competition may be misallocative in cases in which increases in price competition would be allocatively efficient — i.e., since analyses that distinguish the two types of competition may generate different legal and policy conclusions.

Admittedly, proponents of new conceptual systems must bear a considerable burden of proof. This paper has outlined the case for my conceptual systems in the hope of inducing you to read the articles which I believe establish my claims for their utility.[31]

Notes

1. For precise definitions of these terms, see the text accompanying Note 5 *infra*.
2. For a description of quality-or-variety-increasing investments and QV investment competition, see the text accompanying Note 10 *infra*.

3. For definitions of the various types of QV investment misallocation, see the text preceding Note 21 *infra*.

4. For a description of the conceptual system I employ in so-called across-the-board pricing situations (in which sellers set a price that applies to all their potential customers), see Markovits (1978), pp. 637–40.

5. A seller X is said to be best-placed to supply a particular buyer Y if he could profit from supplying Y on terms that no-one else would find intrinsically profitable to match. Obviously, since different buyers will have different product and locational preferences in our monopolistically competitive world, the fact that X is best-placed to serve some buyer Y1 implies little about the likelihood that he will be best-placed to supply other buyers Y2 . . . N.

6. See Markovits (1978), pp. 611–58 and (1979) pp. 603–13.

7. See Markovits (1974), pp. 738–40 and (1976c) pp. 933–5.

8. See Markovits (1976b), pp. 57–79.

9. In fact, such increases in product quality may be misallocative where decreases in price would improve the allocation of resources. See Markovits (1976a) p. 26.

10. See Markovits (1975a), pp. 682–90.

11. See Markovits (1978).

12. See Markovits (1978), pp. 687–8.

13. See Markovits (1975b), pp. 1037–45.

14. For a more detailed treatment, see Markovits (1975a), pp. 683–90.

15. 'Market' is in quotes to reflect the fact that none of my legal and policy proposals presupposes the possibility of defining markets in a non-arbitrary way. See Markovits (1978), pp. 593–603.

16. The text will ignore the possible oligopolistic investment disincentives (0*) an established firm will face when it realises that none of its rivals would invest if it did not, while some would expand if it initiated an expansion. For an explanation, see Markovits (1978), p. 667.

17. Where these exceptional conditions are fulfilled, the established firms may prefer to allow the best-placed potential competitor to enter since the investment they would have to make to keep him out might harm their original projects more than his modest entry. In this case, the rate of return the established firms will be able to realise in equilibrium on their most profitable project will equal the lower of $(\pi_D+R+S+L)$ for the second-best-placed potential entrant and $(\pi_D+R+S+L)$ for the best-placed potential entrant not on his best project but on the first additional QV investment that the relevant barriers deterred him from executing.

18. Where $(\pi_D+R+S+L)_N < (\pi_D+R+S+L*)_E+M*$, the entry-preventing level of QV investment is determinative because it is higher than the entry-precluded, expansion-barring QV investment level — i.e., because the presence of potential competition will preclude the established firms from taking advantage of the ability they would otherwise have to restrict their own QV investments. On the other hand, where $(\pi_D+R+S+L*)_E+M*<(\pi_D+R+S+L)_N$, the entry-precluded, expansion-barring QV investment level will be determinative because it is higher than the entry-barring QV investment level — i.e., because the established firms' inability to restrict their QV investments will preclude them from taking advantage of the opportunities the existing barriers to entry present.

19. See Spence (1976).

20. Ibid., pp. 1034–5.

21. Thus, the relevant imperfections in price competition may be offsetting in relation to relative unit output misallocation and inter-industry QV investment misallocation and compounding in relation to quantity-vs-QV investment misallocation. See Markovits (1975b), pp. 1074–6.

22. To my knowledge, only one other economist has attempted to address such multiple imperfection / lack of information issues in a sophisticated, theoretical way. See Ng (1975, 1977).

23. In what follows, the phrase 'consumer surplus' imperfections will replace the normal 'public goods' imperfection: unfortunately, even in an otherwise Pareto optimal world, consumer surplus can lead to resource misallocation in circumstances in which no public good is involved (see Markovits (1976a), p. 33); human error includes both individual non-maximisation and individual non-sovereignty; the phrase 'imperfections in competition' refers to monopsony and monopolistic or oligopolistic investment disincentives as well as to imperfections in price competition.

24. Fortunately, this process is straightforward in additive cases. Unfortunately, it is extremely complicated in non-additive cases. For an example of such an analysis, see Markovits (1975b), pp. 1053–4, note 132.

25. See Markovits (1976b) on oligopolistic pricing; Markovits (1975b), pp. 1041–2 on horizontal mergers; Markovits (1979), pp. 629–30 on deconcentration proposals; and Markovits (1980a) on tie-ins and reciprocity.

26. See Markovits (1976d).

27. See Markovits (1975b), pp. 1045–59.

28. See Markovits (1980b), pp. 840–7.

29. See Markovits (1975b), pp. 1015–29.

30. See Markovits (undated).

31. All of the work described or referred to in this paper grew out of my doctoral dissertation, which was written under Basil Yamey's supervision and successfully submitted to the University of London in 1966. The dissertation and the work it spawned profited immensely both from Basil's encouragement and from his ability to predict whether particular ideas were worth pursuing. I am therefore particularly pleased to contribute this piece to a volume in his deserved honour.

References

Markovits, R. S. (1974) 'Injurious Oligopolistic Pricing Sequences: Their Description, Interpretation and Legality Under the Sherman Act,' *Stanford Law Review, 26*, 717–71

Markovits, R. S. (1975a) 'Potential Competition, Limit Price Theory, and the Legality of Horizontal and Conglomerate Mergers Under the American Antitrust Laws', *Wisconsin Law Review, 1975*, 658–95

Markovits, R. S. (1975b) A Basic Structure for Micro-economic Policy Analysis in Our Worse-than-second best World: A Proposal and Related Critique of the Chicago Approach to the Study of Law and Economics', *Wisconsin Law Review, 1975*, 950–1080

Markovits, R. S. (1976a) 'The Causes and Policy Significance of Pareto Resource Misallocation: A Checklist for Micro-economic Policy Analysis', *Stanford Law Review, 28*, 1–44

Markovits, R. S. (1976b) 'The Allocative Efficiency and Overall Desirability of Oligopolistic Pricing Suits', *Stanford Law Review, 28*, 45–59

Markovits, R. S. (1976c) 'Oligopolistic Pricing, The Sherman Act, and Economic Welfare: A Response to Professor Posner', *Stanford Law Review, 28*, 919–56

Markovits, R. S. (1976d) 'The Distributive Impact, Allocative Efficiency, and Overall Desirability of Ideal Housing Codes: Some Theoretical Clarifications', *Harvard Law Review, 89*, 1815–46

Markovits, R. S. (1978) 'Predicting the Competitive Impact of Horizontal Mergers in a Monopolistically Competitive World: A Non-Market-Oriented Proposal and Critique of the Market Definition – Market Share – Market Concentration Approach' *Texas Law Review, 56*, 587–732

Markovits, R. S. (1979) 'Monopolistic Competition, Second Best, and *The Antitrust Paradox*: A Review Article', *Michigan Law Review, 77*, 567–640

Markovits, R. S. (1980a) 'Tie-Ins and Reciprocity: A Functional, Legal (Competitive Impact), and Policy Analysis', *Texas Law Review, 58*, 1363–445

Markovits, R. S. (1980b) 'Legal Analysis and The Economic Analysis of Allocative Efficiency', *Hofstra Law Review, 8*, 811–904

Markovits, R. S. 'Monopoly, the Allocative Efficiency of Production Process (Cost-Reducing) Research and Antitrust Policy: A Distortion Analysis' (unpublished manuscript)

Ng (1975) 'Non-Economic Activities, Indirect Externalities, and Third-Best Policies', *Kyklos, 28*, 507

Ng (1977) 'Towards a Theory of Third-Best', *Public Finance, 32*, 1

Spence (1976) 'Product Selection, Fixed Costs, and Monopolistic Competition', *Review of Economic Studies, 43*, 217

PART SIX

INTERNATIONAL TRADE

9 THE IMPACT ON EXPORTERS OF IMPORT RESTRICTIONS*

Richard H. Snape
Monash University

1. Introduction

Most theoretical analyses of trade restrictions have looked at the effects on the country imposing the restrictions. Thus it is argued, for example, that if the objective of policy is to increase domestic production, production subsidies tend to impose a smaller efficiency cost on the importing country than do import tariffs or import quotas. Alternatively, if the objective is a specified reduction in imports, import tariffs or quotas will achieve the objective at lower cost than production subsidies.

In this paper the emphasis is on the effects on exporting countries of trade restrictions imposed by importing countries. These effects are much in the minds of trade negotiators. Such negotiators must often take as given the domestic objectives of their trading partners and will be concerned to ensure that these objectives are pursued at least cost to themselves. This is the real world in which cuts in trade restrictions are more often regarded as 'concessions to foreigners' than as corrections of policy errors.

One reason why little academic attention has been given to the effects of various trade restrictions on foreigners is the common assumption that the terms of trade are given. Occam's Razor provides the usual justification for this assumption when the focus is the effect of trade restrictions on the country imposing them. The optimal policies to secure gains from improved terms of trade are well known and it is often useful to assume constant terms of trade so as to isolate other effects of policy. But the implication of this assumption is that foreign exporters will be indifferent as to whether trade is restricted by 1 or by 100 per cent by the country in question. They will also be indifferent between various instruments of policy used by importing countries. In short, unless the rest of the world's terms of trade can be affected by the country in question, the rest of the world is indifferent to trade with that country.

In this paper we rank the losses caused to exporters by the

imposition of various types of trade restrictions in the importing countries. A basic proposition for the analysis is that the greater the restriction of import demand, the worse it is for trading partners. Krueger and Sonnenschein (1967) consider various welfare propositions concerning the gains from greater or less price divergence, as compared with autarchy, and from greater or less improvement in the terms of trade (using fixed weights for calculation of terms of trade). When one considers a world of more than two commodities, quite limited conclusions can, in general, be reached. Here it is assumed that (at any vector of prices) greater demand for one export commodity will not be accompanied by lesser demand for another. With this assumption it appears clear that, on the usual Samuelsonian potential welfare criterion, the greater the export demand (and terms of trade improvement), the better.

It is possible that distortions within exporting countries may be such that economic welfare may be reduced by an improvement in the terms of trade. Such an immiserizing effect could occur if a production subsidy on an exportable had increased exports of this commodity beyond a free trade level. An increase in the price of this commodity would benefit the country if production of this good did not change; however an improved price would tend to lead to even more production of the subsidised commodity. The loss coming from this latter effect could outweigh the aforementioned benefit.[1] But as we are concerned with 'potential' welfare in exporting countries, this line of enquiry is not pursued further.

To simplify the analysis we assume that the country imposing the trade restriction does it in pursuit of some objective other than an improvement in the terms of trade. The analysis could be in terms of the pursuit of two objectives — the terms of trade gain plus some other objective — but this would complicate things unnecessarily. Thus we are assuming that the terms of trade effect is ignored by the importing country but that it is the relevant consideration for exporters. We also assume that the products under consideration are relatively small in the economy of the importing country, so that we can ignore the income effect of alternative restrictions on the demand for imports.

In considering the differing effects of various trade restricting policies on exporters, the objective of the importing country must be clearly specified. Much of the analysis below has a good deal in common with the literature on the equivalence of tariffs and quotas (e.g. Bhagwati, 1965 and 1968, and Shibata, 1968). Rachel McCulloch (1973) has emphasised the importance of specifying the policy objective in this context. The various objectives considered here are:

(a) encouraging a desired level of domestic production of the commodity in question;
(b) securing a target internal price for producers of the product;
(c) securing a desired degree of protection for domestic producers (i.e. a desired proportionate excess of the price for producers over the international price of the product);
(d) obtaining a desired reduction in the level of imports; and
(e) reserving a specified proportion of the domestic market for domestic producers.

Many — if not all — of these targets are pursued by some governments. Thus, for example, the European Common Agricultural Policy uses variable import levies to secure target internal prices for producers, many governments use import quotas to maintain production and employment in the clothing, textile and footwear industries, and the Australian government uses import quotas to reserve 80 per cent of the Australian motor car market for Australian-produced cars.

A number of weapons could be used to pursue each of these targets. We consider *ad valorem* production subsidies, *ad valorem* and specific tariffs, and quantitative restrictions on imports as weapons. In some circumstances it is possible for exporting countries to take action that would meet the importing country's objective, and such a policy weapon is also considered. The policies are examined first in a comparative static framework, and then some dynamic considerations are introduced. Standard profit-maximising assumptions are used throughout, for the usual methodological reasons.

We examine the impact of the various instruments under the alternative market structures of competition and of monopoly both in production (in the country imposing the restrictions) and in international trade. With regard to international trade there may be monopoly or competition both in importing and in exporting. Trade monopoly in the importing country is likely to arise from the imposition of import quotas or from the granting by the government of exclusive importing rights to a private trader or to a state trading enterprise. With respect to exporting countries, monopoly elements may arise from there being a small number of private exporters. Alternatively, trade monopoly may be due to government influence on exports where there is a small number of exporting countries. Thus we have a large number of alternative combinations of targets, instruments and market structures: fortunately it is not necessary to consider all in detail. In Part 2 we analyse various possibilities under the section headings:

(i) Competitive Production and Trade
(ii) Monopolistic Production with Competitive Trade
(iii) Competitive Production with Monopolistic Importing
(iv) Monopolistic Production and Importing
(v) Monopolistic Exporting

In Part 3 some dynamic considerations are briefly addressed.

2. Comparative Static Analysis

(i) Competitive Production and Trade

Consider first the pursuit of the objective of a desired level of domestic production, assuming competitive production and trade. Import restrictions, whether by quota or by *ad valorem* or specific tariff, encourage production but simultaneously discourage consumption. Production subsidies, on the other hand, achieve the production-expansion effect but without the by-product of reduced consumption. Imports would therefore be greater with the production subsidy and thus would be preferred by the exporting country or countries.[2] This preference by the exporters for a production subsidy rather than any form of trade restriction would also exist if the objective of the importing country were for a particular price for producers, or for a desired degree of protection (i.e. proportionate excess of the price for the producer over the international price), or for reservation of a particular share of the domestic market for domestic producers. In all cases the objective can be met by a production subsidy without restricting demand.

If the objective of the importer's policy were the reduction of imports to a particular level, the exporter would of course be indifferent between production subsidies and the various forms of restrictions on international trade. This indifference as to the weapon used to meet an import target applies throughout Part 2, except when there is monopolistic exporting. Thus this objective is not mentioned again until section (v).

So far we have not distinguished between import tariffs and quantitative restrictions on imports. Import quotas can be designed to have effects identical to import tariffs, as is well known. (Bhagwati, 1965.) In the absence of retaliation and uncertainty, and assuming that both quotas and tariffs are imposed to secure the same level of imports, competition in production and trade will ensure that the restrictive impacts of tariffs and quotas are identical. Competitive auctioning of the quotas can ensure that the distribution of income will be the same as with tariffs, with the economic rent from the imported good passing to the government. Under these conditions the effects on both the importers and exporters will be identical, irrespective of the objective of the trade restrictions.[3]

Relaxing the assumptions of competition in production, trade and quota-holding, a number of differences may occur between tariffs and quotas and care needs to be given to the concept of 'equivalent' (e.g. Shibata, 1968; Bhagwati, 1968).[4]

(ii) Monopolistic Production with Competitive Trade[5]

Some of the analysis used in this rather lengthy section is elaborated geometrically in Appendix 9A: in the text the main argument is presented verbally with the support of summary diagrams. For simplicity, linear relationships are assumed, but the results generalise to a wide range of non-linearities. (It is, however, important that the various marginal revenues decline as sales increase.) We need not enquire why there is monopolistic domestic production, but it *could* be due to economies of scale, for decreasing average (and marginal) costs are compatible with the analysis of this section.

Production Target. Consider first that the objective of the importing country is to expand domestic production to a desired level, and that an *ad valorem* tariff is used to this end. This tariff reduces imports and expands production. Now assume that the tariff is replaced by an import quota that yields the same quantity of imports. As is well known (Bhagwati, 1965, p. 59) the monopolist will reduce his output when the tariff is replaced by a quota, for the quota makes the demand for the domestically-produced product less elastic. In order to induce him to expand output back to the target level, a smaller import quota (i.e. larger demand for the domestic product) will be necessary. Thus to achieve a target level of output, an *ad valorem* import tariff will yield a higher level of imports than will quantitative restrictions on imports, and therefore will be preferred by exporters.

A similar argument can show that a specific tariff will be preferred by foreigners to an *ad valorem* tariff. Again assume that an *ad valorem* tariff is used to secure a desired level of production. Now replace the *ad valorem* tariff with a specific tariff that achieves the same production level. The monopolist's ability to raise the domestic price is, of course, constrained by demand for his product; the higher the domestic price, the lower is total demand and the greater the supply of imports. A specific tariff yields a more elastic (tariff-inclusive) supply of imports than does an *ad valorem* tariff and thus gives a more elastic demand for the domestically-produced output than an *ad valorem* tariff.[6] The specific tariff thus provides less monopoly power so that, at a given level of production, the domestic price would be lower with the specific tariff. With the same level of production under both tariff systems, imports will be higher with the specific tariff than with the *ad valorem* tariff.

Finally, it is clear that a production subsidy will be the most preferred policy for, just as when there is competitive production, the production subsidy increases output but does not reduce demand.

Figure 9.1 summarises the results outlined above. P_f is foreign price, which varies directly with imports by the country imposing the policies; Y_D is domestic output of the commodity in question. $\hat{P}_f$ and $\hat{Y}_D$ are the values of P_f and Y_D existing in a free trade situation: thus point A indicates the free trade position. The lower is P_f (and therefore imports), the worse it is for foreign exporters. $\bar{P}_f$ is the international price that would exist if the country imposing restrictions ceased to import. We may note the following:

(a) In Figure 9.1 it is assumed that an import quota *can* achieve a level of production greater than that obtained with free trade. However as the elasticity of demand for the domestic product is reduced by the imposition of import quotas, it is possible that no level of import quotas will expand production

Figure 9.1: Monopolistic Production and Competitive Trade — Effects of Alternative Policies on Domestic Production and Foreign Prices

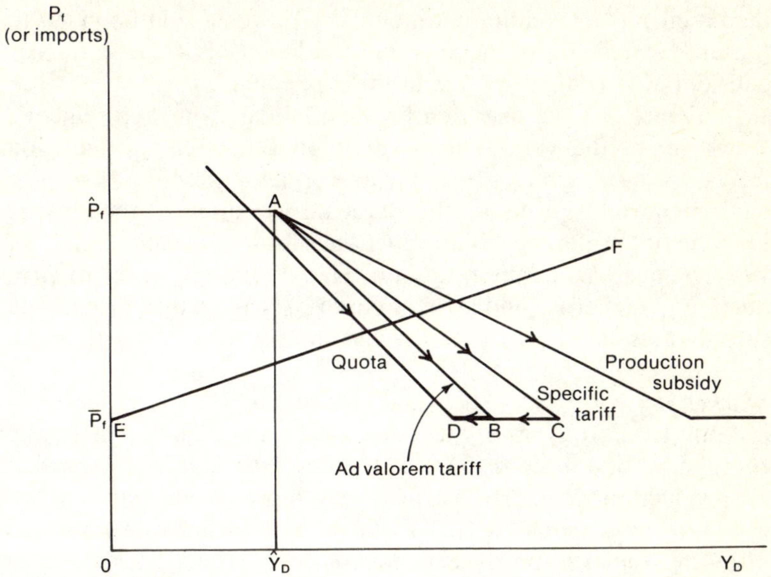

Note: Arrows indicate the direction of movement for increased application of the policy weapons

beyond the free trade level. If this were the case the line labelled 'quota' would be further to the left and point D would lie to the left of $\hat{Y}_D$. The import quota would be of no use in securing a production target.

(b) Imports can be greater in the presence of import quotas than under free trade. Assume there is free trade and then impose an import quota for the same level of imports as that achieved with free trade. With a less elastic demand for the domestic product, the producer can now raise price (and lower production) unconstrained by *additional* imports. A larger import quota would remove some, but not all, of this monopoly power, and imports would rise to fill the larger quota. Thus imports with an import quota can be greater than with free trade. (As a quota larger than free trade imports could not result in a level of production greater than that existing in free trade, such a quota could not be used to achieve a production objective. However it could be used to secure a domestic *price* objective — see below.)

(c) Points C and B are points at which a specific and an *ad valorem* tariff, respectively, just exclude imports. With the tariffs increased further, additional monopoly power would be given to the producer, and production would be reduced. There is further consideration of these points in the Appendix.

In Figure 9.1 we see clearly the ranking from a foreigner's viewpoint of the various instruments in achieving a production target. At any point on the Y_D axis — and assuming that each instrument can be used to achieve the target output — the ranking in order of preference is production subsidy, specific tariff, *ad valorem* tariff and import quota. That is for any level of production, a higher P_f (and level of imports) is given by a production subsidy than by a specific tariff, and so on.

Market Share Target. The ranking is the same if the objective is a desired ratio of imports to domestic production — that is, the reservation of a desired share of the domestic market for domestic production. With the vertical axis representing imports, we can draw rays (such as EF) from point E which show various ratios of domestic production to imports — the flatter the ray, the higher the ratio. We see the ranking of policies is the same as before.

Price Target. Now consider the use of the alternative weapons to achieve a domestic price target. We must first specify the way in which the instruments are applied to obtain the target price. If this price is achieved by means of a continually *variable* weapon (tariff, quota or production subsidy) such that a given internal price will exist irrespective of the international price or the reaction of producers, then the ability of the domestic monopolist to influence price is removed, and his marginal revenue will be equal to this target price. The result is the same as with competitive production, analysed in section (i) above. Foreigners will be indifferent between quotas and tariffs but will prefer production subsidies for they will allow greater imports, as they do not raise prices to consumers.

If, on the other hand, the internal price objective is pursued by means of a policy instrument that is fixed rather than continually variable then we can proceed by using the analysis presented under the 'production target' heading. Consider a particular domestic price that is achieved by a (non-variable) *ad valorem* import tariff. With the domestic price given, domestic demand is determined. With an import quota that allows the same quantity of imports as would the tariff, domestic production will fall and the internal price will increase. In order to reduce the domestic price back to the target price, the import quota will have to be *increased*, the effect of which will be to reduce the monopoly power of the domestic producer. Thus an import quota would be preferred, by exporters, to an *ad valorem* import tariff.[7]

By a similar argument one can show that the specific tariff is worse, from a foreigner's point of view, than the *ad valorem* tariff. Consider a certain internal price that is achieved, alternatively, by an *ad valorem* tariff and by a specific tariff. The demand for *domestic* product, at this price, will be more elastic with the specific than with the *ad valorem* tariff. Thus at this price marginal revenue facing the domestic producer will be greater with the specific tariff, as will be the domestic production level at which the producer equates marginal revenue and marginal cost. Hence imports will be lower with the specific tariff.

Consider now the pursuit of the internal price objective (for producers) with a production subsidy. If a production subsidy were to be used to achieve the same producer price objective as an *ad valorem* tariff, it would yield the same marginal revenue as the tariff (at least in the linear case) and thus the same level of production. Demand and imports would be greater with the production subsidy than with the tariff while the production subsidy cannot be ranked relative to an import quota. Obviously as there are some price objectives at which imports are greater with a quota than with free trade, the quota would be preferred (by the foreigner) to the production subsidy for these prices. There are other, higher, prices at which the production subsidy could be preferred.

In Figure 9.2 a summary is provided. The vertical axis is the same as in Figure 9.1 but the horizontal axis, P_D, now represents the domestic price received by producers (which is equal to the price paid by consumers, except in the case of a production subsidy). The points A′, B′, C′ and D′ may be compared to points indicated by similar unprimed letters in Figure 9.1. $\hat{P}_D$ is the free trade domestic price and is equal to $\hat{P}_f$. Point A′, the free trade situation, is on a 45° line from the origin. We can see that, for

Figure 9.2: Monopolistic Production and Competitive Trade — Effects of Alternative Policies on Domestic and Foreign Prices

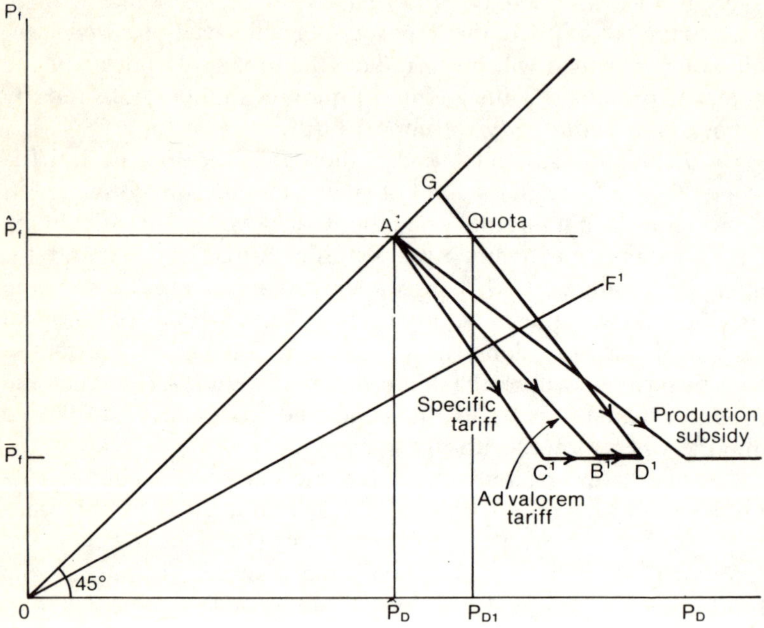

Note: Arrows indicate the direction of movement for increased application of the policy weapons.

pursuit of any domestic price target (P_D) which is achievable by each weapon, foreign exporters would prefer an import quota to an *ad valorem* tariff, and the latter to a specific tariff. A production subsidy would rank above a quota for some high price targets but a quota would be preferred for some lower targets.

We might note that there are some price targets — relatively small increases above the free trade level — that cannot be achieved by an import quota. Price P_{D1} is the price that would be charged if an import quota were imposed equal to free trade imports. Increases in this quota would raise imports and the foreign price and would *lower* the domestic price. At point G the internal and external prices are equal — further increases in the quota would not be utilised.

The horizontal sections of the curves in Figure 9.2 are explained in the Appendix.

Degree of Protection Target. With the aid of Figure 9.2 we can also analyse the pursuit of a policy designed to give a desired degree of protection — i.e. a desired ratio between the internal and external price. Consider a ray from the origin in Figure 9.2. The flatter this ray, the higher the ratio of P_D to P_f, and the higher the degree of protection. Thus the ranking for this objective is the same as for the domestic price target. Surprisingly an import quota is preferred — by foreigners — to both types of tariffs and even, for relatively small degrees of protection (such as represented by OF′), to a production subsidy. Of course the ranking may be different from the point of view of the country imposing the restriction, but here we are concerned only with the ranking from the foreigner's point of view.

(iii) Competitive Production with Monopolistic Importing

The existence of a domestic monopoly in importing could be attributable to government action either by the granting of a legal monopoly to a private trader, as often occurred under the mercantilist 'system', or by granting similar rights to a state trading enterprise. A monopolistic importer that seeks to maximise profits will restrict imports until the marginal cost of imports is equal to the marginal revenue obtained from selling the imports on the home market (i.e. after allowing for the response of domestic producers as well as consumers). This restriction of imports will of course raise the domestic price to both producers and consumers and will encourage domestic production. (Creating such a monopoly thus might be a way of achieving a desired internal price, or level of production, or other objective, though it would be fortuitous if an unregulated monopoly succeeded in precisely attaining one of these objectives. If such an objective were achieved then the creation of such a trade monopoly could then be regarded as a trade policy similar to those considered above in section (i).) If the domestic target is for a higher price than is obtained with an import monopoly or for a higher level of production or higher degree of protection, then an import tariff (*ad valorem* or specific), an import quota, or a production subsidy could be imposed and these would be ranked by foreigners in the same way as in section (i) — that is all trade weapons would be ranked equally by foreigners, and would be ranked as inferior to a production subsidy.

It is possible that a monopoly in importing may be created by the allocation of import quotas — that is, the quotas may all be issued to, or may be acquired by, one trader. In such a circumstance there will be a range of price (and production) objectives that will not be attainable with import quotas as the weapon — objectives that could have been achieved if the quotas had been held competitively. This is because of the monopoly power given by the quotas. If the import quotas allow for more imports than a monopolist importer would choose to undertake, then the quotas will not be fully used (Bhagwati, 1965, pp. 60–2) and thus quotas could not achieve an internal price lower than that which the trading monopolist would choose if he had full control over imports. A *smaller* import quota would raise price (and domestic production) above this level, but a *larger* quota would not lead to a lower price and level of domestic production, unless the monopolist importer were to be regulated.

(iv) Monopoly in Both Production and Importing

We now join together the assumptions of the last two sections and consider the case in which one monopolist is both producer and importer. (The case in which a monopolist importer is not also the monopolistic producer is not considered, as this would imply duopoly, with the outcome dependent on particular strategies.)

We first consider the case of rising (or constant) marginal cost, and then that of decreasing costs. In Figure 9.3 we illustrate the profit-maximising behaviour of a monopolist producer who also has a monopoly in importing. Total demand is D, MR the marginal revenue, S_M the supply of imports, MC_M the marginal cost of imports, and MC the marginal cost of domestic production. $MC+MC_M$ is the horizontal sum of the two marginal costs. The profit-maximising configuration is total sales of OA (at a price of OE), OB being imports (obtained at a price of OC) and domestic supply being BA(=OF). If the monopoly is created by an import quota, and if the import quota is greater than OB, then the quota will not be fully used as only OB will be imported. If the import quota is less than OB, the quota will be fully used and the

Figure 9.3: Monopolistic Production and Importing

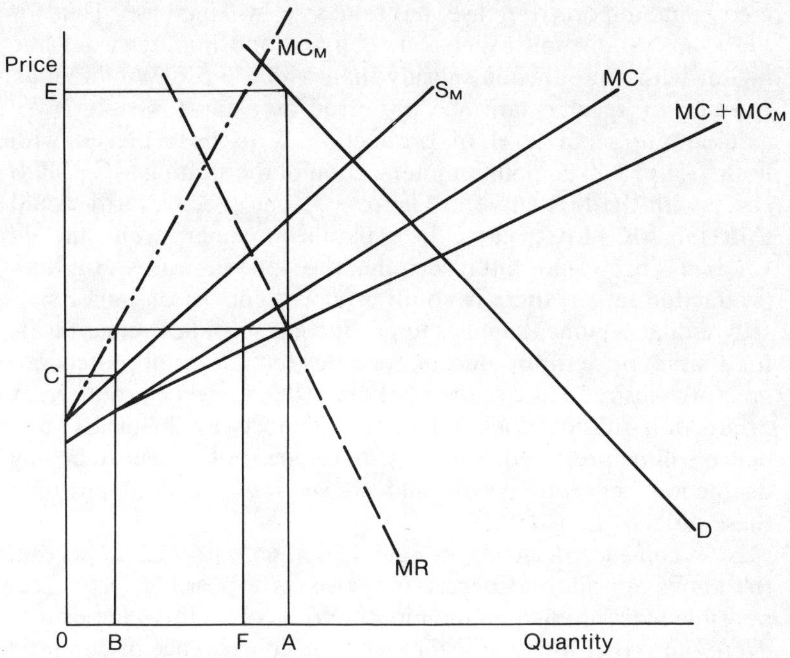

monopolist will not have effective control over imports — control lies with those who determine the size of the quota. In this latter case the analysis of the effects of the pursuit of various objectives is the same as when there is monopoly production and competitive holding of quotas, considered above in section (ii).

But now assume that the quotas are not fully used, or that the trading monopoly exists independently of the quotas, so that the producer is able to secure the full profit-maximising outcome by equating the two marginal costs with marginal revenue (as in Figure 9.3). Import quotas on their own could not be used as a weapon to achieve objectives other than the price/output configuration shown in Figure 9.3. But tariffs or production subsidies could be, for they could alter the marginal cost of imports, on the one hand, and the marginal cost of domestic production on the other. Consider a production target. A tariff would raise the marginal cost of imports MC_M in Figure 9.3, and shift the $MC+MC_M$ line upwards. Production would increase and imports would decline. A production subsidy, on the other hand, would lower MC and shift $MC+MC_M$ downwards. Production will increase and imports decrease, but total sales will increase. Thus for the same production expansion, demand and imports would be higher with a production subsidy than with a tariff. Would an *ad valorem* or specific tariff be preferred as a tariff weapon? We assume the same level of production is to be achieved with both — i.e. a given point of intersection of the shifting $MC+MC_M$ curve with the MR curve in Figure 9.3. The specific tariff would shift the $MC+MC_M$ curve in a parallel manner, while the *ad valorem* tariff would shift it such that the slope increases. But for a production target, there is no difference in impact on imports.

A similar argument applies to production subsidies versus tariffs for a target price for producers, for a desired degree of protection, and for a desired share of the market for the domestic producer. A production subsidy does not restrict imports as do tariffs, and hence will be preferred. Similarly there does not appear to be any distinction between specific and *ad valorem* tariffs in pursuing these objectives.

Now consider declining marginal production costs. In section (ii) above we allowed decreasing costs as a possible factor responsible for a production monopoly. With competitive importing, decreasing costs were consistent with the co-existence of domestic production and imports. However when the same monopolist controls both production and imports, imports and domestic production will not co-exist when there are declining production costs: the monopolist will use only one source, depending on which has the lower average cost for the level of sales required.

If there is a switch from imports to domestic production as domestic production is encouraged, the switch will occur at a higher level of imports when a production subsidy is the weapon than when the weapon is a tariff. This is simply because as a tariff is increased from zero, imports will decline until, at some tariff level, production will commence and will fully replace the imports. On the other hand, as a production subsidy is increased from zero, there is no effect on imports until the switch-over point is reached, at which point the free-trade level of imports is replaced by domestic production. But this is little comfort to foreign exporters; if the switch-over point is reached, imports are zero with any of the policies.

(v) Monopoly in Foreign Supply

We have assumed so far that competitive pressures among or within exporting countries prevent them from capturing the economic rents associated with the policies under discussion. However, if foreign exporters are able to restrict their exports below a competitive level to the country in question, such restriction may secure some of this rent while, at the same time, furthering the importer's objective. We now assume competitive conditions in the importing country so as to sidestep questions of bilateral monopoly.

First consider a restriction of trade designed to achieve a particular level of imports. Given that trade is to be restricted in this way, it is clearly to the advantage of the exporters to impose the restriction — by export taxes, export quotas, or by cartelisation of exporters — so that they collect the rent from the quotas or control (or the revenue from the export tax) that would otherwise pass to the importing country.

Consider now the objective of a particular level of production or price for producers, a target degree of protection or share of the market. Again if these targets are to be achieved by trade restriction it is, from the exporters' point of view, preferable that they impose the restriction themselves. Such a ranking is not clear if the alternative is a production subsidy in the importing country — to achieve a given level of production, trade is reduced less by a production subsidy than by a trade restriction. If the trade restriction required is not greater than that required by an optimal export tax, then an export tax or other restriction on exports will be the preferred policy of the exporter. However to the extent that the required restriction is greater than this, the production subsidy in the importing country will be the better policy from the exporters' point of view — more trade is to be preferred to less, once the point of optimal trade restriction is passed.

It is well known that exporting countries are prepared — given of course that some restriction is to occur — to countenance, and indeed encourage, trade restrictions by importing countries that facilitate the development of monopoly power by exporters. (See Shibata, 1968, p. 141, Caves and Jones, 1977, p. 227.) Export taxes or export quotas are effective if all exporters apply them, but there is an incentive for each exporter to undercut the others' taxes, or to expand its own export quota. The effective formation of cartels by exporters is secured more readily by country-specific quotas or country-specific 'voluntary' export restraint, or brand-specific quotas, as in the case of differentiated goods such as motor vehicles.[8] These are common devices in the contemporary trading world. In international commodity agreements, minimum import quotas are often supplemented by maximum export quotas for individual countries — again a device that facilitates the transfer of the rent to existing exporters.

3. Dynamic Considerations

Leaving aside uncertainty, the two additional considerations brought by time are (i) changing comparative advantage, and (ii) price instability.

(i) Changing Comparative Advantage

It is often argued that import tariffs (or production subsidies) are preferable to import quotas because they allow additional access to markets if comparative advantage moves in favour of exporters.[9] In considering access over time, care again needs to be given to the objective of those imposing the restrictions. If the objective is specified only for the beginning of the time under consideration, weapons that permit additional trade as conditions change will be preferred by foreigners (unless the expected gain in trade is small relative to the rent-transfer that is possible with export quotas). Tariff restrictions and production subsidies are indeed to be preferred to import quotas from this point of view. The preference will be particularly strong for new exporters whose ability to compete with old exporters may be limited by quotas, particularly by quotas allocated to countries according to exports in a base period. However, additional access over time will not necessarily be achieved if policies are adjusted so as to achieve, despite changing comparative advantage, a fixed domestic or trade objective.[10]

When the economic rent arising from trade restrictions that are designed to achieve a fixed domestic or trade objective remains in the importing country, any improvement in productivity by exporting countries will yield a pure transfer to the importing countries. Resources devoted to securing increased productivity (or export subsidies) will, from the point of view of exporters as a whole, yield a negative rate of return, as far as international trade is concerned. This does not mean that the return to particular exporting countries, or to particular exporters within those countries, will be negative, for they may be able to displace other exporters. But for the exporters as a whole the benefits pass wholly to the importing country. (See Sampson and Snape, 1980.) Both sets of countries, it appears, would be happier if the export prices could be raised to the level to give the desired result in the importing country — the importers would not have to impose restrictions and the exporters could take life easy (or cease subsidising exports).

(ii) Price Instability

There is a considerable literature relating to the destabilising effects on other countries of insulating one country from instability. There is also a large literature on whether greater or less stability is good or bad for exporting countries. This latter subject is ignored here.

In looking at instability there is an important distinction between those policies that attempt to achieve an objective at all times so that the weapon is adjusted continually, and those that attempt to achieve an objective in an 'average' sense — say over several years. Examples of the latter are constant *ad valorem* or specific production subsidies, constant *ad valorem* or specific tariffs and constant import quotas. In the former category are deficiency payments that make up the difference between the price received in a market and a target price, and variable import levies, variable import quotas, and state trading that achieve fixed domestic objectives.

The general point is that adjustable weapons export instability, whether the instability arises within the importing country imposing the policy, or in the rest of the world, while fixed weapons permit some absorption of instability within the policy-imposing country. An exception is a variable policy weapon that maintains constant imports in the face of domestic supply variation in the importing country, for the constancy of imports prevents the export of instability.

4. Conclusion

With the specified assumptions, and in the absence of monopoly power, production subsidies will be preferred by exporters to trade restrictions as the means by which importers pursue objectives relating to domestic production, share of market, domestic price, or degree of protection, and exporters will be indifferent between various types of trade restriction.

When there are monopolistic forces present, the picture is more complicated. If the only element of monopoly is in domestic production and if the objective is to achieve a particular level of production (or share of the market) for the domestic producer, then the ranking of the policies considered from the exporters' point of view is: (1) production subsidy, (2) specific tariff, (3) *ad valorem* tariff, (4) import quota. On the other hand, if the domestic objective is a particular price for the producer (or a desired degree of protection) the ranking changes. There is no general ranking of production subsidies and import quotas as the preferred policy; the other two policies can be ranked (3) *ad valorem* tariff, (4) specific tariff.

When there is a monopoly in importing with or without a production monopoly, there would be a general preference by exporters for production subsidies over other forms of intervention.

Except when there are elements of monopoly among exporters, exporters will be indifferent between the various policies if the objective of the policy is to reduce imports to a target level. When there is such monopoly power, exporters will tend to favour those policies that facilitate the exercise of this power. Such policies are quota restrictions and the negotiation of 'voluntary' export restraints. Objectives of the importing countries may be met by action by exporters; if trade is to be restricted, it is better from the exporters' point of view if they impose the restrictions themselves.

The dynamic considerations touched on are market access over time as comparative advantage changes, and price stability. To evaluate various policies in relation to access, one must consider whether importers' weapons are fixed or variable. If they are fixed then those policies that allow additional access over time (i.e. production subsidies and tariffs) will tend to be favoured over those that do not (i.e. quotas). If policies are adjusted frequently so as to achieve targets then the comparative static analysis, summarised above, is applicable.

In looking at price stability on international markets, the crucial distinction is between those policies that allow absorption of some of the world's instability, and those that insulate from it.

Appendix 9.1: The Geometry of a Production Monopoly with Competitive Trade

In Figure 9A.1(a) let D be the demand curve and MR the marginal revenue drawn to this demand curve, MC the marginal costs (which could be rising, constant, or falling), and S_M the supply curve of imports under free trade (drawn with positive values to the left of the vertical axis). $D-S_M$ is the demand for the home produced product under free trade; that is, the demand net of free trade import supply. MR_{FT} (the subscript of FT indicating free trade) is the marginal revenue derived from the $D-S_M$ demand curve. The profit-maximising output is OA (where MC = MR_{FT}), with price P_1 and imports of AB(=OC).

As drawn we may note that production with free trade is less than production with an import quota of zero. If an import quota of zero were imposed the demand curve facing the producer would be D, with marginal revenue of MR. Production would be OL where MR and MC are equal, and this level of output is greater than OA. If the S_M curve were higher, this point 'L' could be to the left of 'A' — that is, free trade output would *exceed* the output with a zero import quota. Apart from implying that an import quota could not be used to achieve a production objective, this possibility does not affect the analysis.

(a) Production Target

Referring to Figure 9A.1(a), assume that there is a target domestic output of OF. This could be achieved by a tariff such that marginal revenue with the tariff equals marginal cost at the output OF. This is shown in Figure 9A.1(b). S_{MT} is the supply curve of imports with an *ad valorem* tariff and $D-S_{MT}$ is the demand curve for the domestic product. MR_T (T indicating tariff) is marginal revenue related to the demand curve $D-S_{MT}$. Output and imports are OF and FE respectively.

Now assume that the tariff is replaced by an import quota that yields the same quantity of imports, FE. As mentioned in the text above, the monopolist will reduce his output when the tariff is replaced by a quota. In Figure 9A.1(b), D−Q is the demand curve net of the import quota and MR_Q the marginal revenue curve related to this demand curve. The profit-maximising monopolist will reduce output to that at which MR_Q = MC. In order to induce him to expand output back to OF (which, it will be recalled, is the

Figure 9A.1: Monopolistic Production and Competitive Trade — Effects of Import Tariffs and Quotas

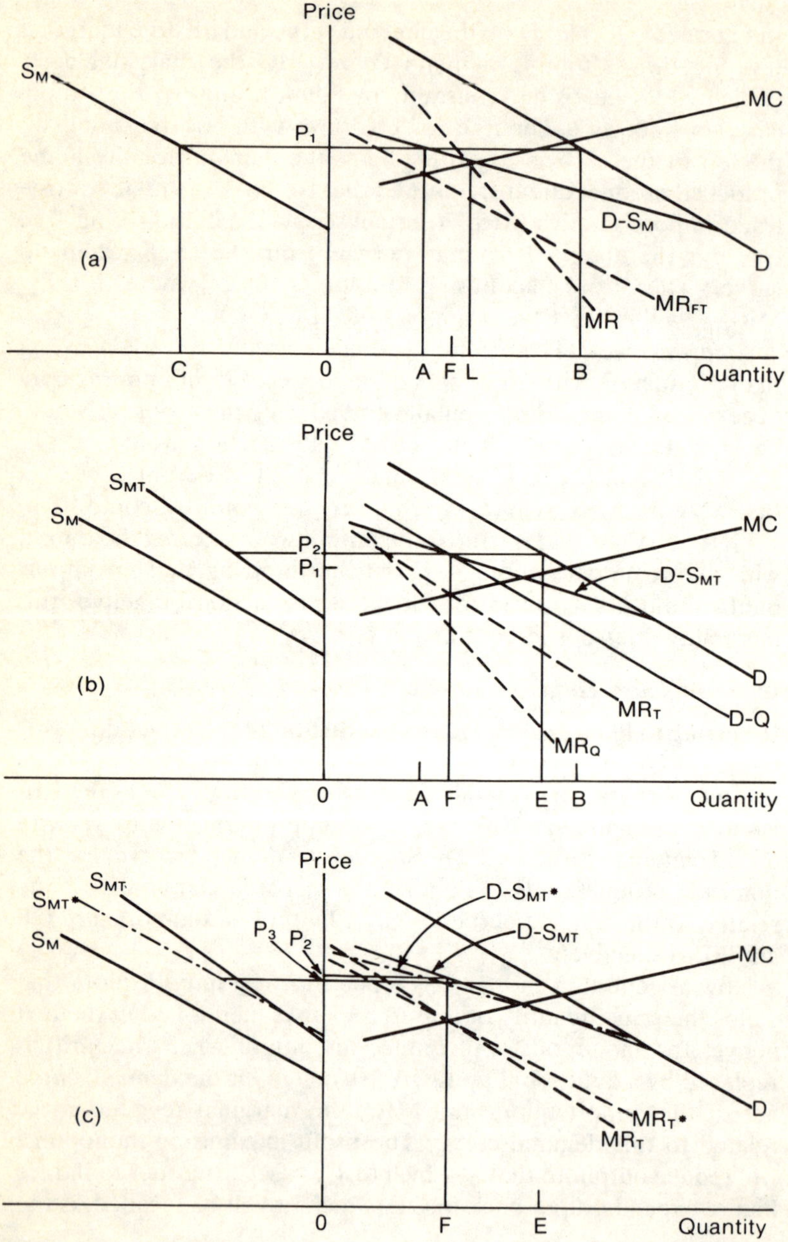

target output) a smaller import quota is necessary. Thus to achieve a target level of output, an *ad valorem* import tariff will yield a higher level of imports than will quantitative restrictions on imports.

If a specific rather than an *ad valorem* tariff had been used to achieve the production target OF, the tariff-inclusive import supply curve would be S_{MT*} (Figure 9A.1(c)), which is parallel to S_M. The demand for the home-produced product is $D-S_{MT*}$ and the associated marginal revenue curve is MR_{T*}, which cuts the MC curve at the target output of OF (as does the MR_T curve). With the more elastic demand for home production ($D-S_{MT*}$), the profit maximising price (P_3) is lower than with the *ad valorem* tariff (P_2), and imports are greater.

A production subsidy would, of course, achieve the target production level OF, without raising the price to consumers above P_1.

(b) Price Target

In Figure 9A.1(b), assume that P_2 is the target price, achieved by an *ad valorem* tariff. Imports are FE. Now, as before, impose an import quota of FE to replace the tariff, so that the demand curve for the domestic product is $D-Q$. With this quota, production will decline and the domestic price will be increased. In order to reduce the domestic price to P_2, the quota will have to be increased. It is not clear in general whether a production subsidy would lead to more or less imports than the quota — it would yield both a higher level of domestic production and a higher total demand.

Looking now at a specific tariff, recall Figure 9A.1(c) in which the production level OF was achieved alternatively with an *ad valorem* and a specific tariff. The former also yielded what we are specifying as the target price P_2, while a specific tariff gave the lower price P_3. To give the price P_2 the specific tariff would have to be increased, yielding a higher level of domestic production. With the same total demand (i.e. at price P_2), imports would be lower with the specific tariff than with the *ad valorem* tariff.

(c) Increasing Tariffs above the 'Just-prohibitive' Level

Consider the points B, C, D, and B′, C′ and D′ in Figures 9.1 and 9.2, respectively. Assume that a specific tariff is being increased until imports are just eliminated — the home production just satisfies total demand. The ability of the producer to raise prices further (and reduce production) is limited by the threat of imports. A higher specific tariff would remove the immediate threat of imports and give some latitude to the producer to raise price and reduce production. Thus we have the horizontal section in Figures 9.1 and 9.2 from points C and C′.

A similar argument applies to an *ad valorem* tariff when it just reaches the level that excludes imports — hence the horizontal sections from points B and B′. The argument does not apply to an import quota — when it is zero, potential imports do not constrain behaviour and the quota cannot be reduced further. Thus there are no horizontal sections applicable to a quota from points D and D′.

Why does C lie to the right of B and C′ to the left of B′? Consider again the just-prohibitive specific tariff. At the internal price given by this tariff, the demand for the domestic product is less elastic (for price increases) with an *ad valorem* tariff than with a specific tariff. Thus at this price but with an *ad valorem* tariff, production would be lower and imports would not be excluded. A higher *ad valorem* tariff — and a higher internal price — would be necessary to exclude imports completely. Hence B′ lies to the right of C′. As the domestic price at which imports are just excluded with the *ad valorem* tariff is higher than with the specific tariff, so the level of production at which autarchy occurs must be lower. (That is, price is higher and demand, which will equal production, will be lower.) Hence point B lies to the left of C in Figure 9.1. Raising *ad valorem* or specific tariffs above the 'just-prohibitive' levels will raise price and lower production until the price/production combination of a zero quota is reached (D and D′); further increases in the tariffs will have no effects.

Notes

* The subject of this paper is related to a theme of my PhD thesis, *Protection and Stabilization in the World Sugar Industry*, written twenty years ago under the supervision of Basil Yamey. Basil was a model supervisor and my intellectual and personal debts to him, then and since, are very great. The subject is, of course, related to his interest in international trade and development. It is a privilege to be asked to contribute to this collection in his honour.

Earlier versions of the paper were presented at a conference on US-Asian Economic Relations, sponsored by the Centre for Asian Economic Research at Rutgers University in April 1981, and at the 10th Conference of Economists in Canberra, August 1981. I am particularly indebted to Ted Sieper, and also to Anne

Krueger, Michael Michaely, Ken Tucker, Ed Tower, and to participants at seminars at Monash and La Trobe universities, the universities of Western Ontario, Minnesota and Melbourne, and at the World Bank.

1. I am grateful to Ted Sieper for this point, and also for developing a rigorous proof. This specific case is not considered in Bhagwati (1971) but is consistent with the propositions developed in Bhagwati's paper. This immiserizing effect will not arise if the only distortion is failure to impose the optimum export tax, for with free trade the utility possibility frontier with greater export demand will lie wholly outside the frontier with the lower demand.

2. Thus the ranking of these policies is the same for exporting countries as for the importing country (ignoring the terms of trade gain for the importing country from the trade restriction).

3. Throughout this paper we have not considered objectives the pursuit of which would turn the importer into an exporter.

4. Sections (i) – (iv) have a clear relation to Bhagwati's paper (1965) on the equivalence of tariffs and quotas. Rachel McCulloch (1973) has results similar to some of those presented below — e.g. 'that a quota will allow more imports from abroad than a price-equivalent tariff' (p. 508).

5. I am much indebted to Ted Sieper for assistance with this section and the associated Appendix — for suggesting the manner in which the basic point could be presented, for uncovering errors (those that remain are my responsibility) and for many of the twists and turns of the analysis.

6. The two alternative tariffs are assumed to yield the same level of domestic production, and elasticities are being compared over the range of prices under contemplation by the monopolist.

7. McCulloch (1973, p. 508) shows that when there are (i) constant terms of trade and (ii) a domestic monopoly in production, an import quota will be preferred by the importing country to a tariff to achieve a domestic price target.

8. The *Far Eastern Economic Review* of 8 August 1975 (p. 35) reported that licences to export knitted shifts from Hong Kong to Australia were being traded for HK$80 per dozen shirts. Export licences were required because voluntary export restraints had been negotiated between the Australian and Hong Kong Governments. The Australian Industries Assistance Commission estimated that restraining trade in knitted shifts by voluntary restraints rather than by additional Australian import tariffs resulted in a transfer to Hong Kong of about one and a quarter million Australian dollars over a nine month period. (Industries Assistance Commission, *Annual Report, 1974–75*, p. 101).

9. Of course comparative advantage in the goods under consideration may move in favour of the importing country over time. But the more common expectation in the world of trade barriers is for the opposite to occur, and attention is directed to these cases.

10. Pursuit of a target degree of protection will, of course, allow additional access if the competitive position of exporters improves.

References

Bhagwati, J. (1965), 'On the Equivalence of Tariffs and Quotas', in Robert E. Baldwin *et al.*, *Trade, Growth, and the Balance of Payments: Essays in Honor of Gottfried Haberler*, Chicago and Amsterdam, Rand McNally and North-Holland pp. 53–67

Bhagwati, J. (1968), 'More on the Equivalence of Tariffs and Quotas', *American Economic Review, LVIII*, (1), 142–6

Bhagwati, J. (1971), 'The Generalized Theory of Distortions and Welfare', in J.

Bhagwati *et al.* (eds.), *Trade, Balance of Payments and Growth: Papers in International Economics in Honor of Charles P. Kindleberger*, Amsterdam, North-Holland pp. 69–90

Caves, R. E. and Jones, R. W. (1977), *World Trade and Payments: An Introduction* Boston, Little, Brown and Co. (2nd edition)

Krueger, A. O. and Sonnenschein, H. (1967), 'The Terms of Trade, the Gains from Trade and Price Divergence', *International Economic Review, 8*, (1), 121–7

McCulloch, R. (1973), 'When are a Tariff and a Quota Equivalent?', *Canadian Journal of Economics, 6*, (4), 503–11

Sampson, G. P. and Snape, R. H. (1980), 'Effects of the EEC's Variable Import Levies', *Journal of Political Economy, 88*, (5), 1026–40

Shibata, Hirofumi (1968), 'A Note on the Equivalence of Tariffs and Quotas', *American Economic Review, LVIII*, (1), 137–42

PART SEVEN

HISTORY OF THOUGHT

10 THE PLACE OF *INDUSTRY AND TRADE* IN THE ANALYSIS OF ALFRED MARSHALL*

Philip L. Williams
University of Melbourne

Judgements of the worth of *Industry and Trade* are divided. Schumpeter encourages the reader to explore it. 'The three volumes [*Principles, Industry and Trade*, and *Money Credit and Commerce*] are all essential: nobody knows Marshall who knows only the *Principles*.'[1] Schumpeter proceeds to explain that Marshall's work in applied economics is located chiefly in *Industry and Trade*. By contrast, Guillebaud seems to be less enthusiastic about Marshall's applied economics; he states his belief that '. . . everything that was important in [Marshall's] thought is to be found in [the first edition of the *Principles*].'[2] Keynes considers the volumes to be a rag-bag containing those snippets of worth which derive from Marshall's work in economic history. 'The most part of it is descriptive. A full third is historical and summarises the results of his long labours in that field. . . . The book is not so much a structural unity as an opportunity for bringing together a number of partly related matters about which Marshall had something of value to say to the world.'[3]

Schumpeter praises *Industry and Trade* for its blend of theory with fact. 'Marshall was, in fact, an economic historian of the first rank, though he may not have been much of an historical technician. And his mastery of historical fact and his analytic habit of mind did not dwell in separate compartments but formed so close a union that the live fact intrudes into the theorem and the theorem into purely historical observations. This shows, of course, very much more obviously in *Industry and Trade* than it does in the *Principles*, . . .'.[4]

This paper explores the relationship between the history and the analysis that is contained in *Industry and Trade*. It argues that the volume is organised around problems which Marshall tries to explain. The facts reported in the volume serve both to illustrate the analysis and to caution the reader from accepting too simple a version of the theory; but the analysis is primary.

Industry and Trade is a volume comprising three separate books. Book I is entitled 'Some Origins of Present Problems of

Industry and Trade'; Book II is entitled 'Dominant Tendencies of Business Organization'; and Book III is labelled, 'Monopolistic Tendencies: Their Relations to Public Well-being'. This paper begins with a section on the structure of the volume as a whole. It then examines the organisation of each of the three books in turn.

The Volume as a Whole

Industry and Trade is a modern book in the sense that it is concerned with questions which have been enjoying a renewed interest from economists in the 1970s and the early 1980s. It is concerned with the organisation of industry. In 1972, Coase (one of the founders of modern interest in the subject) wrote a paper bemoaning the fact that little work was being undertaken in the area.

> What is curious about the treatment of the problems of industrial organisation is that it does not now exist. We all know what is meant by the organisation of industry. It describes the way in which the activities undertaken within the economic system are divided up between firms. As we know, some firms embrace many different activities; while for others, the range is narrowly circumscribed. Some firms are large; others, small. Some firms are vertically integrated; others are not. This is the organisation of industry or — as it used to be called — the structure of industry. What one would expect to learn from a study of industrial organisation would be how industry is organised now, and how this differs from what it was in earlier periods; what forces were operative in bringing about this organisation of industry, and how these forces have been changing over time; what the effects would be of proposals to change, through legal action of various kinds, the forms of industrial organisation.[5]

It would be difficult to give a better summary of the matter of *Industry and Trade*. The title of the volume is informative: Marshall discusses both the organisation of production and the organisation of exchange; and the two are seen to be intimately connected. Indeed, one of the themes of the volume is that expanded opportunities for trade (caused by lower transport costs, lower tariffs, etc.) lead to increased opportunities for the use of methods of production on a larger scale.

As the titles of the three component parts suggest, the tone of the volume becomes increasingly normative as it proceeds. The first two books are concerned to explore, first, the historical processes which have gone to determine the current (1919) organisation of industry. The second book explores those features of the contemporary economic society that influence the organisation of industry. The final book is explicitly normative: it is concerned with the problem of monopoly and appropriate government policy with respect to monopoly. The approach of the whole volume, but particularly the third book, is far more normative than that of the *Principles*.

The most obvious difference between the text of the *Principles* and that of *Industry and Trade* is that the former seems to be more narrowly theoretical than the latter. *Industry and Trade* seems to be a volume of applied economics and, indeed, it is. However, this difference is merely one of degree.

Marshall's earliest work in economics was his most abstract — 'he translated as many as possible of Ricardo's reasonings into mathematics'[6] — and his first-published work — *Economics of Industry* and *Pure Theory* — contains very few facts. Quoting from the Eckstein sketch, Whitaker suggests: 'The key to Marshall's slowness in publishing his theories seems to be his unwillingness to publish them without "the requisite limitations and conditions", because "if separated from all concrete study of actual conditions, they might seem to claim a more direct bearing on real problems than they in fact had."'[7]

With each successive publication, Marshall's output becomes increasingly qualified — as a result of his concrete study of actual conditions. At places in *Industry and Trade* the qualifications and the facts seem almost to swamp the analytical structure. After two chapters on the results of monopoly theory, Marshall devotes four chapters (approximately 80 pages) to competition and monopoly in shipping and railways. However these industries were selected with a definite analytical purpose: '. . . the varying relations of monopoly and competition can be treated in them, with less intermingling of technical considerations peculiar to them than in the case of any other great group of industries. They are therefore used to set the keynote of the present [third] Book.'[8]

In the 1980s, the great bulk of empirical research in economics is comparative. Comparisons across time, across industries, across countries, across firms within an industry may all be utilised to enable sources of variation to be examined.[9] Marshall utilises comparisons across both industries and firms; but *Industry and Trade* is noteworthy for the prominence which it gives to comparisons across nations and across (substantial) periods of time.[10] The selection of these bases of comparison was principally dictated by the building blocks of the analysis. Changes in such variables as antitrust legislation, entrepreneurial spirit, the tariff and the extent of markets may be observed more readily across nations or across substantial periods of time than across industries or across firms. Later economists interested in similar issues (Bain,[11] Bauer and Yamey,[12] Caves[13]) employed international comparisons with great effect. The bases of Marshall's comparisons differ from those used commonly by modern industrial economists because Marshall was interested primarily in testing propositions concerned with the organisation of industry whereas they are interested primarily in testing propositions from price theory or from the theory of the firm.

Book I: Some Origins of Present Problems of Industry and Trade

Book I and its related appendices explore the origins of modern industrial organisation. In particular, Marshall explores how European industrial capitalism came to emerge from the mediaeval system via the transitional stage of mercantilism. Marshall's material is not organised around any one theory of economic evolution. In particular, it is not organised around a Marxist system of classification; but he is concerned to explain the emergence of capitalist methods of production.[14]

The extent of Marshall's indebtedness to the German historical school, the English historical school and even to Herbert Spencer[15] has been raised by commentators but never examined in detail. Shove states that although Marshall was aware of the work of the Germans, he seems to have derived no results of importance directly from them.[16] Whitaker says: 'The question of Marshall's indebtedness to the Historical School — both its major German stem and its minor English branch — is a large one deserving detailed treatment. I am inclined to think the debt was small, and that similarities were more a matter of a common starting point.'[17]

Degrees of indebtedness are difficult to ascertain in one of such independence of mind as Marshall. Nevertheless, we do know that he read much of the German school when he was forming his outlook to the study of economics. We also know that he was impressed by much of their work. Whether indebted or not, Marshall's affinity with the Germans means that his approach to the explanation of the organisation of industry is different from the Ronald Coase[18]/Oliver Williamson[19] approach which has enjoyed such a revival recently.

The difference may be explained with the help of Allyn Young.

> These two views, or ways of conceiving the structure of society, are the contractual and the institutional. In the contractual view social arrangements are deliberate contrivances resting upon voluntary agreements — instruments which men use in attaining their purposes. In the institutional view these same arrangements appear as social habits, the products of history, not really shaped by the rational prevision of men, but dominant factors, themselves, in determining what men's purposes and values shall be, and establishing the patterns which human behaviour follows.[20]

Characteristically, Marshall's outlook is neither squarely contractual (like that of Coase and Williamson) nor institutional (like the Germans) but rather a hybrid.

Marshall's ambivalent attitude to methodological disputes of his time has been misinterpreted. Because of the attacks on Marshall by the fiery Cunningham,[21] and because of Marshall's signing of the free trade manifesto of 1903,[22] he is sometimes said to have opposed the work of the historical school. Indeed, a recently-published article[23] argues that the primarily-deductive, even mathematical, school of Cambridge was the *bête noire* of English economic historians at the turn of the century. Far from being hostile to the historical school, Marshall read its work and used elements of its methodology. Further, his pronouncements on method leave no doubt as to his stated position.

> During the generation that is now passing away it has been made clear beyond doubt by many workers in many lands that the true inductive study of economics is the search for and arrangement of facts with a view to discovering the ideas, some temporary and local, others universal and eternal, which underlie them: and that the true analytical study of economics is the

> search for ideas latent in the facts which have been thus brought together and arranged by the historian and the observer of contemporary life. Each study supplements the other: there is no rivalry or opposition between them; every genuine student of economics sometimes uses the inductive method and sometimes the analytical, and nearly always both of them together.[24]

Despite this catholicity, Marshall was critical of bad economic history. In particular, historians who claimed to be able to do without economic theory were either disingenuous or else were deluding themselves.[25]

> . . . facts by themselves are silent. Observation discovers nothing directly of the actions of causes, but only of sequences of time. It may find that an event followed on, or that it coincided with, a certain group of events. But this gives no guidance except for other cases in which exactly the same set of facts occurs over again, grouped in just the same way. And such repetitions never occur in the life of man; nor indeed anywhere save in physical laboratories: history does not repeat itself.[26]

But strictures such as these were not directed generally at the historical school. Even its more extreme representatives could teach some things.[27]

> As a whole, the German historical school was peculiarly valuable. It would be difficult to overrate the value of the work which they and their fellow-workers in other countries have done in tracing and explaining the history of economic habits and institutions. It is one of the great achievements of our age; and an important addition to our real wealth. It has done more than almost anything else to broaden our ideas, to increase our knowledge of ourselves, and to help us to understand the evolution of man's moral and social life, and of the Divine Principle of which it is an embodiment.[28]

Book I of *Industry and Trade* shows Marshall's close affinity with the German historical school (particularly with its earlier representatives such as List) in many ways. We shall catalogue three of these. In the first place Marshall stresses the importance of the quality of the work force in the process of economic development. Secondly, the primacy of the abilities of the work force leads to an analysis of national characteristics. Finally, prescriptions for economic development, particularly tariff policy, are dependent on the nation's stage in its historical development.

Quality of the Work Force

In the summer of 1875, Marshall visited North America. His purpose was to study the effects of protection in a new country.[29] In particular, Marshall wished to assess the arguments of List and his American followers. Marshall returned to Cambridge with a vivid impression of the mobility and of the independence of mind of American entrepreneurs.[30] Such 'exceptional force of character of the people' and the 'stimulus which those energies derived from exceptional opportunities for bold and rich enterprise' contributed more to the development performance of America than did her natural resources.[31]

Although, characteristically, Marshall in Book I points to a 'consilience' of factors as causing industrial development, one set of factors is stressed far more than the others — the drive and ability of the people who make business decisions.[32] List calls these characteristics the productive powers of labour.

> *The power of producing wealth* is therefore infinitely more important than *wealth itself*; it insures not only the possession and the increase of what has been gained, but also the replacement of what has been lost. This is still more the case with entire nations (who cannot live out of mere entails) than with private individuals. Germany has been devastated in every century by pestilence, by famine, or by civil or foreign wars; she has, nevertheless, always retained a great portion of her powers of production, and has thus quickly reattained some degree of prosperity; while rich and mighty but despot- and priest-ridden Spain, notwithstanding her comparative enjoyment of internal peace, has sunk deeper into poverty and misery.[33]

Characteristics of Nations

Just as List had spoken of an 'interchanging sequence of action and reaction' between moral and material forces,[34] so Marshall, also, makes this a theme of Book I of *Industry and Trade*.[35] The qualities of those who make decisions are partly determined by, and partly determine, the social environment within which business takes place. Their emphasis both on personal qualities and on the interaction between these qualities and the social environment causes both Marshall and List to adopt the nation-state as their prime unit of analysis. The system of formal education, the extent of restrictions on freedom to contract, the proportion of the population composed of recent immigrants, all go to influence the characters of the people who make decisions. Because these features of society are determined largely by the state or by state-wide institutions, the personal characteristics in which Marshall is so interested tend to differ across national boundaries. Consequently, Book I comprises chapters devoted to the analysis of the characteristics of the businessmen of particular nationalities, the effects which these characteristics have on patterns of economic development, and the ways in which various social institutions have influenced those personal characteristics.

Marshall's belief that the interaction of personal characteristics and social institutions was something to be explained is the basis of his public altercation with Cunningham. In his review of Marshall's *Principles*, Cunningham had objected to an implicit assumption which he discerned in the *Principles*.

> The underlying assumption against which I wish to protest is never explicitly formulated by those who rely on it; but it may, I think, be not unfairly expressed in some such terms as these. That the same motives have been at work in all ages, and have produced similar results, and that, therefore, it is possible to formulate economic laws which describe the action of economic causes at all times and in all places.[36]

Marshall replied that he had made no such assumption. Indeed, his purpose had been to explain the variability in human motives which Cunningham had accused him of assuming contant. 'The whole volume is indeed occupied mainly in showing how similar causes acting on people under dissimilar conditions produce more or less divergent effects. The leading motive of its argument is the opposite of that which Dr. Cunningham ascribes to it.'[37]

Cunningham did not entirely deserve this rebuke. If Marshall tries to explain the effects of social institutions on human motives then he must be assuming that there is some constantcy in mankind which causes people to react to a particular set of social institutions in a predictable manner. This difference between Marshall and Cunningham was not so much as to whether human motivation was a constant. Rather the difference was over what should be taken as given. Marshall considered that to attribute an arrangement to custom is really to say that we do not know its cause.[38] Marshall wanted to investigate the causes of human behaviour rather than merely attribute it to custom. And in order to do this he needed to assume that people will react to social institutions in predictable ways.

Relativity of Economic Policy

When he discusses state policy towards monopolies in Part III of *Industry and Trade*, Marshall hesitates to provide any simple rules. This hesitancy to give simple advice on policy probably stems from his early work on foreign trade and economic development. In Chapter 3 of Book I and in Appendix D, Marshall tries to explain mercantilism rather than to argue against it. Indeed, he argues that mercantilism was appropriate to the stage of England's development.

Appendix D reflects Marshall's affinity with the German historical school (particularly with the work of Schmoller) but it utilises many of the original sources. Its balanced judgement of Adam Smith's criticism of the mercantilists is notable for its historical perspective: policies which may be appropriate for one phase in economic development need not necessarily be appropriate to another.

Marshall's strong sense of the relativity of economic policy can be seen in his attitude to the tariff. His views on tariff policy have been misunderstood because of his signing of Edgeworth's free-trade manifesto. 'Marshall entered the lists on behalf of free trade, of course. He had been a supporter of that policy for thirty years — ever since 1875, when he had visited the United States for the purpose of studying protection in operation on the spot.'[39]

With free trade, as with most areas of public policy, simple statements of Marshall's opinion generally are misleading. He believed that the worth of a policy depends on the particular circumstances.

> [The Germans] resented the way in which the English advocates of free trade tacitly assumed that a proposition which had been established with regard to a manufacturing country, such as

> England was, could be carried over without modification to agricultural countries. The brilliant genius and national enthusiasm of List overthrew this presumption; and showed that the Ricardians had taken little account of the indirect effects of free trade.[40]

> List and Carey, the great German and American founders of modern protective policy, insisted on two fundamental propositions: one was that Free Trade was adapted to the industrial stage which England had reached, and the other that State intervention was required on behalf of pioneer industries in less advanced countries. Had English Free Traders appreciated fairly the force of the second of these positions, their powerful arguments that Protection was an almost unmixed injury to England would perhaps have been accepted by the whole civilised world. As it was, their one great error put many of the most far-seeing and public-spirited statesmen and economists in other countries into an attitude of hostility to their position as a whole. It has caused, and it is causing today, able men to deny, directly or indirectly, economic truths as certain as those of geometry; because English predictions, suggested by this one great error, have proved both misleading and mischievous.[41]

List argued that tariffs on manufactured commodities were appropriate for nations which were at that stage in their development when they were developing a base of manufacturing industry. Although the tariff would involve a temporary loss (by forgoing comparative advantage), this loss would be outweighed by a gain because the productive powers of the economy would be developed.

The productive powers of the nation consist primarily of the qualities of the work force. These will not be developed in an agricultural economy.

> In a country devoted to mere raw agriculture, dullness of mind, awkwardness of body, obstinate adherence to old notions, customs, methods, and processes, want of culture, of prosperity, and of liberty prevail. The spirit of striving for a steady increase in mental and bodily acquirements, of emulation, and of liberty, characterise, on the contrary, a State devoted to manufactures and commerce.[42]

The benefits from the development of productive powers are not confined to manufacturing industry. Improvements spill over to agricultural industry — particularly if the two types of activity are within close geographical proximity and enjoy a stable trading environment.[43]

The role List assigned to the tariff was limited to manufactures and was limited to a particular stage of development. Within these confines, the tariff should not be specific to particular industries: it was not that the industry was in its infancy, but rather that the productive powers of the work-force were underdeveloped.

As was shown above, Marshall had great respect for these arguments. This is not to say that he favoured tariffs (he even considered that the America of 1875 was probably more harmed than helped by tariffs);[44] but, rather, he considered that a particular regime of tariffs may be appropriate for a particular stage in the economic development of a nation.

Characteristically, Marshall's enthusiasm for the work of List was not uncritical. In the first place, Marshall considered that List had attributed a power to manufacturing industry which he should have attributed to whatever branch of industry is at the frontier of the development of knowledge. List had made this mistake because, at the time he was writing, manufacturing filled that position. 'It is true that economic development passes generally through three stages: but List's assumption that manufacturing is necessarily superior to other industries seems to mistake accidentals for essentials.'[45]

Marshall's second quibble was that political realities make the working of a tariff policy very difficult.

> I came back [from America] convinced that a protective policy, in fact, was a very different thing from a protective policy as painted by sanguine economists, such as Carey and his followers, who assumed that all other people would be as upright as they knew themselves to be, and as clear-sighted as they believed themselves to be. I found that, however simple the plan on which a protective policy started, it was drawn on irresistibly to become intricate, and to lend its chief aid to those industries which were already strong enough to do without it. In becoming intricate it became corrupt, and tended to corrupt general politics. On the whole, I thought that this moral harm far outweighed any small net benefit which it might be capable

of conferring on American industry in the stage in which it was then.[46]

Finally, Marshall extended the reasons given by List as to why a business may be unable to internalise all the benefits which accrue as a result of its developing the productive powers of labour. (Such externalities have become a necessary component of all respectable modern versions of the infant-industry argument.) In his manuscript on The Theory of Foreign Trade, Marshall states:

> If in the course of a year's work a workman has received training in intelligence, in trustworthiness, in power of self control, and in technical skill and efficiency, the results of the training are the property of the workman and of the state; but not, save to a small extent and indirectly, the property of his employer. The workman can demand from his master an addition to his wages equivalent to the increased value of his services and in a free market his demand will be, within certain limits, successful. It is true that workmen are attracted towards occupations in which they can obtain training of such moral and economic advantages to themselves in the future. But they are likely to estimate such remote advantages at less than their full value unless they or their parents have already attained a somewhat high standard of intelligence and morality.[47]

We have seen that Marshall's study of the emergence of modern industry in Part I (and the related Appendices) of *Industry and Trade* betrays a strong affinity with the German economists — and, in particular, with List. Marshall's historical sense can be seen in his analysis of the influence of social institutions on the motivation of those who make business decisions. It can also be seen in his advocacy of economic policy and in his view that the optimal policy depends on the stage of development of the particular nation which is under consideration.

Book II: Dominant Tendencies of Business Organisation

Book II breaks from history to the time of writing. Whereas Book I sought to explain differences in human nature across nations and across time, Book II explicitly assumes human nature to be constant. It seeks to explain contemporary trends in the organisation of industry. In particular, it explores possible reasons for the growth in the size of the representative firm. The analysis of Book II is conducted on the assumption of open competition. Openness is a necessary condition for competition to be free.

Marshall's notion of free competition is a direct descendent from the English Classical Economists.[48] Marshall deliberately avoided associating the words perfectly or perfect with competition so as to minimise any confusion between free competition and the increasingly-popular Cournotesque concept of perfect competition.[49]

Two conditions are necessary and sufficient for Marshall's free competition. The businesses must be acting independently — each seeking to maximise its own profits. Also, there must be no impediments to the tendency of resources to move in response to opportunities to earn a higher reward. This second requirement means that if someone is earning a higher return than others, the others will be able to replicate the activity of the first so as to equalise net returns. If this second requirement is satisfied, competition is said to be open.

However, two factors may delay this process of replication.

> These obstacles are mainly much capital and effort in setting up the plant and organization, suited for competing on nearly even terms with a strong business, already in possession of the field. Few are able to do it: and fewer still are willing to take the heavy risks involved in it. . . . The second obstacle to the setting up of efficient competition with a business, that has acquired a conditional monopoly, is the *vis inertiae*, the opposition to change, which is inherent in human nature and in human conditions.[50]

The business will estimate the extent of these obstacles; and its estimate will influence the price it sets.

> As things are, its monopoly being conditional and not absolute, it is not likely to have ventured to put its charges up to the highest monopoly levels: but it may on the whole conclude that its position will be less endangered by raising its charges a little nearer to those levels, than by stinting expenditure for the confusion of any assailant whether actual, or merely anticipated.[51]

In the case of standardised commodities, a business may have a group of customers bound to it by goodwill — even though that goodwill may not enable the business to command any premium on the standard price. In the case of non-standardised products, a business may well extract a premium on the standard price from its special group of customers.

> Everyone buys, and nearly everyone sells, to some extent in a *general* market, in which he is on about the same footing with the others around him. But nearly everyone has also some '*particular*' markets; that is, some people or groups of people with whom he is in somewhat close touch: mutual knowledge and trust lead him to approach them, and them to approach him, in preference to strangers. A producer, a wholesale dealer, or a shopkeeper, who has built up a strong connection among purchasers of his goods, has a valuable property. He does not generally expect to get better prices from his clients than from others. But he expects to sell easily to them because they know and trust him, . . .[52]

> The general position is, then: Every manufacturer, or other business man, has a plant, an organization, and a business connection, which put him in a position of advantage for his special work. He has no sort of permanent monopoly, because others can easily equip themselves in like manner. But for the time being he and other owners of factories of his class are in possession of a partial monopoly. The prices of the stock, which they put on the market, will be governed by the demand for that market relatively to that stock, nearly in the same way as if they had a true monopoly. Nearly in the same, but not quite: for in the case of a permanent monopoly consumers will seldom gain much by waiting for lower prices; whereas, if prices rise above the cost of production in an open trade, those consumers, who can do so conveniently, will wait for the effect of competition in bringing down prices.[53]

It is important to summarise (because Marshall has frequently been misrepresented on this matter). Marshall views monopoly as a matter of degree because it takes time before one producer can replicate the activities of another. The higher the barriers to replication, the more like absolute monopoly and the less like open competition is the market within which any producer operates. So when Marshall states that monopoly and competition 'shade into one another by imperceptible degrees'[54] one should not say that he is anticipating the models of Chamberlin and Joan Robinson;[55] because the matter of degree for Marshall is not the number of firms or the degree of product differentiation but rather the ability and/or speed with which others can replicate the activities of any particular business.

For his analysis in Book II, Marshall assumes that competition is open. Analysis of the effects of obstacles to the ability to replicate the activities of others is reserved for Book III. Within Book II, Marshall is particularly interested in why, even in openly-competitive markets, the size of the representative firm is growing. Before his analysis is discussed, the concept of the representative firm should be explained.

Marshall invented his representative firm as a heuristic device to assist in his exposition of long-period industry supply price.[56] The representative firm was devised primarily because equilibrium of the constituent firms was not a necessary condition for equilibrium of the industry. The representative firm is merely the industry aggregate divided by the number of businesses. As such, it adds nothing to Marshall's price theory. It is intended to aid those readers whose imagination is so limited that they cannot absorb Marshall's aggregate equilibrium for the industry. For those who lack such imagination, Marshall supplies a micro analogue to the industry: the representative firm.

Equilibrium for the industry does not require equilibrium for each participant firm because each firm is, to some extent, a monopolist. If the monopoly is in an industry producing a standardised product, and the monopoly is merely the goodwill which distributes the market among the businesses, the monopoly gives the business very little discretion as to price and so businesses must operate at a scale not much less than minimum efficient scale if they are to survive. However, if the product is not standardised businesses can survive at scales much less than minimum efficient scale — particularly if by operating at a small scale the businesses incur only a small cost disadvantage when compared with larger firms.

> There are many trades in which an individual producer could secure much increased 'internal' economies by a great increase

> of his output; and there are many in which he could market that output easily; yet there are few in which he could do both. . . . For in most of those trades in which the economies of production on a large scale are of first-rate importance, marketing is difficult.[57]

Because of his explanation of the determinants of the size of firms in the *Principles*, together with his emphasis on the ubiquity of monopoly in *Industry and Trade*, Marshall's explanation of the growth in the size of the representative firm cannot be confined to technological factors. Three sets of factors are analysed. Chapters II to IV are devoted to technological influences, Chapters V and VI to problems of marketing, and Chapters VII to XII to the influence of changes in methods of internal organisation. Each of these three sets of factors will be examined in turn.

Technological Influences

The three chapters dealing with technological influences on the changing organisation and, in particular, on the growth of the representative firm point to many trends in methods of production. However, the factor to which Marshall gives primary emphasis is standardisation. By standardising products, or components of products, businesses were becoming able to utilise economies of scale. The emphasis is placed on product innovations rather than on process innovations. But the innovations in product design were intended to achieve, and frequently did achieve, a change in the relevant production function. The change in the production function presented the opportunity to utilise economies of scale.

But the process of standardisation and accompanying growth in the size of the representative firm does not eliminate the 'small man with a comparatively small capital.' Indeed, to some extent his survival is facilitated by the process — both as a producer of standardised commodities and as a purchaser of standardised inputs.

> He looks to selling his standardized product without inordinate expenses on advertising, or in building up business connections with individual firms. And, what is often more important, he can enter into any process in which the standardized products are used, with a fair certainty that he will be able to buy them, as he needs them, at a low cost.[58]

Although much of Marshall's analysis of technical influences on the changing pattern of industrial organisation is concerned with the horizontal expansion of business units, he is careful to distinguish horizontal expansion from vertical expansion. Although a firm can often lessen risk by vertical integration, such expansion tends to be lumpy and can, therefore, be constrained by the availability of finance to a greater extent than horizontal expansion.

> The upper stages of mixed works have little anxiety about their supply of material, for it consists mainly of half-finished products from the lower stages of the same works: and the lower stages are generally secure of a vent for their products in the upper stages. But a firm with limited capital can seldom undertake considerable vertical expansions with success; for such expansions are not easily made by gradual steps.[59]

The Growing Size and Complexity of Markets

The three chapters devoted to the ways in which changes in marketing were influencing the structure of industry point to two sets of factors. In the first place the representative retailing outlet was expanding not because cost functions were changing but because increased rivalry meant that, increasingly, only retailers of at least minimum efficient scale could survive.[60] Co-operative retailing was eliminating some of the market fragmentation noted by J. S. Mill.[61]

The entry of large department stores, cooperatives, and multiple-outlet retailers to retailing markets was being assisted by increased branding of goods. The anonymous retailers did not offer goods backed by their own recommendation; but, rather, they offered goods backed by the name of the manufacturer.[62]

The second way in which marketing was influencing the structure of industry was that economies of scale in marketing were becoming increasingly important. In this way branding was influencing the structure of markets. In the case of branded goods, the public image created by one product extends to other products carrying the same brand. Branding was therefore enabling the firms which produced successful products to use that success to assist the launching of other products.[63] Thus an emerging economy of scale in marketing was enlarging the size of the representative firm in manufacturing industries.

But the feature of marketing to which Marshall gives most prominence is the expansion in the sizes of markets caused by technical advance in transport and communications. In this connection, Marshall lavishes praise on Lardner's *Railway Economy*.

> But the area of a circle varies as the square of its radius. Therefore improvements in the mechanism or the organization of transport, which increase the distance over which trade in certain goods can be carried at a given expense, are *prima facie* likely to increase in the square of that ratio the area over which the trade can be conducted profitably. This rule may be called *Lardner's Law of Squares in transport and trade*, for convenience of reference.[64]

The other feature of marketing which Marshall stresses as influencing the structure of industry is the bearing of risk, in particular the risk associated with guessing the extent to which the market will wish to purchase one's product. Because there are different preferences and because there are economies of scale in the bearing of risk, markets have emerged which perform the useful function of concentrating risks among those who are willing to bear them at least cost. 'But the greater part of business risks are so inseparably connected with the general management of the business that an insurance company which undertook them would really make itself responsible for the business: and in consequence every firm has to act as its own insurance office with regard to them.'[65]

Internal Organisation

Although the risks associated with the making of business decisions cannot be transferred to an insurance company they can be transferred by means of joint-stock organisation.

> Here it may be observed that the directors of a company are, strictly speaking, employees of it. Except in so far as they are themselves shareholders, they run no risks from its failure, beyond some loss of prestige; and a possible loss of employment, which they share with other employees. The shareholders bear the risks, but delegate nearly the whole of their functions, as owners of the business, to the directors and other employees.[66]

The increasing prevalence of the joint-stock form of organisation (and the consequent divorce of ownership from control) lowered the important financial barrier to expansion.[67] This had an important consequence for the size of the representative firm. In early editions of the *Principles*, Marshall had claimed that the size of a firm was a function of its age. A business could not necessarily establish itself at minimum efficient scale because it may have needed to build a market and to accumulate the finance needed to reach such a scale. Joint-stock organisation largely removed the obstacle of finance, so firms were much more likely to survive long enough to achieve minimum efficient scale.

> It is obvious that, under this tendency [of increasing returns] a firm which has once obtained the start of its rivals, would be in a position to undersell them progressively, provided its own vigour remained unimpaired, and it could obtain all the capital it needed. In old times there was often much difficulty on this score: but that has diminished greatly during the last three or four generations. It seems therefore that, if there were no other difficulty in the way of the unlimited expansion of a strong manufacturing business, each step that the firm took forwards in supplanting its rivals, would enable it to produce profitably to itself at prices below those which they could reach. That is, each step would make the next step surer, longer and quicker: so that ere long it would have no rivals left, at all events in its own neighbourhood.[68]

Although the spread of joint-stock organisation was removing a barrier to the growth in the size of the representative firm, the problem of the motivation and control of individuals remained. Large businesses may encounter certain managerial diseconomies. Managerial problems arise in large businesses because members of management lose when they make a mistake but they may not gain when they are successful. Workers may not gain by hard work because problems of monitoring work performance are greater in larger organisations. Marshall had a cautious faith that the methods of scientific management might overcome these joint problems of motivation and control in large business.

> Scientific Management is in the main a method of redistributing and reorganizing the functions and the mutual relations of the

> personnel of a great business with the purpose of increasing aggregate efficiency by narrowing the range of responsibility of most of its employees, and bringing careful studies to bear on the instructions given in regard to the simplest manual operations.[69]

The minimum efficient scale of many businesses was expanding because of technical advances, the increasing complexity and scale of markets, and because of changes in methods of internal organisation. The joint-stock method had lessened the extent to which time influenced the size of firms so that increasingly over time firms in industries which were producing standardised products could only survive if they produced at least at minimum efficient scale. This analysis of the growth of the size of the representative firms was conducted on the assumption of open competition. However, if that assumption were changed, other influences on the organisation of industry could be analysed and evaluated.

Book III: Monopolistic Tendencies: Their Relations to Public Well-being

The first two Books of *Industry and Trade* emphasise the past growth and the current tendency for growth in the size of the representative firm. Book I is concerned with the emergence of capitalist methods of production. Book II is concerned with the tendency of the size of the representative firm to grow under capitalism, given the assumption of open competition. Book III is much more normative. It argues that these trends in the structure of industry need not impair market performance. Indeed, trends will not impair market performance providing the state provides a correct competitive environment.

It argues that the growing size of the representative firm need not create problems for market performance. In particular, to ensure that market performance is good the state should ensure that each of four conditions is met. It should keep competition open. It should regulate collusion among firms — paying particular attention to collusion on price. It should prevent large businesses from using their bigness or their monopoly in particular markets as competitive weapons. Finally, it should try to promote a business environment of aggressive rivalry. Each of these factors will be discussed in turn.

Openness of Competition

At the beginning of the discussion of Book II it was noted that openness (the freedom of economic agents to replicate profitable activities of others) and an absence of collusion were the two conditions which were needed to classify a market as freely competitive. In his discussion of free competition and monopoly, Marshall emphasises that monopoly and free competition are matters of degree. But Book III argues strongly that free competition tends to produce good market performances.

As Schumpeter remarks, it is a pity that the more-recent theory of trade practices policy should have stemmed from J. M. Clark's notion of workable competition rather than from Marshall.[70] For Marshall had a much more workable notion of competition than was provided by the theorists of imperfect competition.

The principal problem with the use of the openness of markets as a standard for antitrust policy is the problem of identification. The problem of identification arises largely because openness is a matter of degree and, as Marshall stressed repeatedly, the degree of openness depends on one's time horizon.

Marshall illustrates this problem of identification by detailed discussion of railway pricing. 'But incomparably the largest and most instructive experiences which the world has had of semi-monopolistic power, sufficiently strong to raise problems of public interest, have related to railways.'[71] The basic analytical problem is that any railway company offers a variety of services which share common costs. As we know from J. S. Mill the most competitive pricing under such conditions of joint costs is very difficult to distinguish in practice from pricing by a multi-product monopolist.[72] (This problem of identification was the subject of a protracted debate between Taussig and Pigou[73] and it is characteristic of Marshall's attitude to the usefulness of public debate among economists that he makes no mention of it in the course of his lengthy discussion of its substance.)

Although Marshall's particularisation of barriers to openness was mentioned above, Marshall adds an extra factor when he discusses America's experience of trusts. He notes that '. . . many monopolies owe much to the partial exclusion of foreign competitive products by a protective tariff . . .'.[74] He expresses the fear that German and British cartels will pressure their respective national governments to erect tariff barriers against the imports which otherwise would be resumed after the war.[75]

Combination

> There are three classes of producers who are not tempted to restrictive combination: those who produce for their own consumption; those who produce things for sale in a large open market in such small quantities, that current prices will not be appreciably affected by anything they may do or abstain from doing; and lastly the owners of absolute monopolies.[76]

Of the rest, some are tempted more sorely than others. If products are not standardised across producers price collusion is difficult because commonly an array of prices rather than a single price needs to be agreed.[77] Further, the lower the number of firms, the more likely is agreement to be reached.[78]

It may be noticed that Marshall places the adjective restrictive before the noun combination. The reason for this juxtaposition is that Marshall did not consider all combinations to be restrictive. It is a logical confusion to argue against combinations '. . . on the ground that free competition was a good, and that combination, being opposed to free competition, was, for that reason, an evil.'[79]

Collusion on price is difficult to detect because (even without a statutory prohibition) it is frequently tacit.

> In primitive civilizations people of the same calling or the same locality have generally acted together by habit and instinct, rather than by any formal convention. And, though the overt action of gilds, and other trade and professional associations, has often shown deliberate and elaborate strategy in dealing with the outsider; yet a great part of that collective selfishness, which is thinly covered by some unselfish devotion to the interests of a trading group, has worked through tacit and indefinite understandings.[80]

Although most combinations have some redeeming features, collusion on price is to be condemned.

> The present chapter and the next will be chiefly devoted to various forms of cooperation, in which there is some con-

> structive purpose; though the desire to get the better of others in buying and selling plays a considerable part in many of them, and develops a strong and even antisocial temper in a few of them. Associations for the purpose of marketing are known to be specially prone to such morbid development: and it is important to insist that they nearly always do some important constructive work; and often do no other.[81]

Marshall lists three types of constructive purpose to which combinations may be directed. The first is standardisation. It will be recalled that, when Marshall discusses economies of scale, he gives a great prominence to standardisation. Standardisation prevents unjustified product variety. Indeed, the standardisation of inputs will give the manufacturer increased choice and reliability of supply. Associations may distribute information on costing techniques and other methods of scientific management which may lead to standardisation of methods of production.[82]

Co-operation in research and development may also be constructive. On this issue, Marshall may be undecided or he may have changed his mind between 1890 and 1920. In *Some Aspects of Competition* (1890) Marshall notes that large firms have a great advantage over their smaller rivals in their power of making expensive experiments, yet he considers that many small firms generally constitute a more progressive industry than a few large firms. 'But on the whole observation seems to show, what might have been anticipated *a priori*, that these advantages count for little in the long run in comparison with the superior force of a multitude of small undertakers.'[83]

When he comes to *Industry and Trade*, Marshall seems to be more impressed by the economies of scale which pertain to scientific endeavour. 'Throughout this volume reference has frequently been made to the need for associated action in regard to the applications of science to industry.'[84]

Where cooperation on research and development is costly, large firms may result.

> . . . it seems that the growth of a considerable number of great firms in all heavy industries, and especially in heavy steel industries, is to be welcomed: the present age offers ever increasing scope for large experiments, of vital importance to progress, which cannot easily be arranged cooperatively; while

> yet they involve outlay and financial risks too heavy to be borne by any but a giant business.[85]

The final variable on which cooperation may be constructive is marketing. Marshall considered that much of the resources devoted to competitive marketing could be used better. 'If the concentration of marketing could be attained by methods that are free from cumbrous negotiations and effort, it would be a great social gain: for marketing is not wholly constructive work; and, the less energy is devoted to it, the better for general well-being.'[86]

Although Marshall gives illustrations of successful joint-marketing schemes, they do not receive a blanket endorsement. In particular, they are likely to foster collusion on price. However, economies of scale in marketing are so great compared with the sizes of many overseas markets, that cooperative schemes for export marketing may be justified on that ground.[87]

Unfair Competition

If competition were reasonably open and cooperation among businesses were limited the economy would approach free competition. However, this would not be sufficient to ensure good performance.

> More perhaps than any other country, [America] has learnt that general propositions in regard to either competition or monopoly are full of snares: and that some of the most injurious uses of monopoly, being themselves extreme forms of competition, are not to be restrained by the advocacy of free competition. Consequently, she is now engaged in leading the world in the very difficult task of restraining such methods of competition, as are aimed at narrowing the basis of competition.[88]

One competitive method roundly condemned by Marshall is the various forms of tying contract. He is opposed to the use of monopoly power in one market to gain a competitive advantage in another market. Because he is always alert to the dimension of time, deferred rebates are classified as a tie through time and therefore are to be condemned along with ties across products at any particular juncture.[89]

Marshall gives no other practice such an unqualified damnation. Even resale price maintenance, we are informed, is capable of defence![90] Standard competitive weapons such as price-cutting and price discrimination may be used to decrease competition — if they enable a firm to eliminate another because of the difference between the financial strength of the two. (It will be recalled that Marshall listed access to finance as one of his two sources of domestic barriers to openness.)

As with forms of non-price collusion, Marshall stressed that the judgement of the goodness or badness of competitive weapons is complicated. An informed student of business needs to make delicate judgements of the motive of the suspected firm. A strict verbal interpretation by a Court of Law is unlikely to suffice. Rather, administrative tribunals, peopled by skilled students of business, need to be employed.[91] The American Federal Trade Commission receives messages of congratulations at many places in Book III.

Marshall not only prefers control by administrative tribunal to control via the courts of law, he also prefers such control to public ownership. The reason for this latter preference is that government departments are considered to be less adventurous even than joint-stock companies. And, as with his assessment of tariffs, government discretion is thought to produce politically-flavoured business policy.[92]

Even this preference is not unqualified. Because of differences in human temperament across nations, public corporations may suit some countries better than others.`Public corporations may be acceptable for Europe, but not for America or England.

The Business Environment

Marshall's advocacy of direct controls by an administrative tribunal within a framework of legislation which promotes freedom of competition is contingent partly upon the effects which he considers that these policies will have on the general business environment. In Book I, Marshall canvasses possible explanations of differences in the business environment across nations. In Book III he warns that cooperation among businesses may lessen the spirit of free enterprise.

> The present group of chapters will be much occupied with this class of consideration; because there is reason for thinking that the advantages which some other countries, and especially Germany, have derived from a semi-military organization of

> industry are not in fact as great as may appear at first sight; and because immediate material gains, obtained at the expense of a diminution of the spirit of free enterprise, may prove to have been too dearly bought, even from a merely material point of view.[93]

(Keynes' biographical essay of Marshall established what other investigation has since confirmed: that his basic work on the theory of value and distribution was completed by 1870. By the early 1870s Marshall was lecturing on '. . . Economic History from 1350 onwards, on the lines of the Historical Appendices to the *Principles*. He would give half an hour to theory and half an hour to history. He was keenly interested in Economic History.'[94]

It appears that some of the opening chapters of *Industry and Trade* were written a long time prior to publication. The preface informs us that some of the type was set up in 1904! However, Books II and III contain many references to studies and official reports particularly into problems of monopoly in Britain, Germany and the United States from 1900 to 1916. His search for facts to illustrate, test and modify his hypotheses was pursued up to the publication of *Industry and Trade*.

It is a big volume, organised around three big questions. Why did capitalism emerge in Europe? Why does the size of the representative firm continue to grow? Can the State produce a legislative environment for these large businesses which will preserve competition? Revival of interest in these questions should cause economists to re-read *Industry and Trade*.

Perhaps the greatest problem with the volume is its length. In particular, the wealth of factual detail sometimes seems to overwhelm the structure. Marshall loved to compare the facts of industry with the theory he had developed; and he gleaned these facts from books, reports and observation. The facts illustrate and test the structure. And the structure is analytical. The prime thrust of the book is to explain the structure of industry and to investigate ways in which government policy can influence it for the better.

Notes and References

* I gratefully acknowledge comments by Robert Dixon and by Ken Tucker on an earlier draft

1. Joseph A. Schumpeter, *History of Economic Analysis* (London, Allen and Unwin, 1954) p. 834
2. C. W. Guillebaud, 'Marshall's Principles of Economics in the Light of Contemporary Economic Thought', *Economica*, N. S., May 1952, *XXX*, 111
3. J. M. Keynes, 'Alfred Marshall 1842–1924', *Economic Journal*, December 1926, reprinted in *Essays in Biography*, 2nd edn, New York, Horizon, 1951, p. 212
4. Joseph A. Schumpeter, 'Alfred Marshall's *Principles*: A Semi-Centennial Appraisal', *American Economic Review*, June 1941, *XXXI*, 238
5. R. H. Coase, 'Industrial Organization: A Proposal for Research', in Victor R. Fuchs (ed.), *Policy Issues and Research Opportunities in Industrial Organization*, New York, NBER, 1972, p. 60
6. From Marshall's sketch for his entry in the proposed volume of 'Portraits and Short Lives of Leading Economists' by Eckstein. Reprinted in *History of Economic Thought Newsletter*, Spring 1972, pp. 14–17
7. John K. Whitaker, 'Alfred Marshall: The Years 1877 to 1885', *History of Political Economy*, Spring 1972, *4*, 32
8. *Industry and Trade*, pp. 423–4
9. William James Adams, 'International Comparisons in the Study of Industrial Organization', in A. P. Jacquemin and H. W. De Jong (eds.), *Markets, Corporate Behaviour and the State*, The Hague, Martinus Nijhoff, 1976, pp. 19–31
10. For Marshall's general pronouncements on such comparisons, see *Industry and Trade*, 797n and A. C. Pigou (ed.), *Memorials of Alfred Marshall*, London, Macmillan, 1925, p. 330
11. Joe S. Bain, *International Differences in Industrial Structure*, New Haven, Yale University Press, 1966
12. P. T. Bauer and B. S. Yamey, 'Economic Progress and Occupational Distribution', *Economic Journal*, 1951, *LXI*, 741–55
13. Caves' latest offering in this genre is Richard E. Caves et. al., *Competition in the Open Economy*, Cambridge, Mass., Harvard University Press, 1980
14. See *Industry and Trade*, pp. 507–8
15. Bruce Glassburner, 'Alfred Marshall on Economic History and Historical Development', *Quarterly Journal of Economics*, Nov. 1955, *LXIX*, 586
16. G. F. Shove, 'The Place of Marshall's *Principles* in the Development of Economic Theory', *Economic Journal*, Dec. 1942, *52*, 308
17. John K. Whitaker, 'Some neglected aspects of Alfred Marshall's economic and social thought', *History of Political Economy*, Summer 1977, *9*, 192–3
18. R. H. Coase, 'The Nature of the Firm', *Economica*, 1937, *IV*, 386–405
19. Oliver E. Williamson, *Markets and Hierarchies*, New York, Free Press, 1975
20. Allyn A. Young, 'Economics as a Field of Research', *Quarterly Journal of Economics*, Nov. 1927, *42*, 5
21. John Maloney, 'Marshall, Cunningham, and the Emerging Economics Profession', *Economic History Review*, 2nd ser. 29 August 1976, pp. 440–51
22. A. W. Coats, 'Political Economy and the Tariff Reform Campaign of 1903', *Journal of Law and Economics*, April 1968, *2*, 181–229
23. Gerard M. Koot, 'English Historical Economics and the Emergence of Economic History in England', *History of Political Economy*, Summer 1980, *12*, 174–205
24. Marshall, 'The Old Generation of Economists and the New', in *Memorials*, p. 309
25. Marshall, 'The Present Position of Economics', in *Memorials*, partic. pp. 165–8
26. *Memorials*, p. 166
27. *Industry and Trade*, p. vi
28. Marshall, *Principles of Economics*, Ninth (Variorum) Edition, London, Macmillan, 1961, p. 768

29. Eckstein Sketch, p. 16 (Note 6)
30. See Marshall, 'Some Features of American Industry', in *Early Economic Writings*, Vol. 2, pp. 352–77
31. *Industry and Trade*, p. 158
32. On Marshall's analysis of personal characteristics, see Talcott Parsons, 'Wants and Activities in Marshall', *Quarterly Journal of Economics*, Nov. 1931, *XLVI*, 101–40; Ralph L. Andreano, 'Alfred Marshall's *Industry and Trade*: A Neglected Classic in Economic History', in Andreano (ed.), *New Views on American Economic Development*, Cambridge, Mass.: Schenkman, 1965, pp. 317–29; and Whitaker (Note 17)
33. Friedrich List, *The National System of Political Economy*, translated by S. S. Lloyd, London, Longmans, Green and Co., 1904, 108, his emphasis
34. List, *National System*, p. 40
35. It is also a principal theme of the paper, 'Some Features of American Industry'
36. W. Cunningham, 'The Perversion of Economic History', *Economic Journal*, Sept. 1892, *2*, p. 493
37. Alfred Marshall, 'A Reply', *Economic Journal*, Sept. 1892, *2*, 508
38. *Memorials*, p. 169
39. H. W. McCready, 'Alfred Marshall and Tariff Reform, 1903, Some Unpublished Letters', *Journal of Political Economy*, 1955, *63*, 260
40. *Principles*, p. 67
41. *Official Papers by Alfred Marshall*, edited by J. M. Keynes (London: Macmillan, 1926), p. 388. This quotation comes from the revised version of the 'Memorandum on the Fiscal Policy of International Trade.' The Memorandum was originally written to assist the supporters of free trade within Balfour's Cabinet in the struggle over tariff reform. See John C. Wood, 'Alfred Marshall and the Tariff-Reform Campaign of 1903', *Journal of Law and Economics*, Oct. 1980, *XXIII*, 481–95
42. List, *The National System*, p. 159
43. List, *The National System*, p. 127
44. John Stuart Mill, who probably did more to confer respectability on the infant-industry argument than anyone else, offered the same opinion of the United States in 1866. See *The Later Letters of John Stuart Mill 1849–1873*, ed. by Francis E. Mineka and Dwight N. Lindley, Vol. XVI of The Collected Works of John Stuart Mill, Toronto, University of Toronto Press, 1972
45. *Industry and Trade*, p. 697
46. *Official Papers*, pp. 393–4. Again, Mill expressed similar misgivings. 'As far as I can perceive, those who contend for protection in Australia mean it to be as permanent as any other legislative arrangements & hold to all the false theories on the subject, of which Europe is rapidly ridding itself & which are declining even in America. In such a state of opinion as this I sh^{d} resist, with my utmost strength, any protection whatever, because it is far easier to withstand these false & pernicious doctrines before they have been carried into practice to any serious extent, than after powerful protected interests have been allowed to grow up under their influence.' Mill, Note 44, p. 1420. See also pp. 1520 and 1516
47. J. K. Whitaker (ed.), *The Early Writings of Alfred Marshall 1867–1890*, London, Macmillan, 1975, Vol. II, p. 55
48. Philip L. Williams, *The Emergence of the Theory of the Firm*, London, Macmillan, 1978, pp. 30–3, 102–8
49. See G. J. Stigler, 'Marshall's *Principles* after Guillebaud', *Journal of Political Economy*, 1962, *LXX*, 282–6
50. *Industry and Trade*, p. 398
51. *Industry and Trade*, p. 441
52. *Industry and Trade*, p. 182, his emphasis

53. *Industry and Trade*, p. 196
54. *Industry and Trade*, p. 397
55. Compared with H. H. Liebhafsky, 'A Curious Case of Neglect: Marshall's *Industry and Trade*', *Canadian Journal of Economics and Political Science*, Aug. 1955, *XXI*, pp. 339–53
56. Williams, *The Emergence of the Theory of the Firm*, pp. 100–2
57. *Principles*, p. 286
58. *Industry and Trade*, p. 246
59. *Industry and Trade*, pp. 215–16
60. *Memorials*, pp. 231–3
61. J. S. Mill, *Principles of Political Economy*, 7th ed. 1871, ed. with intro. by Sir W. J. Ashley (London: Longmans, 1909) pp. 246–7. On the impact of cooperatives, see J. Hood and B. S. Yamey, 'Imperfect competition in retail trades', *Economica*, n.s., *18*, 1951; reprinted in K. A. Tucker and B. S. Yamey (eds.) *Economics of Retailing*, Harmondsworth, Penguin, 1973, pp. 115–30
62. *Industry and Trade*, pp. 301–2
63. *Industry and Trade*, pp. 269–72
64. *Industry and Trade*, p. 27, his emphasis
65. *Principles*, p. 398
66. *Industry and Trade*, p. 311
67. *Industry and Trade*, p. 315. Marx anticipated Marshall on this and, indeed, on much of Marshall's discussion of the divorce of ownership from control. See Philip L. Williams, 'Monopoly and Centralisation in Marx', *History of Political Economy*, summer 1982, pp. 14, 228–41
68. *Industry and Trade*, p. 315
69. *Industry and Trade*, pp. 368–9
70. Schumpeter, *History of Economic Analysis*, p. 975
71. *Industry and Trade*, p. 445
72. Williams, *The Emergence of the Theory of the Firm*, pp. 59–60
73. For references, see A. C. Pigou, *Economics of Welfare*, 4th edn, London, Macmillan, 1946, pp. 290 ff
74. *Industry and Trade*, p. 526
75. *Industry and Trade*, pp. 518–19
76. *Industry and Trade*, p. 401
77. *Industry and Trade*, pp. 548–9
78. *Industry and Trade*, p. 550. Compared with Stigler's famous proposition that the lower the number of firms the more likely is the detection of a firm which has failed to abide by an agreement. See George J. Stigler, 'A Theory of Oligopoly', *Journal of Political Economy*, Feb. 1964, *72*, 44–61
79. 'Some Aspects of Competition', *Memorials*, p. 272
80. *Industry and Trade*, p. 400
81. *Industry and Trade*, p. 599
82. *Industry and Trade*, p. 607
83. *Memorials*, p. 280
84. *Industry and Trade*, p. 608
85. *Industry and Trade*, pp. 593–4
86. *Industry and Trade*, p. 553
87. *Industry and Trade*, pp. 613–15
88. *Industry and Trade*, p. 512
89. *Industry and Trade*, pp. 234, 439
90. *Industry and Trade*, p. 547. It is a pity that Marshall does not elaborate this argument. For a careful evaluation of the possible arguments in support of resale price maintenance, see B. S. Yamey, *Resale Price Maintenance and Shoppers' Choice,* London, Hobart Paper, Institute of Economic Affairs, 1960,1

91. *Industry and Trade*, pp. 484, 479, 512, 547
92. See 'Some Aspects of Competition', *Memorials*, pp. 275–6
93. *Industry and Trade*, p. 582
94. M. P. Marshall, *What I Remember*, Cambridge, Cambridge University Press, 1947, p. 20

BIBLIOGRAPHY OF BASIL S. YAMEY

Part 1: Books

1954 *The Economics of Resale Price Maintenance*, London, Sir Isaac Pitman & Sons.

1956 (Editor, with A. C. Littleton) *Studies in the History of Accounting*, London, Sweet & Maxwell, Homewood, Ill., Richard Irwin.

1957 (With P. T. Bauer) *The Economics of Under-developed Countries*, London, James Nisbet & Co, and Cambridge, Cambridge University Press; Chicago, Chicago University Press.

1963 (With H. C. Edey and H. W. Thomson) *Accounting in England and Scotland: 1543–1800*, London, Sweet & Maxwell.

1964 (Editor, with R. Firth) *Capital, Saving and Credit in Peasant Societies*, London, Allen and Unwin; Chicago, Aldine Press, 1964.

1965 (With R. B. Stevens) *The Restrictive Practices Court: The Judicial Process and Economic Policy*, London, Weidenfeld & Nicolson.

1966 (Editor) *Resale Price Maintenance*, London, Weidenfeld & Nicolson; Chicago, Aldine Press, 1966.

1968 (With P. T. Bauer) *Markets, Market Control and Marketing Reform*, London, Weidenfeld & Nicolson.

1973 (Editor) *Economics of Industrial Structure*, Harmondsworth, Middx, Penguin.

1973 (Editor, with K. A. Tucker) *Economics of Retailing*, Harmondsworth, Middx, Penguin.

1974 (Editor, with H. C. Edey) *Debits, Credits, Finance and Profits* (Essays in honour of William T. Baxter), London, Sweet & Maxwell.

1975 (Editor, with O. Kojima) *Ympyn's A Notable and very excellente woorke*, Kyoto, Daigakudo.

1976 (Editor, with B. A. Goss) *The Economics of Futures Trading*, London, Macmillan; New York, Halstead Press.

1978 *Essays on the History of Accounting*, New York, Arno Press.

1978 (Editor) *The Historical Development of Accounting*, New York, Arno Press.

1979 (Editor, with O. Kojima) *The Patheway to Perfectnes in the 'accomptes of Debitour and Creditour by James Peele*, Kyoto, Daigakudo Books.

1981 (With B. A. Goss) *Economia dei Mercati a Termine*, Milan, Franco Angeli.

1983 *Further Essays on the History of Accounting*, New York, Garland Press.

Part 2: Articles

1940 'The Functional Development of Double-Entry Bookkeeping', *The Accountant, 103.*

1941 (With Franklin, N. N.) 'An Enquiry into Some Effects of a Wage Determination in Grahamstown', *South African Journal of Economics, 9.*

'Aspects of the Law Relating to Company Dividends', *Modern Law Review, 4.*

1942 'The Excess Profits Duty in South Africa', *South African Journal of Economics, 10.*

1947 'Notes on the Origin of Double Entry Bookkeeping', *Accounting Review, 22.*

1949 'Scientific Bookkeeping and the Rise of Capitalism', *Economic History Review, 2.*

1950 'The Price Policy of Co-operative Societies', *Economica, 17.*

'Notes on resale price maintenance', *Economica, 17*, 1950.

'Some Topics in the History of Financial Accounting in England, 1500–1900', in W. T. Baxter (ed.), *Studies in Accounting*, London, Sweet and Maxwell, 1950; revised version in W. T. Baxter and S. Davidson (eds.), *Studies in Accounting*, London, Institute of Chartered Accountants in England and Wales, 1977.

1951 (With Hood, J.) 'Imperfect Competition in Retail Trades', *Economica, 18*.

'An Investigation of Hedging on an Organised Produce Exchange', *Manchester Studies, 19*.

(With Bauer, P. T.) 'Economic Progress and Occupational Distribution', *Economic Journal, 61*.

1952 (With Bauer, P. T.) 'Competition and Prices: A Study of Groundnut Buying in Nigeria', *Economica, 18*.

'The Origins of Resale Price Maintenance: A Study of Three Branches of Retail Trade', *Economic Journal, 62*.

1954 'The Evolution of Shopkeeping', *Lloyds Bank Review, 31*.

(With Bauer, P. T.) 'Further Notes on Economic Progress and Occupational Distribution', *Economic Journal, 64*.

(With Bauer, P. T.) 'Economic Aspects of Immigration Policy in Nigeria and the Gold Coast', *South African Journal of Economics, 22*, 1954.

(With Bauer, P. T.) 'The Economics of Marketing Reform', *Journal of Political Economy, 62*.

'Futures Trading in Cocoa, Rubber and Wool Tops', *Three Banks Review, 23*.

(With Bauer, P. T.) 'Economic Progress, Occupational Distribution and Institutional Wage Rigidities: A Comment', *Review of Economics and Statistics, 36*.

'Trade Conspiracies: An Historical Footnote', *Modern Law Review, 17*.

1955 'Bidding Agreements at Auctions', *Butterworths South African Law Review*.

(With Pennance, F. G.) 'Competition in the Retail Grocery Trade, 1850–1939', *Economica, 22.*

1956 (With Wiseman, J.) 'The Raw Cotton Commission, 1948–52', *Oxford Economic Papers, 8.*

1957 (With Hood, J.): 'The Middle-Class Co-operative Retailing Societies in London, 1864–1900', *Oxford Economic Papers, 9.*

'Handson's "Analysis of Merchants Accompts" — An Unrecorded Broadside, 1669', *Accounting Research, 8.*

1958 'The Investigation of Resale Price Maintenance under the Monopolies Legislation', *Public Law.*

'John Weddington's "A Breffe Instruction" 1567', *Accounting Research, 9.*

1959 'Cotton Futures Trading in Liverpool', *Three Banks Review, 41.*

(With Bauer, P. T.) 'A Case Study of Response to Price in an Under-Developed Country', *Economic Journal, 69.*

'Stephen Monteage: A Seventeenth Century Accountant', *Accountancy*, November.

'Some Seventeenth and Eighteenth Century Double-Entry Ledgers'. *Accounting Review, 34.*

1960 'Aggregated Rebate Schemes and Independent Competition', *Oxford Economic Papers, 12.*

'The Development of Company Accounting Conventions', *Three Banks Review, 47.*

(With Peston, M. H.) 'Inter-temporal Price Relationships with Forward Markets: A Method of Analysis', *Economica, 27.*

'A Seventeenth Century Double-Entry Journal', *Accountancy*, November.

'Resale Price Maintenance Issues and Policies', *Three Banks Review, 48.*

(With Bauer, P. T.) 'Response to Price in an Under-developed Economy: A Rejoinder', *Economic Journal, 70.*

1961 'The Word "Ledger"', *Accountancy*, March.

1962 'Some Issues in Our Monopolies Legislation', *Three Banks Review, 54.*

'Accounting and the Rise of Capitalism: Further Notes on a Theme by Sombart' in *Studi in Onore di Amintore Fanfani*, Vol 6, Milan, Giuffre, 1962; revised version in *Journal of Accounting Research*, 1964, *2*; reprinted with addendum in K. A. Tucker (ed.), *Business History: Selected Readings*, London, Frank Cass, 1977.

1963 (With Snape, R. H.) 'A Diagrammatic Analysis of Some Effects of Buffer Fund Price Stabilization', *Oxford Economic Papers, 15.*

1964 (With Bauer, P. T.) 'Organized Commodity Stabilization with Voluntary Participation', *Oxford Economic Papers, 16.*

1965 (With Snape, R. H.) 'Test of the Effectiveness of Hedging', *Journal of Political Economy, 73.*

1966 'Speculation and Price Stability: A Note', *Journal of Political Economy, 74.*

'John Jones's "Diarium Mercatoris", An Eighteenth Century Exposition of Accounting', *Accountancy, 77.*

'Price Maintenance of Books in Britain: The Historical Background' in T. Bagiotti (ed.), *Essays in Honour of Marco Fanno*, Vol 2, Padua, Cedam.

1967 'Fifteenth and Sixteenth Century Manuscripts on the Art of Bookkeeping', *Journal of Accounting Research, 5.*

1970 'Monopoly, Competition and the Incentive to Invent: A Comment', *Journal of Law and Economics, 13*, April.

'Closing the Ledger', *Accounting and Business Research*, 1970.

1971 'Short Hedging and Long Hedging in Futures Markets: Symmetry and Asymmetry', *Journal of Law and Economics, 14*.

(With Caves, Richard E.) 'Risk and Corporate Rates of Return: Comment', *Quarterly Journal of Economics, 85*.

'Jacob de Metz's "Sendero Mercantil": An Unrecorded Book on Accounting, 1967', *Accounting and Business Research*, 1971.

1972 'Predatory Price Cutting: Notes and Comments', *Journal of Law and Economics, 15*.

'Why £2,310,000 for a Velasquez?: An Auction Bidding Rule', *Journal of Political Economy, 80*.

(With Bauer, P. T.) 'The Economics of the Pearson Report', *Journal of Development Studies, 8*.

(With Bauer, P. T.) 'Industrialization and Development: The Nigerian Experience', *Economic History Review, 25*.

'Notes on Secret Price Cutting in Oligopoly', in M. Kooy (ed.), *Studies in Economics and Economic History: Essays in Honour of Professor H. M. Robertson*, London, Macmillan.

(With Bauer, P. T.) 'The Pearson Report: A Review' in T. J. Byres (ed.), *Foreign Resources and Economic Development: A Symposium on the Pearson Report*, London, Frank Cass.

'Do Monopoly and Near-Monopoly Matter? A Survey of Empirical Studies' in M. H. Peston and B. C. Corry (eds.), *Essays in Honour of Lord Robbins*, London, Weidenfeld and Nicolson.

1973 'Algunas Reflexions Acerca de la Politica Britanica contra el

Monopolio y los Acuerdos Restrictivos', *Cuadernos de Economia*, 1973.

'Retail Price Competition and the Origins of the Net Book Agreement' in R. J. Taraporevala, *Competition and its Control in the British Book Trade, 1850–1939*, London, Pitman Publishing.

1974 'Monopolistic Price Discrimination and Economic Welfare', *The Journal of Law and Economics, 17.*

'Luca Pacioli's "Scuola Perfetta": A Bibliographical Puzzle', *Gutenberg-Jahrbuch*, 1974.

1975 'Some Problems of Oligopoly' in M. Ariga (ed.), *International Conference on International Economy and Competition Policy: Papers and Reports*, Tokyo.

'Some Features of Competition Policy in the United Kingdom' in B. E. Hawk (ed.), *International Antitrust, Annual Proceedings of the Fordham Corporate Law Institute, 1974*, New York, Matthew Bender.

'Four Centuries of Books on Bookkeeping and Accounting' in *Historical Accounting Literature*, London, Mansell.

'Notes on Double-Entry Bookkeeping and Economic Progress', *Journal of European Economic History, 4.*

'Two Typographical Ambiguities in Pacioli's "Summa"', *Gutenberg-Jahrbuch*, 1975.

1976 'The Judicial Control of Cartels: The Restrictive Practices Court' in A. Jacquemin and G. Schrans (eds.), *Actes du Colloque sur la Magistrature Economique*, Louvain, Oyez.

'Ralph Davison's Accounting Journal', *Economisch en Sociaal Historisch Jaarboek*, 1976.

(With Bauer, P. T.) 'The Less Developed Countries: Stereotype and Fact' in M. L. Truu (ed.), *Policy and the South African*

Economy: Essays in Memory of Desmond Hobart Houghton, Cape Town, Oxford University Press.

1977 (With Bauer, P. T.) 'Against the New Economic Order', *Commentary, 63*.

'Aspects of Vertical Integration between Manufacturing and Wholesaling' in O. Kojima (ed.), *Studies in Business Economics*, Kyoto, Daigakudo Shoten.

1978 'Vertical Integration and the Size and Growth of the Market' in T. Bagiotti and G. Franco (eds.), *Pioneering Economics: International Essays in Honour of Giovanni Demaria*, Padua, Cedam.

(With Bauer, P. T.) 'World Wealth Redistribution: Anatomy of the New Order' in K. Brunner (ed), *The First World and the Third World: Essays on the New International Economic Order*, Rochester, New York, University of Rochester Policy Centre Publications.

(With Bauer, P. T.) 'The Third World and the West: An Economic Perspective' in W. Scott Thompson (ed.), *The Third World: Premises of US Policy*, San Francisco, Institute for Contemporary Studies.

'I Benefici del Commercio Internazionale e l'Alto Costo del Protezionisma' in F. A. Grassini (ed.), *Industria in Crisi: Soluzione Europea o Nazionale*? Bologna, Il Mulino.

'Pacioli's Pioneering Exposition of Double-Entry Bookkeeping: A Belated Review' in *Studi in Memoria di Federigo Melis*, Naples, Giannini.

1979 'Alucuni Aspetti Economici dell'Integrazione Verticale della Funzione di Ingrosso', *Commercio, 1*.

'Commodity Futures Markets, Hedging and Speculation' in A. Seldon (ed.), *City Lights: Essays on Financial Institutions and Markets in the City of London*, London, The Institute of Economic Affairs.

'The Tobacco War and the Ogden Bonus Litigation, 1901–1906' in *Essays in Honour of Ben Beinart*, Vol 3, Cape Town, Juta.

'Oldcastle, Peele and Mellis: A Case of Plagiarism in the Sixteenth Century', *Accounting and Business Research, 9.*

'Compound Journal Entries in Early Treatises on Bookkeeping', *Accounting Review, 54.*

1980 'The Index to the Ledger: Some Historical Notes', *Accounting Review, 55.*

'Early Views on the Origins and Development of Bookkeeping and Accounting', *Accounting and Business Research, 10.*

'Commercio a Termine: Condizioni per l'Efficiente Funzionamento di un Mercato', *Commercio, 2.*

(With Bauer, P. T.) 'East-West/North-South', *Commentary, 70.*

1981 'Some Reflections on the Writing of a General History of Accounting', *Accounting and Business Research, 11.*

'Two Seventeenth Century Accounting "Statements"', *Accounting and Business Research, 11.*

'The "Partimenti" Account: A Discarded Practice', *Abacus, 17.*

'I Contratti a Termine del Gasolio: un Nuovo Mercato Londinese', *Energia*, 1981.

(With Bauer, P. T.) 'The Political Economy of Foreign Aid', *Lloyds Bank Review*, 1981.

1982 'Accounting' in J. R. Strayer (gen. ed.), *Dictionary of the Middle Ages*, New York, American Council of Learned Societies and Scribner's.

(With Bauer, P. T.) 'Foreign Aid: What is at Stake?' *The Public Interest*, No 68, 1982.

1983 'Basis, Bactavardation e Contango: Le Relazioni tra Prezzi a Termini e a Pronti', Materie Prime, March.

INDEX